Global Oil and the Nation State

Global Oil and
the Nation State

Bernard Mommer

Foreword by
Alí Rodríguez Araque

Published by the Oxford University Press
For the Oxford Institute for Energy Studies
2002

Oxford University Press, Great Clarendon Street, Oxford OX2 6DP

*Oxford University Press is a department of the University of Oxford.
It furthers the University's objective of excellence in research, scholarship
and education by publishing worldwide in*

*Oxford New York
Auckland Bangkok Buenos Aires Cape Town
Chennai Dar es Salaam Delhi Hong Kong Istanbul Karachi
Kolkata Kuala Lumpur Madrid Melbourne Mexico City Mumbai Nairobi
São Paulo Shanghai Singapore Taipei Tokyo Toronto
and an associated company in Berlin*

*Oxford is a registered trade mark of Oxford University Press
in the UK and in certain other countries*

*Published in the United States
by Oxford University Press Inc. New York*

*British Library Cataloguing in Publication Data
Data Available*

*Library of Congress Cataloguing in Publication Data
Data Applied for*

ISBN 0-19-730028-6

*Cover designed by Clare Hofmann
Typeset by Philip Armstrong, Sheffield
Printed by Biddles, Guildford*

CONTENTS

TABLES

FIGURES

ACKNOWLEDGEMENTS

This book is the result of many years of research dating back to the 1970s. During this period governance structures in oil, both nationally and internationally, have been the subject of reform and counter-reform measures. And the tug-of-war continues, with no fundamental reason to expect that the situation will become more stable.

The research for the book continued and was completed at the Oxford Institute for Energy Studies, hence my special thanks to its founder and director, Robert Mabro. I also want to thank all my colleagues for their helpful comments and criticism on earlier versions of the different parts of this book, which I presented in our weekly seminar. Moreover, Juan Carlos Boué, John Mitchell, and Ian Skeet read the last draft of the manuscript and their criticisms have contributed, very substantially, to improving it and making it more readable. I also have to thank Daniel Hellinger, from Webster University (St. Louis), who for many years brought to my attention important and relevant debates amongst political scientists in the United States, which would have otherwise escaped my attention. My special thanks to Angel De La Vega, Universidad Nacional Autónoma de México, and Jesús Mora, Universidad de Los Andes (Mérida, Venezuela), for their interesting and stimulating discussions on everything related to the subject matter; Jesús Mora also read, and commented on, the last draft. I am deeply indebted to Asdrúbal Baptista, with whom a permanent exchange of ideas over the broader issue of 'oil and development' began in the 1970s, when we both were at the Universidad de Los Andes. Last but not least, my special thanks to Alí Rodríguez-Araque for his support and encouragement to work on the subject and his interest in its political dimension since we met in 1970. However, as usual, all opinions expressed in this paper are my sole responsibility.

Vienna, January 2002.

Bernard Mommer

FOREWORD

Control over access to natural resources – and, therefore, to the territories where they are located – has been at the origin of countless conflicts, which can be traced back to the beginnings of civilisation and have continued to exist up to the present. Since ancient times the main reason behind such conflicts has frequently been control over a specific natural resource. This has occurred, for instance, with some minerals that played a significant role in the national and international economy. Territorial control, whether by groups or individuals, leads to the exercise of property rights. Such rights are legitimised over time through their customary use, becoming law, and property rights over a natural resource ultimately materialise in control over access, irrespectively of whether the owner is an individual, a community or a nation. Then, whoever intends to gain access to the resource, may have to pay a patrimonial retribution, or ground rent.

It is, thus, understood that systems of property rights are the expression of relationships among the various groups that interact in society in different periods of history. Feudalism, for instance, laid its foundations on a system of land ownership, which, in turn, responded to a particular set of values, a culture and an ideology. That property right scheme developed under the influence of powerful, opposing forces, which brought about changes eventually leading to the modern economic systems. Those changes, as is well known, were the result of many conflicts, which have at times been solved through negotiations and agreements, but which have also led to the use of force on not just a few occasions.

From the end of the nineteenth century and throughout the twentieth century, another natural resource – oil – entered the political, legal and military arenas where property right issues have been dealt with. Thus, oil has led to a myriad of conflicts – as much as or perhaps even more than land as such – many of which have been resolved through a variety of approaches, but many of which still remain to be resolved.

Bernard Mommer, the author of this book, has dedicated

more than 30 years to passionately researching this topic. He has spent more than half his life as an avid reader and incisive researcher, uncovering and disentangling historical data pertaining to the tense developments in world oil. He has scrutinised data often scattered through, but forgotten by, the mainstream historic and scientific literature. The fruits of this passion are contained in a large number of essays and books; outstanding among them is *La Cuestión Petrolera*, published in 1988, during his days as a researcher in Venezuela.

Now, the publication of his *Global Oil and The Nation State* presents us with new results of greater maturity and strength. Starting from a theoretical discussion about ground rent – an economic, legal and political expression of land ownership – Mommer goes on to describe and to analyse the different relationships emanating from oil activities *upstream*, as he accurately tells us from the first line. It is gaining access to the natural resource that the relationship with the owner develops, be it a public or private entity.

However, beyond its theoretical and historical aspects, the particular importance of this book lies in its contribution to the understanding of present-day problems in world oil. Such an understanding can only be found in the complexity of relationships among four actors linked through oil: the owner of the natural resource, whose interest lies in obtaining a benefit from granting access to his property; the producer, who seeks to obtain a profit on his investment; the consumer, who looks for low prices; and finally, the government, conceived as an organic complexity of relationships, which retains the 'eminent domain' over all natural resources.

The book analyses, in detail, the different phases in the development of these relationships, but not only as far as the facts are concerned. The main focus is on how these phases are reflected in the political discourse of the different actors, given that, as the author says: 'The question of natural resource ownership and its relationship to prices is definitely a question of politics and not of economics.' And of course, it is also an ideological issue, to the extent that in current economic literature and, particularly, in literature on oil, the owners of natural resources generally have disappeared as actors exercising their legitimate rights.

It is of particular interest to us to highlight what happened after the wave of oil nationalisations, especially in OPEC member countries. Up to then, as Mommer rightly points out, oil companies were the mediators between the natural resource owners and consumers. Governments of the consuming countries intervened at certain times but only to withdraw again soon. However, after the nationalisations, mediation between natural resource owners and consumers was left to the market. At the political level, this relationship was taken up by the governments of the principal consuming countries, on the one hand, and the governments of most important exporting countries, on the other. The former have been grouped since 1974 under the International Energy Agency, which was born as an anti-OPEC organisation; and OPEC represents, since 1960, the common interests of key owners of the natural resource. And the important achievements of OPEC in the early 1970s – increasing its control over volumes and prices – provoked a very strong reaction by the main consumers. This is expressed in a very harsh, direct manner by Henry Kissinger in his Memoirs: 'Both the Nixon and Ford Administrations had no higher priority than to bring about a reduction of oil prices by breaking the power of OPEC. The strategy reflected not only economic analysis but – even more – political, indeed moral, conviction. ... I outlined our program: consumer solidarity, including a program of emergency sharing; energy conservation: active development of alternative energy sources; creation of a financial safety net' (Kissinger 1999: 668–69).

This goal has been maintained by the principal consuming countries, over time, through a long list of bilateral and multilateral treaties and has continued to be strongly promoted up to the present.

OPEC, meanwhile, has attained a significant degree of success by coordinating the production policies of its Members, dealing with an exhaustible natural resource, thus avoiding a harmful level of competition for market share. This has led to a relative stabilisation of prices. However, OPEC is now facing new challenges. It must avoid harmful competition among its Members for foreign upstream investment, resisting pressure by external factors, as this could undermine the co-operation upon which the very existence of the Organisation is based.

This policy does take into account, of course, the legitimate right of investors to a fair return, a right OPEC has always acknowledged explicitly.

This challenge has also to be faced by oil-producing countries outside OPEC, taking into account their interests, as natural resource owners, to guarantee a level of revenues that will contribute to their national or regional development. This is a principle that applies to all countries, without distinction, developing or developed – as even a quick look at the developed producing countries, states, or provinces easily reveals.

A very important conclusion emerges from the research and analysis presented in the book, namely that the relationship between the natural resource-owning countries and the consuming nations can only lead to market stability if there is a willingness also to recognise and to acknowledge the legitimate rights of natural resource owners to obtain a benefit for granting access to exploit their property. At the same time, consumers must be guaranteed security of supply at a price level that will not have a disruptive impact on their economies, just as stated by OPEC, in 1960, in its Founding Resolution I.1. In this regard, propaganda campaigns against OPEC – trying to disqualify it by calling it a cartel, as if it were an agreement among companies to displace their competitors – have been completely useless. And it would be equally useless to try to disqualify the IEA by calling it a consumer cartel aimed at depressing prices.

The implicit assumption observed in very recent times, which must be made explicit in the near future, is the recognition of the legitimate rights of each one of the parties concerned. This should lead to a new period of stable relationships, with their positive effects on the market and the world.

Bernard Mommer is presenting us with a very important contribution to the understanding of this process. His book will definitely become a reference for theoretical and political researchers looking into one of the most complex issues in the world today.

Alí Rodríguez Araque

Vienna, January 2002

INTRODUCTION

This book is about upstream oil. It is, therefore, about oil as far as it is part of the primary sector of the economy, which includes all activities directly related to nature. These activities must be based on some system of land tenure, which is a complex scheme for assigning and distributing rights, or bundles of rights, in land and is to be found even in the most ancient and primitive of settled human communities. Rules were required about whom, when, where, to what end, to what extent, and at what consideration, rights of access to, and use of, the different parts of the natural habitat were to be allocated. Land had to be set apart for housing, burial grounds, hunting, fishing, agriculture, cattle grazing, mining, roads, and military use. These rules had to be worked out, of course, by the superior authority of the community, the *sovereign*, whether in the form of priests, warriors, the king, or some secular social or political group.

Moreover, a system of land tenure needs to develop and to adjust continuously, whether in response to population growth, economic development, political and social changes, or external challenges. The process of adaptation may be evolutionary, slow and peaceful and, as the sum of many small adjustments, only perceptible in a historical perspective; or the adaptation may result from a more far-reaching and explicit reform movement redefining, reassigning and redistributing rights. Moreover, these changes may happen without any formal changes in legislation, just reinterpreting existing laws and appealing to new court rulings. But adaptation is necessary to guarantee the lasting and successful existence of the sovereign community as such and, therefore, the rights in land always remain subject to its *eminent domain*. The lack of evolution and adaptation, on the other hand, may entail stagnation and decay of the sovereign community, or a new sovereign community may emerge from civil war and revolution. Last but not least, of course, there is also always the possibility of conquest.

By its very nature a system of land tenure is mostly a legacy of the past, albeit transformed and adapted to fit the present. Up to a certain point it has a life of its own, and the same

1

system may coexist with very different economic, social and political realities. What is more, different natural resources – we include all of them in the general term 'land' – due to their individual history may be subject to a variety of arrangements as there is no specific system of land tenure linked to capitalism. This is a very important fact to keep in mind. Of course, there are systems which are incompatible. All that a system requires to be compatible, however, is that it allows for the production of commodities although, in order to be an integral part of capitalism, it also has to allow for free labour. It does not require private landed property. Indeed, strictly speaking, as far as natural resources are concerned, the question is only one of rights of access, although in a modern society, based on private property of the produce of free labour, these rights are called, by analogy, property rights. There is nothing wrong with this usage, though it tends to obscure the fact that land always remains subject to eminent domain rights of the state. In Great Britain the term 'freehold' reminds us of this fact.

The eminent domain rights are essentially three: the right to tax, or to demand contributions in kind such as military services; the right to condemn, i.e. to revoke a right granted or conceded; and the right to police, i.e. to control and regulate. In modern societies these rights are normally used to guarantee that a system of land tenure actually delivers what it is supposed to deliver: the efficient access of producers to the natural resource. One way to achieve this end is to grant private landed property rights, and leave it to the market to sort things out. But this may not always be the best option.

Minerals – we include petroleum under this heading – provide clear illustrative examples of the foregoing. Most of those minerals that are relatively plentiful and are to be found close to the surface have usually been dealt with as part of the surface. However, things are more complex when it comes to minerals in short supply to be found at greater depth, where public ownership of the reservoirs combined with a system of concessions or licences for their development and production is, as we shall see, the better option. Yet due to accidents of history, though some of the deposits may have been in the public domain since ancient times, others have been subordinated to private surface property rights. Moreover, the situation may vary from one country to another, and even from one region to another within the same country. Thus, even if public ownership is the better option, politically it may be difficult if not impossible to achieve. Nevertheless, there has been a trend in the twentieth century towards public mineral ownership. Most importantly, this has been the case for oil and gas. However, both private and public mineral ownership only define different legal forms of access, and these can only be properly understood as part of a much more complex governance structure.

Governance is defined by a set of rules and a group of actors. There are basically four actors. Firstly, there are the holders of the rights to land. These rights often belong to a clearly identifiable group of landlords or property owners, although they may be widespread amongst the population; or, on the contrary, they may be concentrated in the hands of the state. Secondly, there are the producing companies, the investors, who have to secure, or acquire those rights. Thirdly, there are consumers who, at the end of the day, will have to foot the bill and pay the price of the goods in question. Last but not least, there is the government. The government is, obviously enough, the most complex actor. Its special involvement derives from the fact that, on the one hand, it holds the eminent domain rights of the state, but on the other hand it has to take into account all the interests at stake; it has to make sure that the specific governance structure actually delivers the goods at an acceptable price and fits into the general governance of the country.

Of course, defining the group of actors goes hand in hand with defining the appropriate set of rules. Yet once this has been done the governance structure soon develops into a web of legal, contractual, political, and social relations, and thus may become as difficult and costly to change as physical infrastructure. Although the original motivating circumstances may later change, even dramatically, there are very powerful economic, political and social reasons for new individual transactions to follow well-established patterns. To innovate may have a cost possibly too high to be covered by the profits of an individual transaction and may, therefore, require collective action – i.e. the application of sovereign domain rights – which may well be difficult to achieve given the importance and diversity of vested interests.

For example, in the case of private mineral ownership, one part of the cost of governance is the customary ground rent paid to landowners. Perhaps surprisingly, our studies on the governance structures of British coal and American oil – both historically based on private mineral ownership – show that this may not be the most important part of the costs associated with private mineral ownership. There are also legal and administrative costs, which can be very significant.[1] More difficult to measure but no less important are higher production costs and constraints to the development of productivity. The latter may not have been a significant problem in some distant past, when pit or well depths were a few hundred feet, but they may become a serious problem with growing depths. Hence, property rights need to be redefined accordingly. The responsibility for promoting reform usually falls to the producing companies. In the case of American oil they carried it out successfully. In the case of British coal reform failed because of the exceptional importance of landlords in British politics and society. In the end, in 1938, the economic costs of governance of British coal became unacceptable, and coal was taken back into the public domain. Too late for reform, the nationalisation of the natural resource led to the nationalisation of the coal industry a few years later. The latter was eventually reversed, but not the former.

In Mexican oil it was the political cost of private mineral ownership, which, in the midst of an agrarian revolution, became unbearable. Reform failed due to the opposition of a counter-revolutionary alliance of Mexican landlords and foreign companies and governments. Hence, the decision to nationalise the natural resource, taken in 1917, led also to the nationalisation of the tenant companies some two decades later.[2]

Today private mineral ownership in oil only survives in the United States as a historical relic. Moreover, apart from the few exceptions already mentioned, public mineral ownership was established elsewhere before there was any significant production of oil. Thus, for example, in the Third World oil-

---

1.   This also obtains for the surface (Offer 1981).
2.   We omit the example of Romania, where the events in 1947 and 1948 followed similar patterns but were overshadowed by the advent of communism (Pearton 1971).

exporting countries public ownership was the starting point. An international governance structure developed under the leadership of the international oil companies, even though each case had its own national roots. Nevertheless, national governance structures were basically a transplant of the American governance of oil, albeit adjusted to public ownership. In spite of serious problems early on in Iran and the debacle in Mexico, they evolved and even prospered for a while. However, with the end of colonialism and the advent of independence and nationhood, all oil-exporting countries, newly independent or not and in unison with the rest of the Third World, claimed *Permanent Sovereignty over Natural Resources* (United Nations 1962), the right to redefine their role in the governance of international oil. In the early 1970s, after the OPEC revolution the transplants were rejected (Mény 1993), the concessions were condemned, the international tenant companies were downgraded to service providers and, in this sense, they too were nationalised.

In the twentieth century, therefore, we witnessed the collapse of governance structures in the oil-exporting countries, regardless of whether they were based on private or public mineral ownership. Private mineral ownership was clearly intolerable, but public ownership as such was not enough to bring about stable governance. The international governance structure of oil, with the OPEC revolution, broke up into two extremely different systems. One system, dominated by the governments of the exporting countries, relied on their eminent domain rights, which were understood as sovereign national property rights. Collectively they set up a new governance structure. The national companies could be used at will as tax-collecting agents to maximise international ground rent, a role the international companies could not accept. At the other extreme, the new system, also dominated by governments but from the consuming countries, was based on a desperate bid to contain the consequent increases in prices. The formerly dominant players and intermediaries, the international oil companies, were pushed aside together with the old American reference, and the consuming countries redesigned collectively their governance structure in order to achieve lower prices. The ultimate objective of the consuming countries, moreover, is once again to transplant their new governance system into the oil-exporting countries.

This includes the return of private investors but, as we shall see, not the outright privatisation of the national oil companies. After the unexpected collapse and disintegration of the Soviet Union, the first systematic and large-scale experiment has been taking place in the potentially oil-rich and newly independent Central Asian republics. However, the consuming countries have also achieved important breakthroughs in traditional oil-exporting countries, most notably in Venezuela.

Overview

Modern economic science considers the ownership of natural resources irrelevant to the determination of prices. Competition is supposed to shape, and ultimately to streamline, the conditions of ownership in a way that guarantees the free flow of investment. This book, on the contrary, focuses on the role of natural resource ownership, the constraints it may impose on the flow of investment and, ultimately, its incidence on prices. Yet when it comes to governance structures, the importance of a theory, or an argument, goes far beyond being right or wrong in some narrowly defined scientific sense. Hence, in the theoretical parts of this book we will not only develop our own framework, but we shall also bring the relevant economic theory into the context of governance. Then, as we shall see, what modern economic science really does is to send out to the rest of the world a strong message: the ownership of natural resources *should* not matter.

On the other hand, governance structures 'cannot be evaluated with reference to discrete, isolated decisions, but must be assessed in terms of sequences of interdependent decisions taken by a variety of actors over a period of time' (Majone 1989: 98). In the case of oil the relevant period of time is to be measured in decades rather than years. Thus, we have to look through its history, which extends over one century and a half, though this is not a history book. But only history provides us with the necessary sample and sequence of experiments. Still, this is a small sample, in which we shall include British coal amongst our case studies, since outside the United States this is the only fully-fledged example of private mineral governance. It will provide us with useful insights on mineral governance generally.

Thus, Chapter 1 deals with the theoretical background of private mineral governance. Chapter 2 discusses the relevant examples, which are British coal, American and Mexican oil. The three cases have in common the fact that they were rooted in private mineral ownership, though today only one – American oil – still is. Chapter 3 deals with the theoretical background of public mineral governance. Then, in Chapter 4, we cover the first half of the twentieth century with the international oil companies as the dominant players setting up a first international governance structure. The globe was the playground for this game, and the sequences of interdependent decisions to be assessed linked together different parts of the world, and different levels of national and international politics and policymaking. Thus, we shall first give a detailed account of Venezuelan oil. This Latin American country, independent since the early nineteenth century, provides us with an exceptionally rich and varied example of governance in an oil-exporting country. Then we switch to the Middle East where, properly speaking, the first international governance structure of oil emerged after the First World War, with the 'International Petroleum Cartel' (United States Senate 1952) at its centre. This structure was successfully challenged, collectively, by the Organisation of the Petroleum Exporting Countries (OPEC). We deal with OPEC, the association of landlord states, in Chapter 5. As the OPEC revolution also entailed the nationalisation of the industry, it brought onto the stage the governments of the developed consuming countries. It was now their turn to move closer together and to associate in the International Energy Agency (IEA). The development of a new governance structure in the consuming countries is the subject of Chapter 6, followed by cases studies in Chapter 7. The ideal type of this structure emerged first in the British North Sea, a new oil-producing province. However, the implementation of the new structure confronts difficulties in the United States, as the example of Alaska will show. The most important producing and consuming country of the world in the twentieth century finds it difficult if not impossible to overcome its old privately-rooted governance structure. Surprisingly enough, the consuming countries were more successful in exporting their model to Venezuela, a traditional oil-exporting country. On the other hand, they also succeeded in promoting the Energy Charter Treaty (ECT) whose principal purpose is to graft their governance structure onto the potentially oil-rich newly independent Republics surrounding the Caspian Sea and, above all, onto Russia.

In the end we are left with a world divided between two regimes, one of which – that of the consuming countries – is engaged in a struggle to bring down the other. What are the perspectives? Will this story end with the collapse of the OPEC revolution, similar to the collapse of the Bolshevik revolution? Or is this analogy wrong? Indeed, it is. The consuming countries have been relocating sovereignty at global levels, where consumer interests tend to prevail, embodying sovereign rights in international treaties in precedence over territorial sub-divisions. Yet it is hard to see how nations, national and regional communities, and surface dwellers generally, may simply be ignored. History tells us a very different story. The concluding Chapter 8 is as much retrospective as it is an assessment of prevailing trends, and counter-trends, of an ongoing tug-of-war.

1 PRIVATE GOVERNANCE OF MINERAL RESOURCES: FUNDAMENTALS

1.1 Private vs. Public Mineral Ownership

The issue of mineral ownership was the subject of a remarkable parliamentary debate in revolutionary France in 1791. The debate in the National Assembly started from the assumption that the Nation was entitled to fully benefit from all its natural resources. Regarding the surface, it concluded that the best way to achieve this end was by granting private property rights to the occupiers, very much in the spirit of the slogan *the land to the tiller*, and leave it to the market to allocate the land to its most appropriate use. If necessary, to prevent abuses or correct market failures, the state could still rely on its eminent domain rights. Regarding the subsoil, however, doubts were raised about whether this would be enough. There was certainly nothing to worry about as long as the minerals were to be found close to the surface and, hence, within reach of those working it. Accordingly, the Mining Act of 1791 – to this day the basis of the French law of mineral ownership – confirmed the surface owners' rights to mine all minerals that could be worked open-air, in daylight and with excavations down to the depth of one hundred feet. There was no reason to worry about minerals such as sand, chalk, clay, and stone for construction. Their widespread existence guaranteed an abundant supply at a reasonable price. But for other minerals (different kinds of coal or bitumen, for example) which were scarce close to the surface or which were located only at greater depth, two major problems had to be faced. On the one hand, the deeper the mine the more costly and difficult it would be to adjust to the fragmentation of private surface property rights. In the words of Mirabeau:

> The recesses of the earth do not lend themselves to partition; mineral seams, due to their random nature, even less so. As to the surface, the interest of society is that properties should be subdivided, whereas in the recesses of the earth, on the other hand, it would be necessary to bring them together. For this reason, it would be absurd to allow legislation subordinating

9

the property of minerals to the property of the surface and its delineation. (Mirabeau 1792: 443–45)[1]

On the other hand, deeper mining required technical knowledge and significant amounts of capital, hardly available to the individual surface owner:

> To dig pits, to secure them, to push back the water continually; to drill tunnels through the rocks, and to prevent them from collapsing ...; to have sufficient funds for a great number of workers ...; finally, to have at one's disposal sufficient credit to get the huge amounts of capital required, and to be able to secure the deepest knowledge of an art that requires the assistance of nearly every science. Can this possibly be expected from isolated proprietors? Most of them even do not have sufficient resources to cultivate the surface of their land. (Mirabeau 1792: 445–46)

It was the same guiding principle, *the land to the tiller* or, to paraphrase, *the mineral to the miner*, which led to the conclusion that certain minerals should remain in the public domain. The search for and production of these minerals were subject to a permit, licence (British English), or concession (American English), and these activities were declared to be of '*utilité publique*', i.e. directed to the public benefit. Thus eminent domain rights would prevail over private surface property rights, guaranteeing to the permit holders the necessary ancillary rights. 'There is no other purpose or motive for eminent domain rights to prevail but the working of the minerals' (Mirabeau 1792: 441). Hence, if surface owners were qualified and willing to explore and to mine their land, the Act of 1791 guaranteed them the right to do so. 'The owners of the surface will always be preferred. If they desire so, the franchise of working the minerals which may be found in their lands cannot be denied to them' (Mirabeau 1792: 445–46). But, if they were not qualified, or not willing, they had definitely no right to obstruct or to prevent others from exploring and mining their land. The state, accordingly, was not the proprietor of the mineral resources but only their administrator:

> The national assembly decrees, *as a constitutional article*, that metallic and non-metallic minerals, as well as different kinds of

---

1.   All translations are ours.

bitumen, coal, and pyrite, belong to the nation but only in the
sense that they cannot be worked without her consent. (Mirabeau
1792: 491; Italics in the original)

These minerals, which had belonged to the Crown in the pre-
revolutionary past, remained in the public domain. However,
legitimately acquired rights of pre-revolutionary origin were
respected. The rights of existing concessionaires, or their
assignees, were accepted as such if they had actually discovered
the mines they were working. Their rights were to be phased
out over the next fifty years. In the case of open cast mines,
they were required to hold 'a free, legal and written authorisation
from the surface owners' (Mirabeau 1792: 492f).

In sum, regarding certain minerals, private surface property
rights had to be restricted in order to prevent them from
becoming obstructive. 'The nation has the right to the minerals
being exploited. Hence, if they are not, the nation has to
provoke their exploitation' (Mirabeau 1792: 483). Regarding
other minerals, however, there was no justification for public
ownership. 'Society has the right to their being exploited, and
only to that. Hence, society should not intervene whenever their
exploitation is sufficiently granted' (Mirabeau 1792: 489).
Where markets could not provide an efficient allocation of
resources, the government had to intervene. In principle all
natural resources, soil and subsoil alike, were considered free
gifts of nature.[2] This, then, is the *liberal* ideal; accordingly, public
or private mineral ownership only represent different ways to
put it into practice.

1.2 Private Ownership

With private mineral ownership the industry gains access to the
natural resource by virtue of lease contracts. Regarding such
contracts, tenant companies are normally the active, and the
landlords the passive participants. It is usually the tenants who
approach the landlords and, hence, the former have to convince
the latter. One may safely suppose that the tenants will talk a
lot about uncertainty and risk. They will also certainly point

---

2. For a well-documented overview of the historical debate on this subject
regarding the surface, see Guigou (1982).

out that in the case of failure they alone will have to endure the losses, whereas in the case of success the landlords will share in the benefits in one way or another. But time is money, as the saying goes, and nothing is more convincing than cash upfront. Hence, a signature bonus is the most effective device to entice the landlords to sign a lease contract as soon as possible.

Its amount depends, generally speaking, on expectations and probabilities and, of course, the distribution of knowledge between the negotiating parties. Indeed, if we assume a first-time lease, its term is usually divided into two periods. There is a 'primary' period to search for the mineral, actually an exploration permit with a lease option, followed by a 'secondary' period of development and production if exploration is successful. The primary period usually extends – in American oil, for example – over a couple of years, though it may last as long as fifteen years or even longer. During this period there are annual rentals to be paid and, again, their amounts depend basically on the same variables already mentioned regarding bonuses. Anyway, even in the event of complete failure the landlords get some ground rent.

On the other hand, mining companies are continuously looking out for new leases, even though they may already have been successful and their proven reserves may be more than sufficient. The reason is that depletion implies rising costs though not necessarily increasing prices, because the development of productivity, new technologies, and the accumulation of geological knowledge act as countervailing forces; and new geological data derive not only from working existing leases but also from exploring new lands. 'Exploration is needed *to prevent an otherwise inevitable rise in developing-operating costs*' (Adelman 1972: 74. Italics in the original). For this reason, the tenant companies are always interested in acquiring new land as soon as they can afford the ground rent the landlords demand, together with the usual profit.

Hence, there is a permanent flow of investment into new land and, increasingly, once the industry has settled down, the new land tends to be marginal. In these instances the agreed ground rent is likely to equate to the marginal ground rent in old leases. As a result, a customary ground rent will emerge.

Customary Ground Rent

The usual profit rate, an expected minimum below which the tenant will refrain from making an investment, is not specific to mineral ventures, as competition tends to equalise profit rates across the board. The situation is different regarding the customary ground rent, a minimum below which the landlord will not lease his land. This benchmark is specific to each mineral, as there is no alternative use for mineral deposits. On the other hand, the existence of this minimum is actually much easier to prove than the usual profit rate, as ground rent is defined explicitly in the contract whereas profit is a residue. All it takes to identify the customary ground rent is to compare a number of leases. During the primary term (exploration) it consists, as already mentioned, in a signature bonus and a surface rental. During the secondary term (production) there will still be a surface rental to be paid but also, more importantly, a royalty, i.e. a certain amount of money per unit of production (British coal) or a percentage (British coal and American oil). We shall now concentrate on royalty, which is by far the most important single payment.

Both fixed and percentage royalties relate directly to volumes and thus establish a link to the size of the reservoirs and their depletion. The bigger the discovery, the more the landlords get in royalties over the years. Moreover, if the tenant invests and produces faster or slower than was originally forecast, it does not matter too much. Ground rent varies accordingly, and so does, inversely, the remaining size of the mineral deposit. In other words, landlords and tenants share the risk regarding volumes. Therefore the landlords have the right to check volumes and, by the same token, they also have the right to demand a proper treatment of the mineral deposits to prevent them from being over-exploited, which would result in lower recovery factors. Thus tenants are required, contractually, to follow best-established procedures and techniques. With percentage royalties, landlords also share the price risk and, therefore, in this case they also need to check prices, and they usually also have the right to take their royalties in kind. If they do so, the tenants are obliged to hand over the volume concerned according to the instructions of the landlords.

The advantage of percentage royalties in long-term contracts is that they are inflation-proof. The disadvantage is the cost of observing prices, although this cost will be lower the more developed and, hence, transparent the markets are. In my opinion, that is the reason why fixed royalties in British coal represent the earlier form and why they tended to be displaced later, in new regions, by percentage royalties. Fixed royalties were never seriously considered in American oil, a more recent industry that emerged only in the second half of the nineteenth century. Moreover, as in transparent markets observation costs are low, the option of royalty in kind is rarely exercised. The existence of the option is, however, an effective threat to the tenant.

Royalties draw a clear line between landlords and tenants. Landlords have a say regarding the natural resource, including adequate, efficient and modern methods of working them. But for the rest they do not intervene in the management of the producing companies. Prices, on the other hand, are supposed to be determined by markets, not by individual tenants or landlords. Hence investors benefit, or suffer, from the consequences of good or poor management, and the ups and downs of the markets. And there is no incentive problem, since landlords do not share risks regarding profits.

Then there is the question of the royalty rate. For example, in American oil, the customary royalty in most regions is one eighth, or 12.5 per cent, and this has been the case since the late 1860s; in some regions, however, the customary rate is one sixth, or 16.67 per cent. These percentages, the historical outcome of a collective bargaining process, became an accepted datum-point. One may wonder, however, why the tenants have not later tried to negotiate lower percentages. The answer to this question is fourfold. Firstly, there are significant savings to be achieved by not starting the bargaining process all over again in each case. To have a customary royalty rate at hand, enabling the company to tell the landlords that 'that is what your neighbours get', is certainly timesaving. Secondly, if a lease cannot support the customary royalty, it is probably not worth engaging in lengthy negotiations to convince the landlord that this is actually the case. Thirdly, once the reference has been set, it may be dangerous to go for less. The landlady – for instance, a widow, poor, elderly, and ill – who lets herself be talked into agreeing to a lower royalty may later go to court and sue her tenant with a fair chance of winning; or her heirs may do so. Thus the existence of a customary royalty adds to legal certainty, a very important point to investors. Finally, a customary royalty creates a level playing field between tenants. It adds uniformly to marginal production costs and, hence, to prices. In other words, consumers pay for the customary ground rent, and tenants act only as the landlords' ground rent-collecting agents. Though consumers never actually negotiated it, nor were they consulted, they accept the result for very much the same reasons as they accept prices generally provided they are the outcome of competitive markets.

Conversely, one may wonder why landlords have not later tried to negotiate higher percentages. *Mutatis mutandis* the answer would be basically the same. It requires an extraordinary event for a change in customary royalty rates. As we shall see, such a unique event was the OPEC revolution of the early 1970s.

Differential or Ricardian Rents

New mineral lands coming on the market are not always marginal. Technological development and the accumulation of geological knowledge are not necessarily smooth or predictable. Sudden and surprising improvements happen, and land that was sub marginal yesterday may become economic today. One should bear in mind that improvements that are relevant include refining technologies and transportation. The former affects the quality differences between crudes, which may become wider or narrower, and the latter is of particular importance in more remote regions. Moreover, a plot of land may not be able to be leased at a given time, because its ownership is in dispute but later, when the dispute has been solved and it comes on the market, it may become economically attractive. Of course, the opposite may happen; a tract of land may become once again sub marginal because of disappointing results in exploring the neighbourhood, changes in price expectations, and so on.

Anyway, there are always some parcels of land becoming available that may command higher ground rents or profits than usual. These excess rents are generally called economic rents; more specifically, when these economic rents result from the exceptional richness and fertility of nature, they are called differential, or Ricardian, rents. In a competitive market they will accrue to the landlords who appropriate them in the same way as the customary ground rent, i.e. through higher and additional bonuses – payable, for example, when accumulated production has reached a certain amount – higher rentals, and higher royalty rates.

Tenants and landlords may prefer the first two devices. However, if the expected differential rents are large, in lieu of very high payments upfront it may be advantageous to both sides to agree on higher royalties. Yet higher royalties have one important drawback. Adding to marginal costs, they will eventually force an earlier closure of the mines or abandonment of the wells approaching exhaustion. A solution to this might be to apply a sliding-scale royalty based, for example, on output per well. Indeed, on public land in the United States, some experiments in this direction have taken place, but with disappointing results because of a substantial increase in administrative costs:

> The lessor may determine that the lessee is constraining output in order to reduce his royalty obligation and the lessor may want to introduce a production monitoring program to enforce production at a level that maximises current output, subject to physical constraints. All of these problems lead to disputes and to litigation resulting in higher administrative costs for both lessee and lessor, resulting in a reduction or dissipation of the economic rent. (Mead 1993: 241)

Not surprisingly, profit sharing performs even worse. Heavy administrative costs are needed to prevent the lessee from systematically minimising the calculation of the profits to be shared. Indeed, the lessee may 'import' costs from downstream, or even from any other unrelated business or 'export' profits by outsourcing and subcontracting the different activities that constitute production. Thus, profit sharing requires a thorough understanding of the business, which places the landlord at a disadvantage. 'The benefits of the project may accrue primarily or entirely to the lessee firm' (Mead 1993: 244).

Bonuses, rentals, and flat royalty rates may be considered as primitive ground rent-collecting devices, but they have some decisive advantages compared with more sophisticated ones such as sliding-scale royalties and profit sharing. They are relatively cheap and easy to administer, incentive problems are minor, and surveillance costs are reasonably low.

Reversion and Renewal of Leases

With the benefit of hindsight, expectation may have been too high or too low. If the former is the case, the tenant may even not get the usual average profit. This, of course, does not necessarily mean that he will actually cut short the lease. He may carry on, if only to recover part of his initial investment. But if expectation is surpassed, he will enjoy excess profits, at least as long as the first lease contract lasts. For this reason the lease term matters. As tenants normally have the right to surrender the lease at any time, they have everything to win and nothing to lose with longer terms; their motto is 'the longer the better'. By the same token landlords prefer shorter terms and, of course, they have no right to cut short the lease. Yet there is a technically and economically determined minimum. Mining ventures have a lead-time of many years and, once production is under way, to recover the investment with a profit may take even longer. Moreover, mineral deposits or reservoirs may have a long life and, if they do, their efficient working is associated with a continuous flow of investment. This flow may be hampered by the approaching end of the lease term. This is the second reason for the term of the lease being important.

Upon renewal of a lease, landlords may seem to be in a position to collect not only all remaining differential rents but also all economic rents actually created during the first lease term by the tenants. In practice, however, it may be as early as fifteen years before the end of the contractual term that tenants stop making long-term investments or even carrying out maintenance works and, therefore, cause the facilities to deteriorate before they are handed back. The more derelict they are on the day a lease ends, and the more urgent is the need for new investment, the greater the bargaining power of the tenants. Furthermore, while unworked mineral deposits or reservoirs do not require maintenance, when they are partially worked they may be destroyed and lost forever if they are not maintained or worked continuously. Thus landlords have a serious problem, since to survey and monitor effectively the flow of investment and the maintenance of underground facilities is a very costly task. Moreover, at the time of signing the contracts reversion is a long time away, and there is little point in spending a lot of money on detailing such an uncertain and distant event.[3] Thus, both parties tend to settle for a lease term and a good-will clause under which tenants will surrender leases in good working condition. In other words, the market solution is, strictly speaking, not to solve the problem but to postpone it by renegotiating contracts a number of years before their expiry date, though this practice may still have a deleterious effect on productivity.

Beyond the market, however, there is the world of politics, the law and the courts, where the problem of reversion may be settled. Indeed, for American oil the lease term was simply extended, in the 1880s, until the exhaustion of the reservoirs. In other words, reversion disappeared to the benefit of tenants and consumers. For British coal, on the other hand, landlords were successful in preventing such an outcome.

Conservation

The most important problem of private mineral property rights with growing mine depths is the fragmentation of the surface. Optimal production methods require that mineral deposits be worked as geological units. Hence, technical co-operation between landlords and tenants on the same structure is necessary for their efficient working. By not co-operating, or even by refusing to lease a strategically located piece of land, landlords may cause very significant damage. Worse, the fragmentation of the surface tends to generate a mirror image of tenants equally fragmented and unwilling, or unable, to co-operate.

There are, of course, differences from one mineral to another. There is no case for co-operation more convincing than natural gas, able to migrate over large distances. It is followed quite

---

3.   This is a general rule. As Laffont and Tirole have pointed out, 'one would expect the part of the contract concerning the near future to be more complete than that concerning the distant future'. (Laffont and Tirole 1993: 3)

closely by crude oil, a liquid. Hence, landlords and tenants on the same reservoir are strongly tied together, willingly or unwillingly, for better or for worse. But the importance of co-operation even in the case of solid minerals should not be underestimated. Prevention of flooding and water pumping generally makes up a significant part of expenditure in deeper mines. Both can best be tackled if there is co-operation. Moreover, with increasing mine depths the optimal location of shafts becomes more and more important and, precisely because solid minerals do not migrate, this is even more important than the case of oil and gas wells.

There is, then, a clear case for governments to encourage landlords and tenants, if not to compel them by law and regulations, to co-operate as far as required by geology. Both are still supposed, of course, to compete in their respective market places, for lease contracts or for markets of the mineral produced. Moreover, as we are dealing with scarce minerals – scarce almost by definition, as they have to be searched for and lifted from great depths – the question is not only one of costs but also of quantities. Co-operation also increases the recovery factor. When a deposit or reservoir is abandoned and said to be exhausted, the mineral recovered may represent only a modest percentage of the mineral *in situ*. Hence, *waste vs. conservation* is the catch phrase by which these issues of co-operation are known.

Whatever their form, conservation policies always amount to restricting the landlords' property rights who, not surprisingly, tend to react with mistrust. Individually, and even collectively, landlords may actually lose out. Certainly, the recovery factor will increase, but lower costs will entail lower prices. Hence, out of each reservoir, though more royalty oil will be produced, it will be paid for at lower prices. The reduction of costs does not directly favour landlords but their tenants. The tenants, on the other hand, as already pointed out, though they will certainly benefit collectively from lower costs, will not all benefit individually. Some may lose out too and, anyway, to adapt to and to implement new laws and regulations also entails additional costs before generating benefits. Moreover, ill-conceived regulations may entail higher costs than benefits.

Consequently, policy debates on conservation are complex,

and may be quite confusing. The driving forces behind the scene are normally the tenants with the landlords in opposition, but there is no clear-cut line. In the realm of politics, it is the professionals who come to the fore, to stress the technical character of the issues at stake and to dissociate them from individual interests. As consumers are ultimately the true beneficiaries of successful conservation policies, one might expect them to be sympathetic to necessary legal reforms and regulations. However, they are usually passive, at least as long as the mining sector in question is able to cope with its problems and to deliver a reasonable result. All in all, this has been the case in American oil; in British coal, however, it produced a deadlock.

1.3   Economic Science and Natural Resource Ownership

In the early days of political economy landlords and natural resources, not surprisingly, played a major role. To Turgot, writing in 1766, all surplus value was still ground rent whereas profits and wages were not distinguished. Land and labour were the two original factors of production (Turgot 1898). However, hardly ten years later Smith distinguished systematically between land, labour and capital (Smith 1950). By 1817, Ricardo had already started to dismantle the trilogy and to reduce it to the binomial of modern economics, labour and capital (Ricardo 1821). Land had been 'assimilated to capital' (Blaug 1968: 78).

Natural resources had been taken out of the visible hands of the landlords and placed into the invisible hands of the market. Hence, they became a commodity to be bought and sold like any other. It was no longer deemed necessary to consider private landed property to be a category of its own. From the viewpoint of bourgeois economic theory at least, the revolutionary transformation of Europe was over. In practice, of course, it was a protracted process extending well into the twentieth century, and the outcome was full of compromises.

Ricardian Rent Theory and Private Landed Property

The alleged irrelevance of private landed property in economics is based on the assumption that it has no bearing on prices. Smith still believed, on the contrary, that in some cases and, most importantly, in the case of corn, private landed property was able to impose a customary ground rent, thus causing higher-than-otherwise prices. But Ricardo believed Smith to be wrong, and constructed a theoretical model, which, known as 'Ricardian rent theory', is an unquestioned part of modern economics. In its current version it states that the price of natural resources is determined, like that of all other goods, by its marginal production cost including, of course, the usual profit, with no role at all for the 'appropriation of land and the consequent creation of [ground] rent' (Ricardo 1821: 45). However, as lands of different qualities, or additional investment in the same lands at decreasing productivity, are required to satisfy demand, *economic rents* appear even on lands of poorest quality. Hence, tenants can always afford to pay some ground rent. In other words, the empirical fact that tenants always pay some ground rent is compatible with the assumption that the marginal ground rent on production is zero. Moreover, competition amongst tenants will drive those economic rents, in the form of ground rent, into the pockets of the landlords; but, because of competition in the product market, there is a limit to what can be paid. Therefore, once lease contracts have been signed, the tenants will be compelled to invest, and expand production, as long as it is profitable to do so, i.e. up to the point where long-term marginal production costs are equal to market prices.

Yet the crucial question is not the marginal ground rent on production. Even if it were zero in all *existing* leases, this does not exclude the possibility that some lands may not have been leased because they cannot command the ground rent the landlords were asking for. If this were systematically the case, demand would have to be met by additional investments into a reduced area, and necessarily at higher marginal production costs. The outcome would be higher prices. It is true that one may argue that the landlady who in the end does not lease her land loses out, yet it is equally true that the landlady who accepts a low ground rent will not be able to take advantage of a better opportunity later on.

But there is worse. Ricardo's model depends on the *form* of ground rent. If it is a fixed annual payment, at his time already the most usual form in British agriculture, there is no problem, in the sense that one can imagine the marginal produce paying no ground rent. Yet if we suppose that the tenants are sharecroppers, the ground rent consisting of a certain percentage of the harvest whether paid in cash or kind, then there is no marginal produce that does not pay ground rent and, *a fortiori*, there is a positive marginal ground rent on all investment. And contrary to Ricardo's expectations, sharecropping has not disappeared completely in agriculture. Though it is, indeed, an ancient form of ground rent, it is also a modern one. It is even quite widespread in thoroughly modern countries like the United States. Moreover, in mining the equivalent of sharecropping, i.e. royalty, has remained the dominant form of ground rent.[4] In other words, Ricardian rent theory in these cases is simply not compatible with reality.

Smith did in fact report some examples of this kind, for instance forests in Norway and coalmines and stone quarries in Scotland and England. Ricardo, in order to invalidate them, resorted to redefining ground rent in a very peculiar way:

> [Ground] rent is that portion of the produce of the earth, which is paid to the landlord for the use of the original and indestructible powers of the soil. (Ricardo 1821: 67)

Accordingly, fixed or percentage royalties were paid in 'consideration of the valuable commodity' (Ricardo 1821: 67) taken out of the land, and they were not ground rent at all. Thus, 'royalty is *not* a [ground]rent', wrote Marshall in 1890, but the price for 'the sale of stored-up goods', albeit 'stored-up by nature' (Marshall 1961: 483; Italics in the original). Hence, there is no denying, 'the marginal supply price of minerals includes a royalty in addition to the marginal expenses of working the mine'. Moreover, Marshall stated explicitly, and quite ingeniously, that this was due to the fact that those goods stored up by nature were 'now treated as private property'. Thus, it is the institution of private property that determines the existence of royalty, the price to be paid for a natural

---

4.   Marx apparently shared Ricardo's prejudice against sharecropping and royalties as medieval and incompatible with capitalism (Marx 1966: 795ff).

resource. This ignores the question of its quantity to which Marshall has no answer. He only remarks that:

> Royalty ... when accurately adjusted, represents the diminution in the value of the mine, regarded as a source of wealth in the future, which is caused by taking the [mineral] out of nature's storehouse. (Marshall 1961: 483)

Indeed, once a mineral deposit or reservoir is 'assimilated' to capital, a wasting asset, royalty may be associated to depreciation. Regarding royalty rates, however, this analogy is of no help, as the 'value of the mine' – i.e. the minerals deposit, the natural resource as such – is nothing but the net present value of future royalty payments. Marshall's reasoning is circular.

Marshall had British coal in mind. In American oil, Davidson followed the same reasoning. After acknowledging the fact that there is indeed a customary royalty of one eighth he argued:

> Nevertheless, since royalties provisions are fixed at the outset and depend upon expectations of the future income stream from the well, royalties are, in the long run, price-determined rather than price determining. (Davidson 1963a: 90)

Once more we are sent from pillar to post. It is noteworthy, however, that although American economists agree on Ricardian rent theory as far as it states the irrelevance of private landed property, they do not agree on Ricardo's, or Marshall's, conception of royalty. They are less accommodating regarding the landlords than their British counterparts. Thus, in Davidson's opinion 'oil lands are obviously analogous to the Ricardian case of agricultural lands of differing fertilities' (Davidson 1963b: 126), and 'the lease bonus and royalty payments are ... Ricardian rent payments' (Davidson 1963a: 104). Indeed, royalties may be regarded as an approximation to Ricardian rents. Though ground rent 'under conditions of perfect competition, which assumes perfect knowledge' would be equal to Ricardian rents, 'in the real world of imperfect knowledge' (McDonald 1979: 36) things are somewhat different:

> Royalty affects the margin of land use for mineral extraction and also, to a degree, the price of extracted minerals. This seems to contradict our earlier repeated assertion that rent is price determined, not price determining, but it does so only by

> appearance. Pure economic rent … does not affect price, but a
> fixed royalty as a contractual rent form … does not coincide
> precisely with pure economic rent. It is the nature of the contract,
> not the nature of economic rent, that causes the rent payment
> to affect price. (McDonald 1979: 36)

Yes, indeed, the 'nature of the contract' that causes ground
rent payments to affect prices stems from the fact that one of
the two contracting parties is the proprietor of the natural
resource. But as there is a fundamental consensus in economics
that private landed property doesn't matter, the professional
economists looking at the real world through the lenses of
Ricardian rent theory discover, at best, not that there is
something wrong with the theory but that the real world is
imperfect.

Landlord–tenant relationships and the question of ground
rent in the end disappeared from economics. Jevons' *Coal Question*
(Jevons 1965) dealing with the British coal industry, published
in 1865, does not once mention the words 'rent', 'royalty', or
'lease'. Similarly, the economic literature on the American oil
industry usually mentions the fact that the industry is based on
leases only *en passant* and, preferably, in a footnote.[5] I am aware
only of one feeble, and failed, attempt by an economist ever
trying to explain the existence of a customary royalty.[6] The
landlords have been willed away so consistently and radically
that even the specific vocabulary has disappeared. Rent, at the
time of Smith and Ricardo, meant ground rent. Today,
according to *The New Palgrave* it means more or less any kind of
income.[7] Ricardian rents are considered just an example of
economic rents, which occur wherever there are market
imperfections, whether in the primary, secondary or tertiary
sector. Therefore, to prevent any misunderstanding, we use in
this book the more cumbersome but less equivocal term 'ground
rent'. Moreover, it may be worth pointing out that *The New*

---

5. See, for example, De Chazeau and Kahn 1959.
6. See the debate in Davidson 1963a, Campbell 1963, and Davidson 1963b.
7. 'Rent is the payment for use of a resource, whether it be land, labour,
   equipment, ideas, or even money. Typically, the rent for labour is called
   'wages'; the payment for land and equipment is often called 'rent'; the
   payment for use of an idea is called a 'royalty'; and the payment for use
   of money is called 'interest'.' (The New Palgrave 1998)

Palgrave has no entry for 'royalty'. Indeed, the use of this word in mining is of relatively recent vintage. At the time of Smith and Ricardo 'royalty' still referred exclusively to ground rent paid to the Royals. They never used this term in their writings (Nef 1932: Vol.1, 318f). In modern economic literature on mining, especially in American literature, all ground rent payments are frequently referred to, all-inclusively, as 'royalties'. On the other hand, the word 'mine' may refer to both, to the mineral deposit as well as to the system of excavations in the earth for their exploitation. Hence the term 'mine owner' may refer indiscriminately to landlord or tenant.

Similarly confusing is the fact that in modern economics, as we have seen, there are actually *two* versions, or further developments, of Ricardian rent theory. One version takes no position regarding minerals, and is broadminded enough to disregard the nature of royalties as ground rent and to accommodate them as a compensation for a wasting asset. It reflects the practical necessity of compromise, to live and to let live. Still, it is only a practical compromise; royalty is only tolerated in disguise, as the counterpart of a wasting asset. The second, more radical version brings royalty into the realm of differential rent, as an approximate solution worked out by the market.

Taxation. Pure economic rents, by definition, do not affect the flow of investment or, ultimately, production. And as landlords, according to Ricardo, did nothing but collect them as ground rent, they were not responsible for the high price of corn. Apparently he was defending the landlords. However, he developed his argument further and concluded that for this very reason they were actually ideal targets for taxation (Ricardo 1821: 173). The idea that ground rent should be subject to special taxes, which would allow lower taxes elsewhere, is as old as political economy itself. French Physiocrats already advocated it in the eighteenth century. Moreover, there was debate on the convenience of taking all natural resources into the public domain, to be administered through a system of licences or concessions. Yet according to Ricardo, public or private landed property were all the same, and it was only taxation that made a difference.

Once 'assimilated' to capital, peace was made with private landed property and the idea of special taxes was not taken further. On the contrary, as soon as lands were regularly sold and bought, ground rents appeared as 'capital gains', which are frequently subject to lower tax rates than ordinary profits or rents. In the case of minerals, on the other hand, by conceiving royalties as the counterpart of a wasting asset a more convincing case can be made for tax privileges. In the United States, for example, minerals enjoy, as we shall see, a unique tax privilege known as 'depletion allowance'.

Free Trade. Yet Ricardo was serious about the importance of competition in the product market. In particular, he opposed the British Corn Law of 1815, which prohibited imports of corn if prices fell below a certain level. The Law was finally repealed in 1846. With free trade, imports from all over the world brought lower prices weakening the British, and more generally European, landlords. However, the first response to lower prices was the development of productivity, an increase in investment per acre, and not a fall in ground rent per acre. The full weight of the developing world market, spurred on by new transportation technologies, was only felt in the last quarter of the nineteenth century, when landlords finally had no other choice than to adjust downwards the customary ground rent (Marx 1966: 734 ff; Kautsky 1899: 80). Similarly, after the First World War the increasing costs of private mineral rights were one important reason for American oil companies to seek concessions abroad (United States Senate 1952: 39f). This did not affect landlord–tenant relationships as such, but did contribute to lower prices and to containing the increase in ground rent.

The effect of competition in the product market on landlord–tenant relationships depends largely on the nature of the contracts. In agriculture with short-term leases and fixed annuities, price variations may possibly induce with relative ease an adjustment regarding the customary ground rent.[8] In mining, on the other hand, with long-term royalty-based contracts and high sunk costs, it may take a much longer and more significant

---

8.   Though I have to confess my ignorance. I could never find a study on this question.

variation in prices. Shorter-term variations of prices may only lead to incorporating new or abandoning old marginal lands, without any change in the typical lease contract. To induce a change in the contractual structure itself, and to bring up or down the customary ground rent, may be beyond the reach of market forces. It can still be done, but it requires a purposely-designed policy. Radical Ricardian rent theory provides the policy makers with a simple, consistent and persuasive model for their confrontation with landlords.

Marxist Rent Theory

Marx sided with Smith against Ricardo on two counts. Their definition of ground rent covered all natural resources, including minerals. Royalty is just one form of ground rent. And both agreed on the question of private landed property and prices. Under certain circumstances landlords were strong enough to impose what Marx called an absolute rent, and what we have called a customary ground rent (Marx 1966: 756ff).

By representing a customary ground rent as an additional burden on the working class on top of capitalist exploitation, the aversion of Marxists for landlords was, of course, exacerbated. Nevertheless, after the First World War ground rent disappeared also from Marxist economics. Lenin, for example, based his *Agrarian Programme* (Lenin 1964), written in 1907, on Marx's rent theory. But ten years later, in 1917, in his book on *Imperialism* (Lenin 1934), he did not mention the term ground rent again. Land disappeared as a factor of production both in bourgeois and Marxist economics, albeit with a certain time lag. As a matter of fact, Marx himself was interested in absolute ground rent only from a historical perspective – the transition from feudalism to capitalism. As a historical category, he concluded, it was bound to disappear with the further development of capitalism. With the growth of productivity in the primary sector and worldwide competition, natural resources would become more abundant and the landlords would be weakened. Engels, who published posthumously, in 1894, the third volume of *Das Kapital* (which contains Marx's rent theory) supported this viewpoint, presenting as evidence the fall of ground rent in Europe at that time.

On the other hand, Marx did not elaborate on mineral ground rent. His political interest concentrated on the peasantry as a possible ally of the working class, to whom the question of land tenure was of paramount importance. *The land to the tiller* was a popular bourgeois revolutionary device, appealing to a peasantry eager to work its own piece of land. But the mine workers were confronting modern industrial mine owners. The workers in the mines cared very little about land tenure. *The mineral to the miner* could not be a popular slogan. Thus, regarding mining, Marx was content simply to signal that absolute rent had to be explained in the same way as in agriculture.

Nevertheless, Marx was careful to point out that absolute ground rent – i.e. customary ground rent – may also exist under capitalism, independently of and beyond the process of transition from feudalism to capitalism (Marx 1966: 772). His followers completely ignored this point. It took only a few decades for Ricardian rent theory to be accepted in practice also in Marxist writings: Marx had been right in his time to claim that Ricardo was wrong; but Ricardo was now supposed to be right.

Governance, Factors of Production and Natural Resources

Governance of private mineral ownership develops in two phases. There is a first period when mining industries settle in, during which the game is, strategically, about defining the set of actors, the basic rules, and a customary ground rent – thus setting up a governance structure. A second period follows, where the game is, on the one hand, only about differential or Ricardian rents and, on the other, to make this structure work as efficiently as possible. In this second period the structure may still, and has to, evolve and adapt to changing circumstances, but the basic outcome of the first period is preserved. The latter may only be changed by really exceptional circumstances, strong enough to impose and to justify the economic, political and social costs of demolishing the old structure and setting up new governance.

Modern economics only deals with the second period. The first one belongs to its forgotten pre-revolutionary past, to what today is known as classical political economy. In modern countries, where land is subordinated to developed markets, land tenure is a non-issue. In consequence, the question of natural resource ownership and its relationship to prices is left to politics. It is up to policy makers, whoever they may represent – consumers, the tenant companies, or landed property owners – to deal with it. And though Ricardian rent theory theoretically aimed at denying even the possibility that customary ground rents might exist, it turned a blind eye to them whenever they showed up in practice. It thus offers a menu of models, to cover up, and to justify, the existing compromise, a legacy of history or, on the contrary, to question its very nature. Policy makers are thus free to deal with the real world. The restriction in modern economics of the factors of production to just capital and labour, and not land, tends to be reflected, politically, in a left-right divide. But, as a matter of fact, 'left' (labour) and 'right' (capital) coincide in their position against ground rent (Marx 1974: 38ff; Guigou 1982). Both would prefer the cake to be divided into two and not into three.

The governance of natural resources is a much more elementary issue than the left-right divide suggests, though it may be politically beneficial to stick the label 'right' or 'left' on whichever is the other party and whenever some related problems have to be dealt with. Regarding mineral governance, its proper dimension is the physical divide above–below, i.e. the tension that necessarily exists between those who work and live on the surface, and those who make their living out of the subsurface.

2 CASE STUDIES IN PRIVATE GOVERNANCE

2.1 British Coal

Outcrops of coal used to be widespread in Britain.[1] Nevertheless, as long as there were abundant supplies of wood, coal was disregarded as a fuel. The reason was the poor quality of outcrop coal, and even of coal at a shallow depth, due to its exposure to oxygen. But wood gradually became scarce and it was displaced, at first locally, by coal. Though the costs of digging surface coal were small, transport costs were very high. Eventually a regional and national market for coal developed. Simultaneously, private landed property extended to minerals, with some regional exceptions and the general exception of silver and gold. This development was peculiar to Britain, related to its political evolution and the strong position of the landlords within the monarchy. On the Continent the situation generally evolved in the opposite direction, towards public ownership.

Early Coal Leases

Hence, in Britain, the landlords themselves generally carried out surface digging and coal mining, though leasing was always an option. In the latter case, coal leases followed the pattern of agricultural leases, though from the beginning depletion was taken into account by limiting volumes tenants were allowed to produce. 'It was usual in letting coal mines ... to limit the number of pits that could be worked, and the number of hewers ... to be employed in each pit. Thus a maximum limit was set upon output' (Nef 1932: V.1, 320). In other cases there were outright volume restrictions.

These primitive restrictions were acceptable to both sides within a traditional environment of short lease contracts of a few years, and of producers supplying only local markets. They were easy to supervise. But once coalmining became a modern, market-oriented activity, this system had to change. First, the

---

1. For a comprehensive history of British coal see the five-volume study sponsored by the National Coal Board.

restrictions simply disappeared altogether, at a time when landlords were weak due to competition from the privatisation of Church and Crown lands. 'The common lease during the period from 1580 to 1640 stipulated for a fixed payment, regardless of the quantity of minerals extracted' (Nef 1932: V.1, 321). At the same time the customary minimum period of tenure became twenty-one years. As this happened when demand for coal was about to take off, the landlords did not immediately share the profits arising from the revolutionary expansion of the coal industry towards the end of the sixteenth century. They had no means of improving their position until the lease expired. In some cases their ground rents amounted to less than half of one per cent of the selling price of a ton of coal. Those who signed later were more fortunate, but wide variations were the rule, and it was the most fertile or best-situated mines that tended to pay the lowest ground rent per unit of coal extracted, since the oldest leases covered them. In new or renewed leases, ground rent started to soar. 'By means of high rents [annuities], frequently by even higher fines [bonuses], the owners sought to recoup what they no doubt regarded as their losses during the period when the industry had expanded so rapidly' (Nef 1932: V.1, 322–24). In the period of depression that followed, it was the turn of the mine owners, now unable to make sufficient profits to pay their rents, to complain.

Modern Genesis of Royalty

Only after both landlords and tenants realised that these Elizabethan contract terms might be to their disadvantage were they in a mood to adopt a different method of calculation, which would establish a definite relation between ground rent and volume of coal extracted:[2]

> The system of assessing royalties at a fixed sum per unit of coal produced ... apparently originated in the English coal mines. Before 1700 many landlords throughout the country had adopted it. ... And, while the new system was not general at the end of

---

2.   Rougher approximate solutions, for example linking rent to the number of pits worked, the number of hewers employed, and so on, were earlier versions. (Nef 1932: V.1, 321; Flinn 1984: 43–4; Hatcher 1993: 273ff).

the seventeenth century, it was everywhere gaining ground. (Nef
1932: V.1, 324–25)

Nef stresses the fact that royalties in coal were *not* a legacy of
ancient times. They developed, independently, as a modern
ground rent-collecting device in mining. 'Though it is possible
to trace the influence of the medieval lead and tin miner in
certain colliery practices ... still, these are survivals largely of
academic interest' (Nef 1932: V.1, 298).

In the new coal leases royalties were combined with fines
and annuities; the latter were called *certain rents*. This was a
minimum to be paid in the event that royalty payments
amounted to less. Fixed royalties became predominant, but in
some regions – in South Wales and Scotland, for example –
percentage royalties were reported from the middle of the
eighteenth century. In my view, the reason for percentage
royalties appearing later and then becoming more popular can
be explained by the development of a more transparent market,
which facilitated the observation of transport costs and prices.
Fixed royalties survived in those regions where they had
previously been solidly established. In other words, where coal
production and leases developed first, a fixed royalty became
traditional, and where they developed later, a percentage royalty
developed as a new, later to become traditional, form. This
explanation seems to fit well in the case of Scotland, where
landowners were themselves involved in coal mining for longer
than anywhere else, and in the case of South Wales, a region
that became an important producer relatively late.

In a fully developed and competitive market a percentage
royalty entails only a moderate increase in monitoring costs
and, as already pointed out, has the advantage of adjusting
automatically to inflation as well as to differences in quality and
location. Although historically inflation was low by modern
standards, there is no denying that the average royalty per ton
tended to diminish in terms of real purchasing power during
the eighteenth and nineteenth centuries. Thus, landlords everywhere should have been interested in switching to a percentage
royalty. In practice, percentage royalties progressed very slowly,
and I suspect this may have been due to the opposition of the
tenants. Indeed, the most powerful tenants of the North-east,

historically by far the most important producing region of the country, had been operating a cartel since the sixteenth century – the Company of Hostmen of Newcastle-upon-Tyne, later giving way to the Grand Alleys. As a cartel they were certainly not interested in disclosing their pricing policy, and with a fixed royalty inflation worked in their favour.

Yet as inflation became more and more important in the twentieth century, one may wonder if fixed royalties would have become simply unacceptable to the landlords and percentage royalties would eventually have displaced them – if the mineral resource had not been nationalised before this happened.

Evolution of Royalty Rates

According to Nef, fixed royalties were at their highest in the century following the Restoration (1660). In the second half of the eighteenth century they began to fall. In Adam Smith's days a royalty equivalent to one tenth of pithead prices was common.

> Since that time the fall has been marked. In Durham and Northumberland between 1824 and 1834 comprehensive statistics of the Coal Trade Committee of 1836, the royalties average about one fifteenth of the selling price; in 1889 the average was about the same; during the last two years of the Great War [the First World War] about one thirty-sixth (Nef 1932: V.1, 326–27).[3]

Yet the very low percentage at the end of the First World War was also due to exceptional price levels.

As for percentage royalties, a consultant – or a viewer as they were known in the coal industry – while at Leslie in Fife in 1773, found that it was usual 'to pay a forth part of gross output for level free coal near the sea or city that affords constant sale or a good price, one fifth for level free coals that have not the above advantages, one seventh for coals wrought by a water engine and one tenth when wrought by a fire engine' (Flinn 1984: 45). In the late eighteenth and early nineteenth centuries the most frequent percentage royalty seems to have been one

---

3.   See also Hatcher (1993: 280) and Flinn (1984: 46).

eighth (Flinn 1984: 44–45). Originally this percentage may have been more or less in line with fixed royalties, yet due to inflation towards the end of the nineteenth century it became much more advantageous to the landlord.

In earlier times different royalties reflected, partially at least, Ricardian rents. Nevertheless, they did so very poorly. Mining conditions evolved fast and the state of the market for coal fluctuated from month to month, while leases were drawn for long periods during which royalties were fixed at a definite sum per unit, or percentage, of coal extracted.

Customary Royalty

It is noteworthy that there was no trend towards finer devices of rent collection. On the contrary, the historical trend went in exactly the opposite direction, towards a customary royalty:

> during the last two centuries, there is … a tendency for the tonnage royalties at all British mines to approach a common level. At the end of Elizabeth's reign [1558–1603], the … rents … charged probably ranged from one half per cent to as much as twenty per cent of the pithead price …. During the seventeenth and eighteenth centuries this margin was narrowed considerably; since 1800 it has been narrowed further. In 1836 the maximum royalty in Durham and Northumberland amounted to 1*s*. 3*d*. per ton, in 1889 the maximum was 10*d*., today it is 9*d*. All the representatives for the mineral owners, who testified before the Coal Commission of 1925, agreed that, at the overwhelming majority of mines throughout the country, royalties ranged between 5*d*. and 7*d*. a ton. Thus the average has tended more and more to become the usual charge. (Nef 1932: V.1, 327)

The remaining differences were mostly due to quality. The shrinking differential in royalty rates and their ultimate convergence was a complex process. Ricardian rents due to location, on the one hand, came down as a consequence of a sharp reduction in transport costs. On the other hand, depletion, i.e. the continuous movement towards greater depths and new lands, brought down Ricardian rents due to the different productivity of the mines themselves. Last but not least, and related to the foregoing, as landlords withdrew from coal mining, there ceased to be marginal producers who did not pay any ground rent.

Transportation. In earlier times the ease of communication with markets and the size of those markets were frequently more important than the costs of raising the coal. If coal was not to be consumed locally, it had to be produced *and* consumed next to the sea or rivers. This explains the early development of Newcastle with its Tyneside collieries as the most important producing centre, and that of London as the most important consuming centre. Thus, one of the most significant developments in the later seventeenth century, the spectacular growth in the output of collieries located at some distance from the south bank of the Tyne, was only made possible by the provision of wooden waggonways along which the coal could be cheaply transported.

The development of waterways, and finally railways, followed. Yet with the strengthening of private landed property it was not sufficient for coal to be well located; neighbouring landlords asking for wayleaves became extremely important in the second half of the seventeenth century, partly as a consequence of the exhaustion of coal mines along the rivers and the sea. Not surprisingly, the coal owners[4] and their landlords wanted wayleave rents to be paid only according to the damage actually sustained by the transit-landlords, whereas the latter defended the point of view that they were entitled to participate in the profits of the collieries. Wayleaves became extremely oppressive. 'Even the most slothful of conservative landowners could derive a handsome income from the coal trade without dirtying his hands if his land was strategically placed' (Hatcher 1993: 254).

Though the problem of transportation was of special importance to coal, it was one that faced all trade, and obviously tended to divide even the landlords. For this reason it had to be tackled at a national level. In the eighteenth century legislation developed giving the constructor of a public utility such as a

---

4.   The reader should be aware of the somewhat confusing terminology. 'The term 'owners' (or coalowners) in the coal industry was applied to the active owners and senior managers of coalmining enterprise. The owners of the actual coal before it was mined were known as 'royalty owners' or occasionally 'mineral owners'.' (Supple 1987: 23n1).

canal, a turnpike road, or a railroad, rights of compulsory purchase of land. Therefore, calculated by the ton-mile, wayleaves 'tended to reach a peak at the end of the seventeenth or the beginning of the eighteenth century, since which time they have absorbed a steadily diminishing portion of the selling price. Their importance has been largely reduced ... by the introduction of ... railroad transport, the right of way now being secured by the railroad' (Nef 1932: V.1, 334). By the mid-eighteenth century wayleave rents had lost their importance. 'The advent of public railways had the effect of diminishing the need to negotiate rights of way. By 1890, outside the North-east, where relatively lengthy private wayleave lines which had preceded public railways continued to offer cost effective services to colliery owners and merchants, only a small proportion of coal output was subject to wayleaves' (Church 1986: 14–15).

The drastic fall in transportation costs and wayleaves reduced Ricardian rents for well-located collieries, and brought new collieries into a regional, and eventually a national market.

Landlords Become Exclusively Rentiers. Until the sixteenth century it was not unusual for landowners to work their own mines, and even to lease additional ones. Indeed, landowners could be lessors in some cases and, at the same time, lessees in other cases. Even at the time of Adam Smith there were still marginal mines worked by the landlords themselves:

> There are some of which the produce is barely sufficient to pay the labour, and replace, together with its ordinary profits, the stock employed in working them. They afford some profit to the undertaker of the work, but no rent to the landlord. They can be wrought advantageously by nobody but the landlord, who being himself undertaker of the work, gets the ordinary profit of the capital which he employs in it. Many coal mines in Scotland are wrought in this manner, and can be wrought in no other. The landlord will allow nobody else to work them without paying some rent, and nobody can afford to pay any. (Smith 1950: V.1, 166)

Yet as early as the seventeenth century an increase could be observed in the proportion of mineral owners in all parts of Great Britain who leased their mines instead of working them. This eventually became the rule. 'By the 1830s perhaps no more than 10 to 15 per cent of coal production came from collieries worked by landed proprietors, a share which was probably half that figure by the 1870s and fell to a negligible proportion by 1913' (Church 1986: 12, 762). Landowners became rentiers, and at the beginning of the twentieth century many of the largest mineral owners knew 'almost nothing about the origin of their incomes from royalties' (Nef 1932: V.2, 8).

Leases became the rule as coalmining went deeper and deeper and, hence, collieries became increasingly capital-intensive. In earlier times when coalmining was limited to outcrops or coal seams close to the surface, the existence of coal, its quality, and the ease of operation, was almost as well known to landowners and tenants as agricultural land. Later, however, a degree of exploration was required. In the early nineteenth century this was still done by consulting viewers engaged by the landowner. The landowner's choice then lay between financing a colliery himself or, more likely, offering a lease at a royalty, hoping to attract investors on the strength of the viewer's report. However, with increasing mine depths, exploration became a specialised, expensive, and risky undertaking:

> Thus, from the 1860's, when coal was being sought in Fife, and especially in the concealed parts of the coalfield extending from Yorkshire across the East Midlands, a new class of specialised surveying and boring contractors began to emerge. By 1913 several such firms were in operation, obtaining leases or options from landowners and boring and proving the coal before attempting to persuade a colliery company to take over the actual winning of the colliery. (Church 1986: 311–12)

By the end of the nineteenth century the landowners had not only retreated from production, but were even unable to assess the value of their lands. A class of entrepreneurs specialising in exploration arose:

> The pioneering company's income generally came from reimbursement of its costs by the colliery company, to which was added a tonnage payment on coal raised, calculated on the difference between the royalty paid and that which would have been asked had the coal already been proved; sometimes shares were substituted for cash payments. (Church 1986: 312)

The average cost of one borehole in the two decades prior to the First World War has been estimated at £10,000, and normally several boreholes were necessary for a proper assessment of the seam, its richness, inclination, quality, and so on. The landowners were no longer willing, or able, to invest and risk such amounts of money. They had become rentiers, and a customary royalty rate had developed.

The Historical Average. Increasing mining depths indicated depletion and the need continually to acquire new leases on unexplored lands or on deeper unexplored strata combined with the closure of older mines. These new marginal leases had to pay a customary ground rent, i.e. a customary royalty that was still to be determined. The minimum in question turned out to be the average rate of royalties. This average was well known amongst consultants and lawyers and, as such, could easily develop into a *focal point* (Rasmusen 1989: 36). Since the landlord was by now out of the business and thus uninformed, sticking to the average was a good way to reassure him that he was offered a 'fair' deal. On the other hand, ex-ante Ricardian rents had largely disappeared anyway.

Period of Tenure and Renewal

Early leases were short, up to a few years, which was sufficient for small medieval diggings. It was not long enough, however, for more capital-intensive coal mining. Investment in infrastructures – shafts, underground layouts, water pumping, ventilation, and so on – required longer leases in order that the investment could be undertaken and recovered. It was only after the privatisation of Church and Crown lands that the necessary longer lease terms became available. Twenty-one years became the customary period of tenure, though there were many leases lasting longer. As the 'initial sinking of a major pit could take up to four years in the late eighteenth and early nineteenth centuries' (Flinn 1984: 48, 191), a period of twenty-one years as a customary period of tenure seems not to have been too generous. Until the final quarter of the nineteenth century most leases fell within the range of twenty-one to sixty-three years, with an overall trend for leases to become shorter on average. Thereafter they tended to become longer. The new trend 'was clearly associated with increasing mine depths accompanied by the greater capital expenditure necessary for deep mining operations, developments which led colliery companies to insist upon leases of sufficient duration to justify the heavier capital investment associated with long-term mining development' (Church 1986: 13).[5] By the mid-nineteenth century forty-two years was quite usual, and sixty-three years was not uncommon, though there were still plenty of leases with the old twenty-one year term (Mitchell 1984: 253; Nef 1932: V.1, 322n6).

Whatever the period of tenure, however, there was the question of what happened when leases fell in. If the seams were already exhausted at this point, tenants were usually required to restore the surface for agricultural or other uses, and to seal off the shafts to prevent accidents. The lessees would then take with them what viewers used to call the 'live stock', those parts of their capital that were removable and saleable, whereas the 'dead stock' such as buildings would become the property of the lessors without payment of an indemnity. If the seams were not exhausted at the time of the escheating of a lease – as happened quite frequently even with periods of tenure of forty-two years or more[6] – the renewal of the contract could be the opportunity for the landlord to collect *ex-post*, at last, Ricardian rents and, generally, all economic rents created by his lessee. There was no longer any geological uncertainty and risk, and the 'dead stock', which the lessees had to hand over, included not only permanent buildings but the shafts and the underground layouts as well.

Hence, the landlord could claim not only for fines reflecting those rents but also for interest on the capital invested by his lessee during the previous lease term. In some cases, this was successfully achieved. 'It was possible for a landowner's revenue from fines to swell to become a significant proportion of his whole revenue from mines' (Flinn 1984: 46–47). What is more, fines could be agreed on before the termination of the lease. This happened, for example, in the Northeast in the late

---

5.   Church (1986: 8) mentions an example where mine depth reached 715 metres.
6.   By 1925 'about half the work-force was employed in mines more than 40 years old' (Supple 1987: 401). In 1980, on the other hand, 'well over a quarter of the operating collieries had been sunk before 1880' (Ashworth 1986: 113).

eighteenth and early nineteenth centuries, by building into the initial lease provision for renewal every seven years and allowing for the levying of a fine on the occasion of the renewals. With what were called 'filling-up' renewals, the expired term was added to the end of a lease to allow, on payment of renewal fines, for 'leap-frogging' extensions. This system could become very oppressive for the tenants.

With growing mine depths, however, leases became longer and the landlords' ability to enforce favourable conditions upon renewal was considerably weakened. The maintenance of deeper mines is extremely costly – for example water-pumping must be permanent – and if maintenance is not carried out properly, mines may quickly be lost, within a few months or even weeks, and can only be reopened, if at all, at a very high cost. At the same time, observation and enforcement costs for the landlords increased, and the landlord found that he had to reach an early agreement with his lessee for renewal of the contract, since otherwise he had to find a new lessee to take over immediately. In these circumstances it must have been easy for the lessee to undermine, or even to sabotage, any intention by the lessor either to impose high fines, which he considered unfair, or to replace him with a new lessee.

Although information available is relatively scarce on this point, since those 'substantial fines payable on renewals of leases … are not often revealed in surviving records' (Hatcher 1993: 279), overall information is sufficient to ascertain that the customary royalty represented the major part of ground rent payments in modern coal leases. Ex-post Ricardian rents largely remained with the tenants even upon renewal:

> it is clear that in our time the major portion of the additional return from the better situated and more productive mines no longer goes to the landlord, who tends to receive royalties at the same rate in all parts of Great Britain, but to the investors in colliery enterprises. (Nef 1932: 328)

Nevertheless, this does not allow us to jump to the conclusion that the definite period of tenure did not cause serious harm. On the contrary, the perverse incentive problem caused by the approaching end of the lease, by threatening to interrupt an activity that required by its very nature a steady flow of investment and long-term planning, seems to have caused considerable damage. It entailed higher production costs and, more importantly, a short-term investment policy.[7] Its accumulated effects were amongst the principal causes of the crisis faced by the British coal industry in the twentieth century. Although leases became longer towards the end of the nineteenth century, this was too little too late. The fundamental problem of reversion was never addressed. Ultimately, there was a deadlock; landlords were unable to get hold of economic rents upon renewal of the leases, and tenants were unable to develop a system that permitted a steady and unhampered flow of investment for the whole lifetime of the mine.

Nationalisation of the Natural Resource

Fragmentation of Private Landed Property. Optimal exploration strategies, the location of shafts, and the design of underground outlays bear no necessary relationship to the fragmentation of the surface by private landed property. In Great Britain, however, private property prevailed. As Nef pointed out, the exceptional concentration of landed property made the system of privately owned royalties tolerable in Britain. But that was all – it made private mineral property *tolerable* because even in the eighteenth century 'in most collieries … the length of levels was determined … not so much by the difficulty or cost of underground hauling as by the acreage of coal legally accessible to the operator' (Flinn 1984: 81). Regionally things could be worse:

> highly fragmented land holdings at the northern end of the Warwickshire coalfield around Wilnecote prevented mining on all but the smallest of scales during the first half of the eighteenth century. Many leases laid down a strict limit on the number of acres that might be worked, and it is worth bearing in mind that a shaft sunk in the centre of a square twenty-five-acre coal lease would permit levels driven to meet the sides of the square at right angles of no more than 175 yards. (Flinn 1984: 81)

---

7. For a discussion of the related problem of 'second sourcing' in the case of regulated natural monopolies, see Laffont and Tirole (1993: Chapter 8).

For technical reasons – to prevent subsidence – pillars of coal had to be left underground. Additionally, however, coal had to be left to form barriers to separate mines on adjacent properties in order to prevent water flowing between the two. The resulting waste for these and other reasons related to the fragmentation of the surface 'involved the loss of great quantities of coal' (Nef 1932: 341) even in the seventeenth century. Moreover, those barriers implied significant losses in productivity. The drainage of the mines, a problem that should have been tackled co-operatively, 'dwarfed all others … in importance, and determined to a large extent the structure of the seventeenth-century colliery' (Nef 1932: V.1, 353). Yet 'disputes without number could arise where several mine owners depended surreptitiously, and without written agreement, upon the drainage system of a rival. … [A coal owner] estimated [in the second half of the seventeenth century] that, if all the collieries around Newcastle had been operated as a single enterprise, the expense for drainage would have been only one sixth of what it was' (Nef 1932: V.1, 338). By the same token, underground layouts were poor and, according to the Reid Committee Report in 1945, 'had crippling effects on labour productivity' (Supple 1987: 616).

The fragmentation of landed property became more and more serious a problem with the growing depths of mines. In the words of a famous viewer at the beginning of the nineteenth century: 'Where a pit costs from £10,000 to £20,000 sinking, we cannot afford to sink a shaft every ten or twenty acres' (Flinn 1984: 88). Levels had to become longer, crossing beneath several properties. By 1925–6 the Samuel Commission estimated that on average each mine had to secure leases from five mineral owners, a time – and money – consuming enterprise as the following example shows:

> When the Staveley Coal and Iron Company was formed … in 1864 the directors commissioned the leading viewer from Newcastle, William Armstrong, to examine the firm's resource position. The result was his plan to acquire extensive leases on coal bearing land in the Midlands, which became the basis of company policy patiently pursued for some twenty years through tedious and protracted negotiations with a handful of landowners. (Church 1986: 16)

As a matter of fact, in the words of the Samuel Commission, the 'planning of the mines is influenced continuously by surface boundaries. ... But surface boundaries have no relevance at all ... to the proper organisation of the industry underground' (Supple 1987: 405n3).

Nef believed that litigation, engendered by multiple management of the same drainage area, might have been a significant part of the additional drainage costs. Validating private property rights on minerals underground always implies significant legal costs, and coal was no exception: 'Coal mining in all ages appears to have been a peculiarly fertile source of litigation' (Nef 1932: 286). The situation in Great Britain, however, was made much worse by a lack of an adequate legal framework:

> The more we consider the state of mining law in Great Britain in the seventeenth century, the more we are likely to conclude that the coal industry expanded in spite of it. Nor is this impression offset by a consideration of the probable effects of the private ownership of minerals.

> While the transfer of mineral property at the time of the Reformation undoubtedly contributed to the expansion of the coal industry in the Age of Elizabeth, the private ownership of minerals which became a principle of English law at this time was hardly an advantage to the subsequent development of mining. (Nef 1932: 341)

The loss of synergy and, thus, of productivity, were apparent everywhere even in older times. In lieu of co-operation as required by geology, private landed property fostered litigation. Surface boundaries were as arbitrary to coalmining as those imposed by the period of tenure. Both caused serious obstructions to the development of productivity, and more so with growing mine depth, and both required an appropriate legal framework to be tackled. What is more, both problems tended to reinforce each other. Co-operation required a long-term time horizon, common to all participants. Indeed, leases became longer as mine depths increased, yet the legal framework was, and remained, hopelessly inadequate.

'Nationalisation of Royalties'. Nevertheless, even in these conditions the technological development of productivity was vigorous enough not only to make up for depletion, but even for a slow

and steady growth of productivity (measured by yearly output per employee) – up to the early 1880s. Then productivity started to decline. On the eve of the Second World War productivity was back to the same level as in 1830. British coal production peaked, finally and conclusively, in 1913, with 287.5 million tons, and employment peaked in 1920, with 1.25 million people.

The decline of productivity in the British coal industry since the early 1880s was in stark contrast with the development of productivity elsewhere in Europe and the United States.[8] With the exception of the United States, the British resource base remained superior, but with growing mine depths the advantage of public ownership on the Continent made up for the difference.

For some decades prior to 1914 the demand for coal grew worldwide at about four per cent annually but only two per cent in the United Kingdom. Between 1913 and 1937 the growth of world demand slowed down to a mere 0.3 per cent. In the United Kingdom, production actually decreased. Domestic consumption, in 1913, was 183.8 million tons; in 1946 it was nearly the same: 183.5 million tons. Overseas shipment, however, declined from 97.7 million tons to a mere 9.2 million tons. The British coal industry was no longer competitive internationally and had lost its share in world markets.

Private mineral property became critical. The almost complete lack of a satisfactory legal framework is not difficult to explain. Whatever the legal reforms that might have been envisaged, one thing is clear: they would have entailed some kind of restriction to private landed property rights. Yet in the British parliament landlords were strong, and dominant in the House of Lords, able to block any initiative to restrict their property rights. What is more, making co-operation compulsory encountered difficulties not only among the landlords but also among the tenants. This is inevitably the case wherever producers are required by a new law or regulations to co-operate, but it was particularly difficult in the case of British coal since entrepreneurship was as fragmented as private landed property.[9] It was short-term oriented, and it could not be otherwise with leases about to fall in, on average, within fifteen to twenty years.

---

8.   For some data see Church (1986: 774) and Supple (1987: 192).
9.   In 1913, there were over 1400 firms and over 2600 mines. (Supple 1987: 361).

No industrial leadership developed. Tenants, too, failed to promote adequate legislation. For this reason, initiatives finally had to come from outside. This implied that they were bound to come late, only after the problem had become critical even for third parties, i.e. consumers;[10] too late, indeed, given the long lead-times of structural adjustments. It is the lack of evolution in the legal framework of coalmining that eventually led to nationalisation of the natural resource, the take-over of unworked coal into public ownership.

The 'nationalisation of royalties' as it was called, became part of the Liberal Party's programme in the 1880s, and in 1891 the Trade Union Conference called for the nationalisation both of royalties *and* the mines. But only after the poor performance of the coal industry during the First World War and its inability to increase supply even after the war, in spite of extraordinarily high price levels, was it finally recognised that private mineral ownership had become a serious problem. In 1919, the government appointed a Royal Commission of Inquiry 'equally representative of miners [i.e. workers] and owners [i.e. mining companies]' (Supple 1987: 124), which agreed unanimously on the nationalisation of royalties 'on the grounds that the fragmentation of private ownership and decision-making led to inefficiency in the use of a natural resource' (Supple 1987: 136). Prime Minister Lloyd George, a Liberal, announced that the government would seek public ownership of royalties and foster regional mergers of colliery companies.

This was a last attempt to reform, but landlords and tenants successfully resisted all compulsory measures, without which nothing serious could be done. Reform had failed again. Finally, in 1935 the Conservative government committed itself to the 'unification' of royalties, as the nationalisation of coal royalties was officially, and bashfully, called. It was enacted in 1938. To handle the very complex process, 1 January 1939 was established as 'valuation date' but 1 July 1942 as 'vesting date'. Compensation payments amounted to £80.888 million (Ashworth 1986: 25). Over half of the sum went to 114 claimants who received more than £100,000 each; of the rest, almost 8,000 drew less

---

10. Jevons (1865) already foresaw the decline of productivity in British coal and discussed in detail its consequences on the competitiveness of the national economy.

than £1,000 each, and only 1,300 were paid more than £5,000, there being 13,482 claimants in total (Fine 1990: 56).

The Coal Act of 1938 vested the unworked coal in a Coal Commission. Leases continued in force as before, but ground rent had to be paid to the Commission. Since the Commission was also responsible for re-negotiating or renewal of leases, it was in a strong position to promote amalgamations, concentration, and the modernisation of British mines.

Nationalisation of the Mining Companies

In the event, before the Coal Commission was able to act, it was obliged by the outbreak of the Second World War to concentrate on output. The industry's performance was even worse than in the earlier war and this time seriously threatened the war effort. The potentially disastrous decline in production during the war motivated the Ministry of Fuel and Power to appoint in 1944 a Technical Advisory Committee (Reid Committee). It reported in March 1945 'the thorough reorganisation of the Industry requires the examination of the problems on a coalfield basis rather than mine by mine' (Supple 1987: 617–18). In addition, it continued:

> it is not enough simply to recommend technical changes which we believe to be fully practicable, when it is evident to us, as mining engineers, that they cannot be satisfactorily carried through by the Industry organised as it is today. … it is evident to us that it is not possible to provide for the soundest and most efficient development and working of an area unless the conflicting interests of the individual colliery companies working the area are merged together into one compact and unified command of manageable size. (Supple 1987: 618)

All the members of the Committee were mining engineers, most of them with senior managerial experience in the coal industry. Strong public action was certain to follow. Moreover, the general backwardness of the industry also affected working conditions, and coal mining was a highly labour-intensive industry. Industrial relations had been appalling for decades, but had deteriorated further during the inter-war period after big strikes and lockouts. The victory of the Labour Party in the General Election of July 1945 was only the last drop in a glass already full to the brim. The mining companies, then still the most important industry in the country, were nationalised. Royalties had been nationalised too late.

Global compensation payments accorded in 1946 amounted to £394 million. The industry's assets, however, excluding ancillary or subsidiary investment, were officially estimated at £164.66 million (Ashworth 1986: 28). Thus the capital invested in coalmines was, in nominal terms, just twice the amount of the capitalised ground rent, estimated a few years earlier at £80.888 million. In real terms the difference was somewhat less. This is roughly in line with the distribution of profits between landlords and tenants. In the mid-nineteenth century the profit split was still favouring the landlords by a significant margin 60:40; but on the eve of the First World War it had been reduced to 40:60 (Church 1986: 54, 530–32).

Landlords, Tenants and State

The essential features of British coal leases were a customary royalty, fines [i.e. bonuses], certain rents, and rental payments [i.e. surface rentals]. In spite of having evolved over centuries, by 1938 this process was still not complete. In the long run the tonnage royalty would have had to be replaced everywhere by a percentage royalty. Moreover, the problem of reversion was never directly addressed, though lease terms became longer.

Towards the end of the nineteenth century the customary royalty represented, as we have seen, approximately one fifteenth of pithead prices, i.e. 6.7 per cent. According to one author, 'even had royalties been abolished completely … the elasticity of demand for coal … suggests that the long-term consequences would have been unlikely to have afforded an appreciable stimulus to the industry, either by increasing the volume of mineral extracted or by expanding the supply of capital' (Church 1986: 15). From this viewpoint, then, the outcome would have been lower prices and a slight increase in demand. Yet royalties represented only the tip of the iceberg. A successful evolution of the landlord–tenant relationship in British coal would have required an industry able to generate, in a process parallel to the evolution of the contracts, the necessary legal changes required by depletion and increasing mine depths. It is in that political dimension that the landlord–tenant relationship in British coal ultimately failed. Over many decades, and even centuries, inefficiencies accumulated at the economic, legal, social and political level. One of the most important of those accumulated inefficiencies was a shortsighted entrepreneurship as fragmented as private landed property, and as unable and unwilling to promote innovations and reforms as the landlords themselves.

The British coal industry, radically reduced but thoroughly modernised, was re-privatised by a Conservative government in 1994 (Parker 2001). Of course, public mineral ownership was maintained and *never* questioned again. Today, the private industry is based on a licensing system, licences extending over 99 years, the natural resource being a free gift of nature, although the licensees have to pay, symbolically and as a reminder of other times, a peppercorn rent.

2.2   American Oil (1860s–1970s)

In the United States the settlers in their advance westwards appropriated with the surface the minerals beneath (Peele 1918: 1468–74). Conversely, until 1909 anyone could pre-empt a tract of land on the public domain to search for and extract minerals, become its proprietor by investing a certain amount of money in the land (Uren 1950: 188ff). But where oil production began first, close to the populous East Coast, private property was already well established. Hence, the new industry was essentially based on leases. 'Of the total of 1.56 million acres of oil property in 1890 … approximately four-fifths was leased' (Williamson and Daum 1959: 760). The remaining one fifth was bought privately or acquired from the public domain. Farmers engaging in oil production were rare. From the beginning landlords and tenants could clearly be distinguished. The American petroleum industry was from its inception a modern industry.[11]

---

11. In this book we do not deal with natural gas, which acquired commercial value only in the 1920s. After the Second World War it became the second energy source of the United States, crude oil being the first. However, as exploration and production of oil and natural gas were in practice part of one indivisible process, leases from the 1920s onwards always referred to both, and the same royalty rates applied.

The market for crude oil emerged from the demand for kerosene, used for lighting, which was originally derived from coal oil, an intermediate product derived, in turn, from coal. Though kerosene extracted from crude oil was of much better quality, the latter was in short supply as its production was limited to collecting from rare surface leakages. But this changed all of a sudden, in 1859, when the first commercial oil well was completed in Pennsylvania.

Early Oil Leases

The first successful lease, signed in 1859, established a fixed royalty of $4.20 per barrel. It triggered a run on all potential oil lands in the neighbourhood. But in the first twelve months crude oil prices varied wildly, between twenty dollars and ten cents a barrel. The former was a 'net-back' price derived from kerosene produced from coal, which was soon forced out of the market; the latter price was caused by an acute shortage of storage and transportation facilities. Royalty rates and bonuses varied accordingly (Giddens 1975: Part I, 63). However, during the following ten years 50 per cent seems to have been the usual rate, and even at that rate the production of oil was highly profitable. According to one estimate, in 1865 a pumping well yielding twenty barrels per day still broke even at $2.37 per barrel. Taking into account dry holes (at that time four out of every five wells drilled) and the average life expectancy of producing wells (eighteen months) the break-even price rose to about $6.35. Actually, prices ranged in 1865 between a low of $4.00 and a high of $10.00 a barrel. There was enough room for high bonuses on promising prospects, and even higher royalties. In some cases royalty rates reached 75 per cent, with bonuses as high as $2,000 per acre. Later, with a royalty of 50 per cent, bonuses went up to $4,000 and even $10,000 per acre. Furthermore, landowners were powerful enough to reduce progressively a typical leasehold from one to eight acres in the early years, to one half acre, at mid-decade, containing as many as three wells.

A few years later productivity had increased significantly. By 1871 the average life expectancy of producing wells was about three years and only five out of eight wells drilled were dry.

Average production costs had fallen sharply. 'Thus on a 20-barrel-a-day pumping well with a royalty still of 50 per cent, the owner could recoup all expenses, including his 'share' of the incidence of dry holes, with crude selling at $2.20 per barrel, compared with $6.35 ... in 1865' (Williamson and Daum 1959: 159). Prices ranged between $3.25 and $5.25. Hence, pumping wells sometimes yielding less than four barrels per day were still profitable. As a matter of fact, the average daily yield of some 3,275 producing wells was only between five and six barrels.

Producing oil was becoming an ordinary business. Prices gradually came down. 'From 1874–85 the average yearly price of crude per barrel ranged from a high of $2.58 to a low of 78¢; the average for the period was approximately $1.25' (Williamson and Daum 1959: 375). The average life of a well increased to seven years and only one out of eight wells drilled was dry. Productivity developed fast. Moreover, in the early 1860s a small group of landowners was in an extraordinarily strong position, as oil was believed to exist only within the limited area where it had been leaking to the surface. But soon it became clear that oil could be found in many places, though in more remote regions the problem was transportation. Only short gathering lines were in use, and the oil was barrelled and brought to the nearest railway station on horse carriages. This changed radically with the introduction of long-distance pipelines in 1879, which brought transport costs down to a fraction of their previous level. Competition between landlords increased, forcing them to rent their entire property, and the usual royalty rate came down to one eighth. Even wells of small yields – the average was 3.5 barrels daily – could now be profitable.

Ground Rent

Customary Royalty. The first reported though unsuccessful oil lease was signed in Pennsylvania in 1853, on a property where oil was leaking to the surface. It provided for a 50:50 split of profits. Given the really speculative nature of the venture, this is hardly surprising (Rasmusen 1989: 36). In fact, the 50:50 principle is very common in the history of leases generally,[12] and some kind

---

12. In agriculture sharecropping by equal parts was once predominant in

of 50:50 split remained the focal point during the following years. As the production of oil became extraordinarily profitable, a 50 per cent royalty became the standard in the 1860s – a 50:50 split, not of profit but of gross product, with all costs paid by the lessees. But supply of oil-bearing lands increased steadily, and so did productivity, forcing prices and royalty rates down. By 1880 a one-eighth royalty had become well established.

Leases were often executed on standard printed forms available from stationers in most oil-producing regions (Uren 1950: 165). The first printed forms were published in Oil City, Pennsylvania, around 1870, and already contained the one-eighth royalty (Glassmire 1938: 56). It has been claimed that this royalty rate was an overall proxy for a 50:50 profit split: 'Experience shows that a one-eighth royalty takes about half of the profits in the average case' (Uren 1950: 170). But in some other regions, originally of higher natural productivity such as Ohio and Indiana, a customary royalty rate of one sixth developed. American experts advising the Venezuelan government in 1942 claimed that this royalty rate was intended, too, as an approximation to an overall 50:50 profit split (González-Berti 1967: 16). Nevertheless, though those customary rates have survived up to the present, their association with some kind of a 50:50 profit sharing did not. Indeed, the western Pennsylvania wells were small high-cost producers, and the wells of Oklahoma and Texas, where oil was discovered much later, were much more prolific. However, the customary royalty rate of one-eighth became generally accepted. As a matter of fact, in 1959–60 the landlords' share of profits in American oil, including all ground

---

Medieval Europe and experienced the most diverse interpretations and specifications throughout its history: 'The most common division has been that into two equal parts, whereof one belonged to the Peasant and the other to the Proprietor. It is this that has given rise to the name of *Métayer (medietarius)* or Peasant with equal share. In the arrangements of this kind which are to be found in the greater part of France, the Proprietor makes all the advances of the cultivation; that is to say, he furnishes at his own expense the labouring cattle, the ploughs and other instruments of husbandry, the seed and the maintenance of the Peasant and his family from the moment when the latter enters on the métairie until the first harvest' (Turgot 1898: 22). In Germany and England the surnames Mayer (also written as Meier, Maier or Meyer) and Major derive from *metayer*.

rent payments, was estimated to be only between 32 and 38 per cent (Kahn 1964: 290).

Differential Rent. Still, 'once a discovery well has been drilled in a new area, competition is keen for "open leases", not yet signed. The owner of well-situated acreage, who has refused to lease until this stage, may then be in a position to exact a large bonus and a high royalty' (Uren 1950: 172). Indeed, in these cases even royalties as high as 50 per cent and bonuses of $1,000 an acre may still be offered (Davidson 1963a: 103–4). For this reason, the tenants would not normally start exploration without first covering the whole area with leases in order to benefit fully from a discovery:

> most of the larger oil companies are well organised toward this end. Usually this responsibility is delegated to a land department … well versed in the techniques of leasing practices …. When the geological department recommends an area for testing, the land department will be commissioned to negotiate the necessary leases. Landowners in the area will be approached with circumspection in order to avoid undue excitement tending to inflate land values and making the task for negotiating leases more difficult. The landowner being as a rule more or less unfamiliar with the oil business and susceptible to the popular belief that huge profits are the rule is apt to be unappreciative of the risks involved and the great cost of making a test. Accordingly, he is inclined to ask more than his lease is worth. The oil-company agent must patiently explain to the owner the financial risks that are involved and the advantages gained by completing an agreement on terms that will justify a test and, if successful, encourage efficient exploitation. (Uren 1950: 168–69)

Thus, in 1935 93.5 million acres were under lease, but only 9.9 million were 'proven acreage'. There was a permanent flow of new acreage leased and old acreage surrendered, but at that time four or five million more acres were leased each year than surrendered. Such a leasing strategy also permitted the location of exploratory wells optimally according to geology ignoring surface boundaries, though it certainly also entailed the payment of delay rentals over huge areas. In the case of a discovery, it would also lower technical production costs. Moreover, while ex-ante Ricardian rents were normally next to nil, ex-post Ricardian rents would fall to the tenants and not to the landowners. On the other hand, a landowner who did not rent his land at this stage had to take the risk of not receiving any ground rent at all, not even a signature bonus, if explorations on neighbouring lands proved unsuccessful.

All in all, in 1959–60, about 18.5 per cent of total capital expenditure in oil and gas consisted of payment to landowners, or some 10 to 15 per cent of gross revenues, merely for the right to probe beneath their soil. They were thus comparable in importance to royalties, which averaged 15 per cent (Kahn 1964: 290). This is somewhat surprising because usually they are considered to be low and, as far as I know, no study pays attention to them. The problem is, I believe, that perception is biased because in successful leases the customary ground rent in exploration may in hindsight indeed be of minor consequence.

Period of Tenure

Originally, 'leases ran for as long a period as the parties might agree; many of them expired in twenty years; some extended to forty, and a few were granted in perpetuity' (Giddens 1975: Part I, 63). What happened when leases fell in before the reservoirs were depleted? This question found an immediate and radical answer with the escheating of the first leases. The landowners were prevented from taking advantage of reversion by court rulings in the 1880s. Contractual provisions providing that the lessee should not remove machinery and equipment from the land in order to maintain the property in good working condition were declared unlawful:

> The courts held that all machinery, as well as the casings of the wells, were trade fixtures and removable by the lessee within the term. Therefore, while the lessor had the lessee at a disadvantage in contracting for renewal, the lessee might in turn remove all fixtures and well casings, and leave the property in such a condition that the lessor would have to grant a second lease of the premises on terms approximately the same as if the wells had not been drilled. (Williamson and Daum 1959: 762)

Accordingly, though landlords could claim whatever ground rent they wanted, this ruling forbade them to put their hands on the capital of their tenants. Yet this is precisely what would have been necessary to make reversion effective. Hence, backed by the courts, the tenants were now in a position to impose an indefinite period of tenure. Moreover, they were temporarily strong enough to remove from the contracts any specific obligation actually to explore the land. Thus, they could lease plots of land at no cost at all, or at very low rentals, and then monopolise them in perpetuity. In 1900 the Supreme Court declared this practice illegal; a contract, to be lawful, must satisfy the legal requirement of mutuality. Lease contracts were modified accordingly. Now a fixed term called a 'primary term' or 'exploration period' – generally between ten and fifteen years – became customary. If the drilling had not started within a specified period, for example one year, a 'delay rental' had to be paid. If oil was found and production actually began, a 'thereafter' clause provided for a 'secondary term': the lease would remain in force as long as oil was produced in 'paying quantities'. If production did not start before the end of the primary term, or if it were suspended later, the lease would fall in (Sullivan 1955: 69ff). Hence, leases were normally never renewed and remained in force until the final depletion of the reservoirs.

Prorationing and Conservation

Fragmentation of private landed property may be much more of a serious problem in petroleum production than in any other extractive industry. There are huge savings to be made searching for oil according to geology and ignoring property boundaries. Even more is to be gained by exploiting the reservoirs as geological unities. What makes oil different is that it is a liquid, frequently driven by gas pressure, able to migrate over long distances. Hence, oil produced on one property may actually come from surrounding, and even distant, properties.

As initially nobody knew where the oil was coming from, the courts upheld the 'rule of capture'. Hence, it was not entirely correct, as stated earlier, that oil reservoirs in the United States were privately owned; they only had a right of appropriation. As a result property owners and their tenants, covering the same reservoir, were competing to produce as fast as possible and as long as there was any profit above operating costs. It was out of the question to locate wells optimally according to technical criteria. They were located close to the boundaries both to prevent the oil from flowing to the neighbouring lands and to siphon off any neighbouring oil. Instead of co-operation there was destructive competition. Instead of low costs and high recovery factors, there were high costs and low recovery factors. Only a small percentage of the oil underground was actually recovered.

In the beginning not only the fragmentation of private surface property was to blame, but also ignorance. Later, scientific and technological development, most prominently in the field of geology, made it possible to assess with ever-increasing precision the characteristics of each reservoir. It was then possible to exploit the reservoir optimally, i.e. to locate the producing wells according to geology, minimising costs and maximising profits. As a result the percentage of oil recovered from each reservoir was maximised (or, conversely, the percentage of oil lost was minimised) and, with this in mind, the unitisation approach to oil reservoirs became known as *petroleum conservation* (Lovejoy and Homan 1967; McDonald 1971). This became, of course, even more important as drilling depth increased since deep wells were more expensive. However, petroleum conservation became really prominent only after the First World War, when the United States became an oil-importing country, albeit for a short period.[13] At that time an important oil producer, Henry L. Doherty, campaigned for legislation to make unitisation compulsory. But the fear of an oil shortage vanished with extensive discoveries in California, Oklahoma, and East Texas, and with the ensuing collapse of prices, due to the 'rule of capture' which typically generated boom-and-bust cycles. The waste of the natural resource was most conspicuous in East Texas where small landed property prevailed. The economic waste of wells drilled like fences along property boundaries as well as the damage caused to the reservoirs by over drilling was well publicised by the press and documented with aerial photographs. The effectiveness of *petroleum conservation* as a

13. The United States became definitively a net importer of petroleum –
     crude oil and products – in 1947.

political slogan was thus boosted by the unambiguous interest of big producers in 'price stabilisation', and legislation developed in the most important oil-producing states. Its centrepiece was prorationing, and the most famous committee in charge of executing such a policy was the Texas Railroad Commission. Prorationing was enacted first at state level. But in 1935 federal law created the Interstate Oil Compact Commission (IOCC) to control the flow of oil between the states.

Although prorationing was aimed in the first place at price stabilisation, the Supreme Court upheld its legality in 1932 on the ground of its effectiveness as a method of petroleum conservation. The Supreme Court in its verdict ignored the obvious link of prorationing with prices. What is more, as we shall see, it was also linked to the setting up of the international petroleum cartel (Frankel 1946: 116ff). But to acknowledge any link of prorationing to prices might have made the scheme illegal. Market competition was supposed to set prices, not producers – but something had to be done. The fact was that, even beyond the fragmentation of private landed property, oil was necessarily a geographically dispersed industry, and any new large discovery was a potential threat to price stability. Hence, apart from legal problems, it was impossible to control the industry by private agreement. By 1955 the seven major producers – SONJ, Socony Mobil, Gulf, Texas, Socal, Standard of Indiana and Shell – controlled no more than one third of US output, and even the major twenty together only reached 55 per cent. It is worth noting that these figures include royalty oil, which the landowners could sell to third parties if they wished. At the other extreme there were thousands and thousands of small and independent oil companies. It is, indeed, the existence of these companies that characterise the American oil industry. The monopoly power of the big oil companies was always limited, basically, to transportation and refining. In these areas the concentration percentages, in 1955, were as follows: pipelines 57 per cent (the major seven) and 88 per cent (the major twenty), refining 54 per cent and 86 per cent respectively (DeChazeau and Kahn 1959: 18).

With prorationing, legally binding maximum efficient rates (MER) were determined for every single well. Moreover, the output of non-marginal wells could be reduced according to market demand. However, marginal wells were allowed to produce at full capacity, as otherwise they would have been forced to shut down. Thus, there would be not only an irreversible loss of reserves, but also an irreversible loss of profits, whereas in non-marginal wells the reduction of output only delayed production. At the same time legislation developed establishing minimum acreage for new wells. In 1948 this was held to be about 20 acres, but double this figure in 1970. Thus, on small properties no well could be drilled but the landlord would still get his royalty. In other words, the 'rule of capture' was gradually abandoned and royalties paid according to the origin of the oil, as established by experts.

Although unitisation was promoted, it was not compulsory. Moreover, as marginal wells were exempt from prorationing, there was an in-built perverse tendency to replace more productive wells with a number of marginal wells. What might have been achieved with a more radical approach to conservation can be seen from the following examples. In the mid-1950s about nine per cent of US production came from unitised fields, in which the recovery factor was estimated to have increased, on average, from 27.5 to 46.3 per cent. Pressure maintenance techniques were crucial, but they could only be applied under unitisation. Compulsory unitisation could have increased the nation-wide average recovery factor, of 33 per cent, to over 45 per cent (DeChazeau and Kahn 1959: 230–44). More specifically, two large producers of the East Texas giant field proposed in 1962 to reduce the number of producing wells, with unitisation, from 17,200 to 1,500, implying that 15,700 wells were technically superfluous. The Texas Railroad Commission turned down the proposition. The Commission also refused a more modest proposal in 1965 to reduce the number of wells to 9,500 (Lovejoy and Homan 1967: 121). Adelman estimated that half of the 200,000 oil wells in Texas were superfluous (Adelman 1964a: 56). In 1956, according to estimates by Standard Oil of New Jersey, $370 million was spent in new and superfluous wells in Texas alone, representing a cost of 35¢ per barrel (DeChazeau and Kahn 1959: 230–44). As the average wellhead price that year was $2.79, this amount was equivalent to a one-eighth royalty. In other words, the waste of money due to the fragmentation of private landed property

reservoir may extend beneath different leases is not a problem as lessees on public lands are legally obliged to co-operate according to geology.

The first Mineral Land Leasing Law applying to federal onshore land dates from 1920. On unproven land a five-year prospecting permit was granted to the first qualified applicant and, in the case of success, the right to lease 25 per cent of the land paying a 5 per cent royalty and a rental of one dollar per acre per year. Moreover, the lessee was further entitled to a preferential right to lease the remaining 75 per cent at a royalty to be fixed by the Secretary of Interior, but not less than one eighth. Proven oil lands, on the other hand, would be leased to the highest bidder – in a public bidding – in tracts no larger than 640 acres, at a royalty of no less than one eighth and a rental of no less than one dollar per acre per year.[14] The lease term was twenty years, with a preferential right to a ten-year renewal, on terms set by the Secretary of Interior (Ise 1926: Chap. XXIV).

In 1935, the 5 per cent royalty disappeared. From then on the Law established a difference between leases on lands outside and inside known geological structures of producing oil fields. In the first case prospecting permits could be obtained through an application. During the ten-year primary period the rental is US$ 0.50 per acre and carries a flat one-eighth royalty. In the second case the primary period is five years and requires a rental of two dollars per acre per year. Royalties are based on a variable scale from one eighth and one fourth, depending on total production. Both leases have a shut-in royalty of one dollar per acre per year. In other words, this payment can be offset against the one-eighth royalty. This is designed to bring to bear pressure on the lessees to start production as soon as possible. Moreover, the secondary period, following the pattern established on private lands, was extended indefinitely, as long as oil was to be produced in paying quantities.

Regarding bidding practices, basically two systems have been in use: fixed royalty rates and bonus bidding, or fixed bonuses and royalty bidding. In the federal offshore, which became of

---

14. 37.5 per cent of royalties went to the government of the States where these lands were located.

interest in the mid-1950s and which is subject to the Outer Continental Shelf Lands Act of 1953, the government has traditionally fixed royalty at one sixth (though the Law only establishes a minimum of one eighth), and leases are granted to the highest bonus bidder. However, there have also been higher royalty rates and some royalty bidding.

Indian Lands. Indian lands were at times very important to oil production. Most of the big oil fields in Oklahoma, for example, have been found on Indian lands. Since the Indians were wards of the federal government, their lands were governed either directly by federal statutes or by treaties and agreements drawn up under the provision of federal statutes. Thus the first oil leases the US government had to deal with were actually on Indian lands. In 1891 'a law was passed authorising the Indian councils to lease their lands for mining purposes, as far as it was not needed for agricultural purposes, for not more than ten years, on conditions fixed by the agent in charge of the reservation with the approval of the Secretary of the Interior' (Ise 1926: 388). However, such a council did not always exist. For example, at the time when the oil companies became interested in their lands the Navajos had never met as a tribe. 'Non-existent in 1921, by October 1923 a Navajo tribal council was in place, and the government had presided over the first auction of oil leases on the reservation. Oil companies had finally succeeded in imposing their will on Navajos' (Chamberlain 2000: 33). Indeed, together with the Federal government they had created the indispensable sovereign power to grant them titles to the land, a sovereign power restricted beforehand by the Federal government. This council, however, also formed the core of the future Navajo Nation.

Indian land had originally been assigned collectively, as common property of the tribes. Yet by the end of the nineteenth century it was largely converted into private property, which, with some exceptions such as the Navajos and Osage Indians, included mineral ownership. In these latter cases the Nations, not only a few lucky individuals, profited from the oil wealth of their lands. The luckiest amongst them were the Osage who granted their first lease covering the whole of the Nation (1.5 million acres, or 6,070 km^2) in 1896 at a 10 per cent royalty.

On its renewal, ten years later, its area was reduced and a royalty was raised to one eighth, and the same rate applied to one new lease. These leases were still very large, 680,000 acres (2,752 km²) and 350,000 acres (1,416 km²). Moreover, the first one was actually subleased, at a royalty of one sixth. Then in 1915, the Osage tribal council approved a new leasing policy. Those leases would not be renewed, new leases would be limited to 4,800 (19.4 km²) acres each, and they would be sold directly to the companies actually working them, which was approved by the Secretary of Interior. Moreover, in new leases there was a rental of one dollar per acre per year – there had been no rental up to then – and the royalty rate was set at one sixth, or at one fifth where, on average, the output per well was one hundred barrels daily or more. This was their last chance to take advantage of escheating and renewal of leases in order to increase rents and royalties. The Indian Oil Leasing Act of 1924 extended the lease term, also on Indian land, indefinitely, as long as oil and gas was to be produced in paying quantities. Due to public ownership the Osage fared far better than most of the Indian tribes, which received only a customary royalty of one eighth. The Navajos managed to re-negotiate their leases in 1957, when they too got a one sixth royalty. After the 1950s one sixth became the customary royalty rate in new leases on Indian lands, though royalty rates varied according to circumstances between one sixth and one third.

The Osage enjoyed unique supervisory powers over petroleum leasing. The Department of the Interior only provided staff services and support and, because of tribal control, mismanagement problems that have plagued other tribes have been largely avoided (Bradley 1996: 274). The Osage in fact provided a first model of public management of oil and gas lands in the United States.

Depletion Allowance

In 1909 the USA introduced a corporation income tax. Accordingly, income had to be quantified by deducting production costs from gross revenues, including depreciation. Thus the idea that natural resources might be 'associated' to capital became of practical interest. In the case of mineral deposits, since they are depleted as they are worked, this 'natural capital' was indeed 'depreciating'. Regarding oil the 1918 Revenue Act accepted this reasoning (Lichtblau and Spriggs 1952; The New Palgrave 1998). The lucky explorer was supposed to have found a 'natural capital'. However, its quantification was somewhat complicated, until the Revenue Act of 1926 provided a very simple formula. Depletion was set at 27.5 per cent of wellhead price, which was supposed to reflect the diminution in the value of the mine. This so-called 'percentage depletion' simply represented the supposed intrinsic value of the mineral, independently and on top of the accounting for real exploration and production costs. Obviously enough, if oil had an intrinsic value, the same had to be true for other minerals. Thus, in 1932 percentage depletion was extended to them. The percentages were set between 23 per cent (for bauxite, lead, zinc, etc.) and 5 per cent (for stone and sand). Theoretically, these percentages should reflect the different speed of depletion. Oil deposits were depleting faster than all others as evidenced by the continuous and intense exploration effort of the industry. Yet it may also be necessary to take into account the extraordinary political power of oil-related interests. The fact is that oil not only enjoyed the highest percentage; it also enjoyed this tax privilege fourteen years earlier than other minerals.

One might expect, with Marshall in mind, that the recipient of percentage depletion should be the owner of the deposit, i.e. the landlord. Yet this tax privilege was actually shared by both landlord and tenants, proportionally to royalty. If the landlord held a royalty of, say, one sixth, the mining company retaining five sixths, percentage depletion applied accordingly to both of them.[15] The lion's share went to the tenants. The rationale of this split may be found, of course, in the fact that oil reservoirs have to be discovered, which is done by the tenants and not by the landlords. They therefore claim a kind of co-ownership. As a matter of fact, all over the world it is not uncommon for the law to recognise some compensation to the finder of a lost property. Again, this is ultimately a question of power and,

---

15. Typically, in its entry 'depletion' *The New Palgrave* does not mention the landlords. The depletion allowance is only discussed, and criticised, as a tax privilege of the producing companies.

obviously enough, whatever the political importance of royalty-owners at state levels, in Washington they would not have achieved anything without the support of the big oil companies.

At the time percentage depletion was introduced, corporation income tax rates were about 13 per cent, but they rose to 52 per cent after the Second World War. Hence, the tax privilege became more and more significant. To the landlords, subject to higher personal income taxes, the privilege became even more important. By the end of the 1960s the effective income tax rate for manufacturing industry in the United States was about 43 per cent, but only about 21 per cent for upstream oil (Mancke 1978: 84). The annual loss to the Treasury due to percentage depletion was estimated at $1.7 billion (Blair 1978: 193). For decades the depletion allowance was the subject of an intensive and critical debate. It was difficult for the consuming states to accept that mining rents were not only not subject to special taxes but were, on the contrary, actually privileged. For decades the consuming states achieved nothing, but finally, in 1969, they had some success: the depletion percentage for oil was reduced from 27.5 to 22 per cent. Shortly thereafter, however, things changed radically as US domestic oil policy was overshadowed by the 'OPEC revolution' of the early 1970s.

The Decline of US Oil and the OPEC Revolution

Historically, 1970 represents a turning point in American oil. Crude oil production peaked at 9.6 million barrels daily. Notwithstanding the development of productivity, high prices, and the then recent discovery of a new oil province – Alaska – US production has been declining ever since. Today, it is at 6.2 million b/d. As no country in the world has been as thoroughly explored as the United States, there cannot be any doubt that the country is running out of oil. In 1940 it produced two thirds of the world's total; in 1960 it was already down to one third; and it was only one sixth in 1973. Today, it is less than one tenth.

And 1970 marked the beginning of the OPEC revolution. The United States, until the 1960s, still had enough spare capacity – mainly in Texas, controlled by the Texas Railroad Commission – to confront international crises such as the Arab–

Israeli war of 1967. After 1970 spare capacity in the United States disappeared quickly. Thereafter it was only to be found within, and controlled by, OPEC. Until 1970 the governance of international oil could not be understood without a prior understanding of the governance of American oil. Moreover, American oil prices were 'made in USA'. This changed in the 1960s, and OPEC developed its own governance structure. US domestic prices, ever since the OPEC revolution, have been determined by world market prices. The United States, once the biggest oil-exporting country in the world, still breaking even in 1947, at present is the biggest oil-importing country with imports up to nearly 10 million barrels daily.

Thus, after the 1970s the evolution of percentage depletion, for example, has to be considered in the international context. Even the customary royalty rates were shaken by the OPEC revolution. In the 1970s, on private lands these rates 'gave way to whatever the market would bear' (Pierce 1998: 288n2). On public lands the situation became more complex, as one alternative to higher royalty rates was the increase of severance taxes, i.e. an additional royalty imposed by law on private and public land alike, as a tax and not as a contractual payment. In the federal offshore the government maintained its traditional approach with a fixed royalty of one sixth, and bonus bidding.

While *onshore* production was falling, *offshore* production actually increased. Consequently, production from the public domain, which represented only a few percentage points in the 1940s, is now over 50 per cent.[16] 'Discoveries of new major oil and gas reserves on privately owned lands in the United States is becoming less and less likely. The last frontiers for major domestic discoveries are generally believed to be on public lands' (Pierce 1998: 835). Expectations are still high regarding the deep waters of the Gulf of Mexico and Alaska's National Wild Life Refuges, but even in the best of cases they will only slow down, not reverse, the overall trend of falling production. That, however, is a different story, which we will have to take up again later in the context of public mineral ownership and the governance of international oil.

---

16. For detailed information see the American Petroleum Institute: *Basic Petroleum Data Book*, twice-yearly publication.

2.3 Mexican Oil (1880s–1970s)

Private Mineral Ownership

The tradition of public mineral ownership in Hispano-America was upheld with Independence, having been reinforced by the French Revolution and its modern mining law. Yet Mexico, in 1884, included coal and petroleum among the minerals 'of the exclusive property of the surface owner' (quoted in Collado 1987: 32).[17] At that time neither coal nor petroleum was of any significance. It seems likely that this classification was motivated by the example of the neighbouring United States where, based on private mineral ownership, a powerful coal and petroleum industry was developing.[18] However, public ownership of the important minerals of the country – such as silver and copper – remained unquestioned.

The first specific petroleum law, referring to public lands, was passed in 1901. It established an exclusive exploration permit for one year, followed, if successful, by an exploitation permit for ten years. There was a surface tax of five cents per hectare and a 10 per cent tax on utilities paid out to shareholders. The latter was to be divided, on state land, between the Federal (70 per cent) and the relevant State government (30 per cent). In exchange for this special tax, concessionaires were exempt from paying any other Federal taxes with the sole exception of stamp duties. However, regarding customs duty, the exemption was limited to machinery and equipment required to start operations.

Four years later the potential oil wealth of Mexico was already becoming apparent, and two lawyers and members of the Mexican Congress, Lorenzo Elízaga and Luis Ibarra, submitted to the government a draft for a new mining law under which public mineral ownership in coal and oil would have been restored. The government referred the draft to the *Academia Mexicana de Legislación y Jurisprudencia* for an expert opinion

---

17. In the following we rely heavily on Collado's article.
18. Mexico followed thereby the move of Florida, Texas, New Mexico, Arizona, and Louisiana. These territories formerly belonged to Spain, Mexico, and France. Texas, for example, extended private landed property rights to the minerals beneath the surface in 1866, Louisiana in 1870. (Bradley 1996: 290–2, 352)

(Sentíes 1989: 115–17). In the ensuing academic debate the two lawyers supported public mineral ownership with the same arguments put by Mirabeau to the French National Assembly in 1791. They denied that the landlords could legitimately claim ownership on unknown mineral deposits, the purpose of public ownership being 'to activate the coal and oil which the indolence, or the arbitrariness, or the incapacity of the present surface owners maintain concealed in the recesses of the earth or out of the reach of our industrial progress' (quoted in Collado 1987: 39). Accordingly, they said, the petroleum industry should be declared of 'utilidad pública', i.e. eminent domain rights should prevail over private surface property rights, although previously acquired rights would be respected.

The viewpoints of foreign oil interests were determined by two outstanding personalities: Sir Weetman D. Pearson (Lord Cowdray), a British citizen, and Edward L. Doheny, an American. Pearson later founded the Mexican Eagle Oil Company (El Águila) and Doheny the Huesteca Petroleum Company, by far the two biggest companies in the country in the years to come. Pearson was interested in public lands and supported the draft law. He was probably even its promoter. In fact, Elízaga and Ibarra were his legal representatives (Collado 1987: 38). Doheny, on the other hand, from the very beginning was interested in *buying* private land. Not surprisingly, being a proprietor of vast potentially oil-bearing estates, he opposed the initiative of Elízaga and Ibarra, and so did the majority of the *Academia* who deemed the draft to be retroactive and, therefore, unconstitutional. According to its majority, the fact that the mineral deposits or reservoirs were undiscovered or unworked was irrelevant. They had to be regarded and respected as private property. The opportunity to elaborate a modern petroleum law, at a time when vested interests were still very small, was lost.

The first lot of important concessions was granted the following year. The lease term was fifty years. Tax exemptions, including customs duties, applied to the whole period. Although these contracts were obviously contrary to the Petroleum Law of 1901, Congress approved them. In other words, at this stage, none of the parties involved was able to impose a legally consistent oil policy.[19] On the one hand, the companies would later typically insist on their 'faithfully' acquired rights and, on the other, the government would claim that these contracts went through Congress 'fraudulently' being read out quietly to conceal last-minute illegal changes (Gobierno de México 1940: XXX; Collado 1987: 29). These contracts contained another note-worthy feature: the Calvo clause, according to which concession-aires were unrestrictedly subject to Mexican law and courts, waiving their rights to protection by their respective embassies.

This was, then, the legal framework on which the extraordinary oil boom of the following decade, triggered by the discovery of the 'Golden Lane' in 1909, had to rely. Mexico became the world's largest exporter and second largest producer coincidentally with revolution and civil war. After 1914, however, the rest of the world was not peaceful either. War and revolution brought the production of Russia – up to then the world's second largest producer – to a standstill. The world's number one producer, the United States, was not able to keep up with the sharply increasing demand following the invention of the internal combustion engine. The country became a net importer of petroleum, albeit temporarily. Hence, Mexican production soared to maximum levels at maximum prices. In 1920 the average wellhead-price per barrel in the United States was an extraordinary US\$ 3.07. In 1920 Mexico produced 157 million barrels, which amounted to 24 per cent of world output. Virtually all of it was exported, most of it (78 per cent) to the United States (Hall 1995: 13).

The Mexican legal framework was totally inadequate, with respect not only to sub-surface but also to surface rights. 'The confusion of an oil boom in a region where property lines were blurred and informal multifamily ownership was the norm, resulted in a great many leases being suspect. If the land, by chance, yielded a flowing well, later litigation became endless' (Brown 1992: 8–10). Not surprisingly, then, 'a majority of the leases and land were held illegally'. In fact, 'the leasing documents for the first few years were often Spanish translations of the ones that were being used in Texas and other areas of the US'. Worse, beyond litigation, 'given the significance of the prize

---

19. As we shall see, the same situation is still to be found more or less in all Third World oil countries.

to be won, these fights often led beyond legal battles to violence and even murder' (Hall 1995: 104). This situation also entailed, of course, waste and the premature exhaustion of the reservoirs.

Mexican landowners were initially in a disadvantageous position. Ignorant of the potential value of their lands and economically weak, they were confronted with modern, powerful foreign oil companies, and sold out cheaply.[20] When land was leased, rentals of 5 to 25 Pesos *per hectare* and royalties of 5 to 25 per cent were paid. Five per cent was apparently the usual royalty rate by 1914, for example in the region of Tuxpan; but by 1916 it had increased to 10 per cent. At the same time, in the Istmo region royalties were usually between 10 and 15 per cent, and, exceptionally, even as high as 40 per cent. The lease terms were generally between 20 and 30 years. There is no doubt that rents and royalties did increase with competition once the potential oil wealth of the lands was revealed. And the landlords had to depend not only on market forces; the local authorities supported them. In order to strengthen the Mexican lessors, General Cándido Aguilar, son-in-law of President Venustiano Carranza and governor of Veracruz – the state containing virtually all producing oil fields – ordered by decree, in 1914, and again in 1916, that all transfers, sales, leases, or mortgages had to be approved by the local government, thus creating an opportunity to intercede in favour of the Mexican landowners. A contract would not be approved if it 'was unjust and detrimental to one of the parties' and the exploitation of the lands would 'exclusively benefit the companies' (Gobierno de México 1940: 541–42).

Similarly, on public lands the government had extended important tax privileges to its concessionaires, which quickly turned out to be far too generous. In 1910, still under the presidency of Porfirio Díaz, the government increased the bar duty collected at the port of Tampico (Brown 1992: 6). Thereafter, due to revolution and civil war there was a desperate need for additional revenues and now, most conveniently, the *ancien régime* could be blamed for the exemptions granted. As the Mexican government could not convince the companies to

---

20. In 1921 it was estimated that the companies, acquired at an early stage at low prices, owned some 25 per cent of oil-producing lands.

agree to higher taxes, President Madero, in 1912, finally went ahead with a production tax in the form of a stamp duty. The companies paid under protest, but in 1914 the Mexican Supreme Court ruled this tax to be legal (Meyer and Morales 1990: 38). The same procedure was used to decree an *ad valorem* tax of 10 per cent on crude oil exports in 1917. The companies again protested, but to no avail. The fact was that the oil sector was the only really working and still profitable, indeed highly profitable, sector of the national economy.

The international importance of Mexican oil put the sovereignty of the country into jeopardy early on, a fact which brought a new viewpoint into the debate over private *vs.* public mineral ownership. In 1911 rumours spread that Standard Oil of New Jersey (SONJ) was about to take over the British-owned Mexican Eagle. The take-over would have completed the control of Mexican oil by American companies. It was argued in the Mexican Congress that public ownership and an appropriate concession system would provide the tools to prevent this from happening. These rumours turned out to be false, although it was in 1911 that SONJ obtained its first successful concession in Mexico under the same conditions as those granted earlier.

With revolution unfolding, there was also the threat of American military intervention. US military forces went into action twice, though in both cases intervention was limited in its importance and not directly related to oil. Nevertheless, the threat was real. Moreover the US government and the oil companies had a strong bearing on the precarious balance of power in a country torn apart by civil war and revolution. Worse, by the end of 1914 the central government lost control over the oil-producing region – although not over the ports of export – to rebel forces under the leadership of General Manuel Peláez. It remained under his control for the next six years, Peláez maintaining his rebel army with levies exacted from royalty owners and oil companies.

In January 1915 President Carranza intensified the swelling conflict by decreeing the suspension of new drilling,[21] since he considered it necessary to revise radically the petroleum

---

21. These permits were necessary, private property of coal and oil notwith- standing, as the working of the underground was legally subject, in any case, to the regulations applying to mining generally.

legislation of the country, and to regulate the activities of exploration and exploitation. 'So far neither the nation nor the government have had the benefits they are rightfully entitled to' (quoted in Collado 1987: 79). Although under the pressure of the US Department of State Carranza soon granted 'provisional permits', he went ahead with his plan and appointed a *Comisión Técnica de Hidrocarburos*, which would have 'to propose laws and regulations necessary to the development of the industry' (Gobierno de México 1940: 541). The Committee, chaired by General Cándido Aguilar, concluded the following year recommending public ownership of the reservoirs.

Public Mineral Ownership

In January 1917, a new Constitution was proclaimed to become effective on 1 May. Art.27 covered the ownership of natural resources, a central issue for what was, indeed, a peasant revolution. Regarding the surface, while safeguarding eminent domain rights, it sanctioned private ownership; however, minerals were to be kept in the public domain:

> To the Nation belongs the direct dominion of all minerals or substances which in seams, layers, lumps, or reservoirs constitute deposits distinct from the components of the land, such as ... solid mineral fuels, petroleum and all hydrocarbons solid, liquid, or gaseous ....
>
> In [these cases] the dominion of the Nation is inalienable and indispensable, and only the Federal Government may grant concessions ... subject to the condition that they are worked regularly. (Art.27, 1917 Constitution)

The new Constitution also embodied the Calvo clause:

> Only Mexicans by birth or by naturalisation and Mexican companies have the right to acquire the dominion of lands, waters, and its accessories, or to obtain concessions to exploit mines, waters, or mineral fuels .... The State may concede the same rights to foreigners subject to their agreeing with the Ministry of Foreign Relations to consider themselves, with respect to these goods, as nationals and not to invoke the protection of their government. (Art.27, 1917 Constitution)

The Committee in charge of drafting Art.27, in its Exposition of Motifs suggested that the 1884 Mining Law, which had conceded private mineral property rights on coal and oil, was probably null and void from the very beginning 'as no government can possibly have the authority to transfer, generally and permanently, the rights which pertain to a Nation on those goods which are, and always have been, part of its undivided inheritance' (Burgoa Orihuela 1989: 142). Thus, if at one extreme the *Academia* had argued, dogmatically, that private mineral property rights were absolute and not limited by eminent domain rights, at the other extreme the argument, equally dogmatic, was that eminent domain rights on minerals were absolute and, hence, private mineral property rights could never have been legal. Both sides were unable, and unwilling, to understand that these were only differences in governance, as even a careful reading of Art.27 made plain: some minerals belong to the nation when found at greater depths, but not if found close to, or on, the surface.

According to Knight, Art.27 'was the work of a small group of intellectuals and *políticos*, a minority within the minority Constituent Congress' (Knight 1986: 508). One may even suspect that the approval of public mineral ownership by the Constituent Assembly was actually facilitated by the fact that rebels controlled the oil-producing region. Manuel Peláez, the rebel leader in control of the oil fields and himself a royalty owner, not surprisingly opposed Art.27 and supported private property rights (Brown 1992: 16). Similarly, the first Congress of Mexican Industry, in 1917, considered Art.27 'to be retroactive and socialist and ... an attack against property and Human Rights' (quoted in Collado 1987: 98). And even though General Heriberto Jara, a delegate to the Constituent Assembly, welcomed Art.27, he did so in the belief that this was a way to strengthen Mexican landowners against the plundering foreign oil companies (Collado 1987: 85), an idea he shared with General Cándido Aguilar. The latter considered the fact that petroleum properties were usually fragmented in small plots to be consistent with 'the ideal of the distribution of land, sustained by the Revolution'. Accordingly, to diminish or to limit those property rights would always turn out 'to benefit the exploiting capitalists. Thus, the national would be sacrificed in favour of the foreigner' (quoted in Collado 1987: 97).

Aguilar's ideal of small property owners was precisely the nightmare of those 'intellectuals and *políticos*' which, on the contrary, in government publications tried to convince the oil companies, quoting Adam Smith and John Stuart Mill, of the advantages of public ownership and the disappearance of the class of landowners. Joaquín Santaella, a spokesman of the government, made no secret of his feeling regarding private mineral ownership in oil:

> Shall we establish a privileged class of oil rentiers? They have not displayed any contribution of capital, intelligence, or effort in order to obtain an income which no merchant, manufacturer, or professional can possibly imagine ever achieving. (Quoted in Collado 1987: 96)

'One has to make a fundamental distinction', Santaella argued, 'between the oilman and the landowner, because the latter plays the same role in this industry as the dead weight in transport. He is more harmful than helpful to the development of the oil industry' (quoted in Díaz Dufoó 1921: 123n). On the contrary, the industrial investors deserved a special treatment. 'It is in the interest of the Nation to support the industrial investor and to give all kinds of guarantees to him' (quoted in Díaz Dufoó 1921: 260).

Art.27 had to entail negotiations and further legislation. Leaseholders had to become concessionaires, which was *per se* nothing frightening. Technically, a modern concession system could provide an ideal framework for producers. Certainly, to disentangle the maze of landed property rights and leases, converting them into concessions, would require a major organisational, legal and political effort. However, to co-operate in creating such a system could be very rewarding, as sorting out and organising rationally the different interests in the fields would entail large savings and gains in productivity (Hall 1995: 109). Moreover, there was a big prize to be won: a satisfactory arrangement could open up new areas of interest. So far concessions or leases covered only a minor part of the potentially oil-bearing lands in Mexico, and even less had been explored. Theoretically at least, the benefits could help to accommodate everybody, royalty owners included.

Sovereign Taxation. In February 1918 the government decreed taxes on royalty owners. Surface rentals were to be taxed, according to their importance, at 10 to 50 per cent. A flat 50 per cent tax would apply to royalties. These were unusually high rates. For the lands worked by the companies as freeholders, a yearly surface tax of five Pesos per hectare and a royalty of 5 per cent were to apply. Furthermore, owners of oil properties were required to register officially within three months in order to be allowed to continue drilling. Thereafter all unregistered lands would be considered vacant. There is no doubt that this decree sealed the alliance between Mexican landlords and American free holding companies. As Luis Cabrera, an outstanding intellectual, observed, the government 'made the mistake of not seeking the support of the landowners' (quoted in Collado 1987: 107). But could one really expect otherwise, in the midst of a peasant revolution? Moreover, were royalty owners not supporting rebel forces with their 'taxes', willingly or not?

They both refused to pay, and the oil companies generally refused to register. The US, the UK, and the French governments sent diplomatic notes in protest at Carranza's decree in February 1918, on the grounds that it resulted in confiscations of private property and arbitrary losses of property rights (Díaz Dufoó 1921: 270–72). The British note omitted any consideration of the sovereign right to tax; this provoked an angry answer from the Mexican government, pointing out that the British government 'would not accept diplomatic objections due to the contributions, necessarily high because of the war, which the government has been obliged to decree in all its dominions and which also affect foreigners' (quoted in Díaz Dufoó 1921: 277–78). Even worse, the companies operating in Mexico were actually paying taxes to their home countries, in support of the war effort. Though there are no data regarding British companies, there are some data regarding one American company. In 1918 Huasteca Petroleum Company was paying two million dollars to the Mexican government in taxes but five million to the American government, in support of the war effort, in excess profit taxes (Collado 1987: 91). Nevertheless the fact was that, given the circumstances, the question of sovereign taxation and nationalisation of the reservoirs was closely linked.

As the confrontation escalated, the companies decided to join forces in the Association of Petroleum Producers in Mexico (APPM). Negotiations with two representatives of the oil companies led to a decree in August 1918, whereby 'positive acts' realised before 1 May 1917 (i.e. having made some investment) were sufficient to prevent the land from being defined as 'vacant'. In other words, some kind of 'acquired rights' was acknowledged. At the same time, it was suggested that the export tax would be lowered. In exchange, the companies' representatives recognised the principle of public mineral ownership. Then, however, the APPM immediately disavowed the agreement, and the Mexican government, in turn, resumed its policy of confrontation and harassment. Finally, in 1921, the American oil companies sent a high-powered negotiating team to Mexico.

The delegates were five top executives from SONJ, Mexican Petroleum (Huasteca), Atlantic Refining, Sinclair Consolidated, and the Texas Company. They had three major aims: (1) a tax agreement that would be permanent; (2) the freedom to continue exploratory drilling; and (3) the cancellation of harassing regulations. 'They further hoped that the tax agreement would reduce their obligations by about 50 per cent' (Hall 1995: 29). If they could reach an agreement along these lines they would be able to double output and the government would suffer no loss of revenues. All they achieved, however, was a reduction in production and export taxes. On the other hand, Shell, which had taken over El Águila in 1918, protested at having been excluded from these negotiations.

In November the same year, W.C.Teagle (SONJ), who was taking part in the negotiations in Mexico, informed the US Department of State that seven American majors were interested in joining together for combined explorations in Mesopotamia. These were the same five companies negotiating in Mexico, plus two others. At the same time, the five were also interested in a joint venture in Mexico provided that the American government did not object on anti-trust grounds. Initially, President Obregón was enthusiastic about the idea. The existing companies would transfer about one and a half million acres to the new company, and they would agree to pay the government what they considered a generous share – 25 per cent – of the profits. 'In return, they also wanted the government to include all adjacent federal zones ... in the holdings of the joint company' (Hall 1995: 33). Indeed, this was in principle the way the problem had to be dealt with: the companies would convert their leaseholds and freeholds into concessions but, at the same time, the concessions could be reshaped and enlarged according to the underlying geological structure. Joining in one company, reservoirs covered by different concessions would be exploited rationally as a geological entity. Royal Dutch–Shell, also expressed its interest in participating in this scheme.

However, the American companies wanted a one-sided deal. On the one hand, they insisted on a 'permanent' tax agreement with the Federal government protecting them 'from taxation and harassment from state and local authorities' (Hall 1995: 34–35). On the other hand, they refused to accept the conversion of their holdings into concessions and the payment of rents and royalties on what they considered their own land, insisting on Carranza's decrees being declared null and void. As a matter of fact, they were unwilling to agree to anything less than the cancellation of Art.27. The negotiations with the companies had failed.

The US Government. The American oil companies were successful in further delaying US recognition of the Mexican government. But their influence in Washington was diminishing and more voices, with other interests than oil, were to be heard asking for recognition. Finally, in 1922, the American government sent a team of negotiators to Mexico to settle the issue of Art.27. 'Surprisingly, during the actual course of negotiations, the question of subsoil rights was dealt with relatively quickly. ... The discussion of agrarian matters lasted much longer' (Hall 1995: 148). This should not be surprising at all. Agrarian reform implied the expropriation of large estates to be distributed amongst the peasants, in the form of small individual properties or *ejidos*. In the case of the subsoil, Art.27 favoured the miners, i.e. the oil companies, against the private surface owner. In the first case, the problem was to get rid of the landlords, some of them US citizens or Europeans, by paying an indemnity. In the second case, the oil companies had to give up private mineral property rights as far as they were landowners, but would conserve, through concessions, their rights as producers. What is more, the producers' potential rights would be strengthened on lands they did not own. Hence, the problem was only to agree on the definition of a 'positive act' and the extension of existing 'acquired rights'. This was achieved easily as the Mexican government accepted the most generous definition possible of a 'positive act', from having drilled the land to having bought it with the intention to do so. What is more, in the new legislation surface owners were granted a preferential right to obtain a concession. Mexico's sovereign right to tax, however, and Art.27, remained in place. Recognition followed.

The Failure of Reform. Still the American companies were not satisfied. They continued to complain that 'the question of taxes had not been resolved and that no absolute ownership of the subsoil had been granted by the Mexican government. Worst of all, the question of royalties … was left open' (Hall 1995: 152). What is more, they 'had not given up on the possibility of replacing Obregón with someone more malleable' (Hall 1995: 152). It has always been rumoured that they supported the (failed) De La Huerta rebellion, which started at the end of the year in the heart of the oil-producing region, Veracruz.

Any sensible solution would have required negotiations, a balance of rewards and threats. It is difficult to imagine a definitive settlement of that kind, necessarily complex, without some 'arm twisting'. Given the stubborn unwillingness of the big companies, nothing could be achieved without the *American* government assuming a role as mediator, as it actually did, as we shall see, in Venezuela twenty years later. In Mexico, President Plutarco Elías Calles finally went ahead, unilaterally, with legislation.

The long awaited Petroleum Law regulating Art.27 was passed in December 1925. The oil industry was declared to be of 'utilidad pública', i.e. 'the industry will enjoy preferential rights over any use of the surface' (quoted in Collado 1987: 135). A concession would not last more than thirty years, but could be renewed. Private surface owners were granted a minimum royalty of 5 per cent 'as an indemnity' (Collado 1987: 135); the word *royalty* was avoided. On public lands, the situation was basically the same: an indemnity for the use of the surface plus a royalty, to be determined on a case-by-case basis. Those who had worked or leased land for the explicit purpose of producing oil prior to 1 May 1917 would be granted 'confirmatory concessions'. The concession period would be, at the most, fifty years from the day the land had first been worked or leased. Finally, those who did not apply for a confirmatory concession within the following twelve months would forego all rights. Clearly, the definition of a 'positive act' implicit in this law was somewhat more restrictive than the one agreed on in the negotiations with the American government.

The APPM protested, supported by the American Ambassador in Mexico and the Secretary of State in Washington. Nevertheless, most of the smaller companies submitted to the law. The big European companies, after some hesitation, finally lined up with the Americans. The tension eased again when the Supreme Court ruled in favour of the complaining companies. Limiting the period of confirmatory concessions to fifty years was deemed to be retroactive and, hence, unconstitutional. By the same token, non-compliance with the law was not considered to have been illegal. The government retreated and reformed the 1925 Petroleum Law accordingly. In the case of freeholders, the confirmatory concessions would not establish any time limit, and in the case of leaseholders the original period of tenure would remain. What is more, and contrary even to the letter of Constitutional Art.27, the companies would not be obliged to sign the Calvo clause, though the validity of that clause was not questioned either. Again, the companies had to apply for confirmatory concessions within the following twelve months, which they finally did but only under pressure from their own governments (Meyer and Morales 1990: 69). In other words, the companies had succeeded in enforcing their viewpoint, and they had only given way on one *formal* point: they had accepted registration and, by doing so, became *concessionaires*.

Moreover, the companies enforced their will on another point. In 1927 the government repealed Carranza's decree of February 1918. Although never applied, formally at least it had still been in force. This meant in practice that the land-owning oil companies would not pay any rents and royalties even after the conversion of their lands into concessions. On lands leased before 1 May 1917, on the other hand, rents and royalties would be paid, according to the law, to the Mexican landowners.

Consequently, in the mid-1930s only one quarter of output was subject to any state royalty; three quarters was subject to general taxation only (Collado 1987: 211). Regarding the latter, in 1924 Mexico created an income tax. The oil companies were subject to an 8 per cent rate; for royalty owners a 10 per cent applied. There was no protest. Regarding income tax one has to keep in mind that this development was in line with what was happening in the United States and Europe. The international companies could credit the full amount against their income tax liabilities at home. The same applied to the increases in 1933, when a maximum corporate income tax of 12.3 per cent was established; as for rents and royalties, the maximum rate was now 20.3 per cent (Collado 1987: 137–8, 152).

The companies still had something to complain about: the confirmatory concessions were issued very slowly. According to the government, the problem was due to the fact that much of the documentation handed over by the companies was faulty. In 1921 it had been estimated that the companies controlled 2.7 million hectares, two million as leaseholders and 0.7 million as freeholders. Yet by 1933 they held confirmatory concessions on 6.9 million hectares, and 2.6 million as 'ordinary concessions', i.e. concessions granted after 1 May 1917. Many leases were dated a few days before 1 May 1917 (Collado 1987: 151–59).

Modern Governance Frustrated. What was the practical importance of private rents and royalties? According to Philip, 'payment to landowners played a fairly significant part in the overall financial calculations of the companies' (Philip 1982: 28). He quotes a diplomatic source from 1926, stating that the average royalty rate was about 10 per cent, and 'that no less than thirty million pounds [$150 million] had already been paid out to Mexicans in royalties' (Philip 1982: 28). This should be compared with $200m of taxes paid up to 1926 by all oil companies combined. Though this number was never confirmed, Philip concludes that, in any case, 'payments to landowners, law-suits arising out of disputed claims and bribes to settle these were of significant economic as well as political importance in Mexico' (1982: 29).

After 1927 a quite peaceful decade followed, not only in oil but also in US-Mexican relations generally. Moreover, Mexican oil production soon began to recover, due to El Águila's discovery of a giant field in Poza Rica. This was the biggest discovery in decades. The reservoir extended beyond the El Águila concessions and, in November 1937, a new concession was granted covering 13,000 acres, the government receiving royalties in different blocks of between 15 per cent and 35 per cent (Collado 1987: 188). Nevertheless, as far as oil was concerned, this peace was not based on any understanding but rather on the Mexican government's resignation to its fate, at least for the time being. The foreign oil companies had seriously interfered with the institutionalisation of the new Mexican state, and had successfully frustrated the development of modern governance in oil. Ultimately, they had refused formally to acknowledge, and to submit to, Mexico's sovereignty.

The fact that some American oil companies had become big landowners prior to the Revolution played an important role in this outcome. It blurred the lines, which the Revolution was eager to draw, and created an unfortunate alliance between Mexican landowners, concession dealers, and the oil companies. The American oil companies with their national background of private mineral property were particularly ill prepared, but also unwilling, to understand and to submit to modern concessions. British, French and Dutch interests with their European background, largely based on concessions anyway, were in a much better position to understand the problem and, at least in this regard, were also more willing to co-operate. Yet at the end of the day, although they represented a majority interest in Mexican oil, they accepted American leadership and, thus, the route of confrontation.

Nationalisation of the Oil Industry

The share of oil in Mexico's GDP has been estimated, for the year 1921, at 6.92 per cent; eleven years later it was down to 1.62 per cent. Indeed, oil production peaked in 1921 with 193 million barrels but, due to the lack of new investment and the wasteful exploitation of the existing fields, it fell to 33 million barrels in 1932. Prices, which had peaked in 1920, had also come down. Average wellhead prices in the United States may be taken as an indicator. They fell from US$ 3.07 in 1920, to

US$ 0.87 in 1932. Fiscal revenues, however, were more stable. Taxes had increased from US¢ 10 per barrel in 1919 to over US¢ 16 in 1920 and 1921, and thereafter stabilised somewhat above US¢ 20 (Philip 1982: 17). Even though this was still significantly less than rents, royalties, and taxes paid in the United States, with price levels around one dollar per barrel the Mexican fiscal take was significant. However, fiscal petroleum revenues fell with volumes. Total fiscal revenues in oil peaked in the early 1920s, when they amounted to one third of government revenues; ten years later, they only represented about one eighth (Meyer and Morales 1990: 65). Internationally, the loss of importance of Mexican oil was even more striking, from 25 per cent of world output in 1921 to some 2.5 per cent in the mid-1930s. Furthermore, American investment in Mexico had increased significantly with peace, but only a fraction was investment in oil (Collado 1987: 143). Oil accounted for less than 20 per cent of Mexican exports (Hamilton 1982: 217).

From one point of view, however, the importance of Mexican oil actually increased: as an input to the national economy. In 1920, virtually all of Mexican oil was exported. But with the end of Revolution and civil war and with the economy recovering, by the mid-1930s about 40 per cent of the output was consumed domestically. In fact, the expected domestic demand was the main reason why the Mexican government had been seriously concerned with petroleum conservation since the time of Carranza. His successor, Obregón, created 'national reserves' (including some very promising strips of land, such as the tracks of the national railroad sometimes running through producing fields).[22] From these national reserves emerged, in 1933, Petromex, the first national oil company, to produce, refine, and distribute petroleum and petroleum products in the domestic market.[23] It was intended to be a joint venture between

---

22. This was very much in line with what was happening north of the border. Fears of an 'imminent exhaustion of oil led there to petroleum-land withdrawals and the reservation of oil-rich acreage for military use. Four Naval Petroleum Reserves were set aside between 1912 and 1923' (Bradley 1996: 1027).

23. Mexico thus followed the example of Argentina and its Yacimientos Petrolíferos Fiscales (YPF), a public company set up to secure domestic supply at low prices (De Gortari Rábiela 1989: 95).

the government (40 per cent) and the Mexican private sector
(60 per cent). Yet the government would have, according to the
company's bylaws, the power of veto on certain questions such
as production volumes and subcontracting. The national private
sector, however, did not respond as expected, leaving the
government with the majority of the shares. It has been claimed
that the lack of interest from the private sector was due to the
government's veto power (España 1993: 82–83). However, one
may wonder if there was not a more fundamental reason, which
had led the government to insist on its veto power in the first
place: the smouldering confrontation with the foreign companies.
Was there any other way to ensure that the national oil
entrepreneurs would not become allies of the foreign companies,
as had happened with Mexican royalty owners?

Anyway, in 1936 Lázaro Cárdenas went ahead with the
project, though the company would now be wholly state-owned.
As it turned out, this company would soon be quite helpful.
Indeed, the following year saw the beginning of the famous
confrontation between petroleum workers and the industry,
which led to its nationalisation. The two parties being unable
to reach an agreement, the Sindicato de los Trabajadores
Petroleros de la República Mexicana (STPRM) brought the
dispute before the Junta Federal de Conciliación y Arbitraje
(JFCA). The Junta grasped the opportunity not only to
pronounce judgement on the issue at stake – a labour dispute –
but also on the role the foreign oil companies had played since
the Revolution. Amongst other things, the verdict stated that
the principal oil companies 'have never been connected to the
country and their interests have always been foreign and on
occasion in effective opposition to those of the nation'. It accused
the companies of selling their products in Mexico at prices considerably higher than those at which the same products were
sold abroad, thus creating an obstacle to national economic
development. Most importantly, however, the verdict concluded
that the oil companies had obtained 'very considerable profits'
and, consequently, they were 'perfectly capable of accepting
the demands of the STPRM up to a value of approximately 26
million *pesos*', i.e. US$ 7.2 million (Philip 1982: 218; Collado
1987: 196).

The oil companies rejected the verdict and appealed to the

Supreme Court, where they lost again. Nevertheless, they continued to refuse to comply with the verdict, convinced that they could still impose their will as they had done in the past.

Economically, however, they were now much less powerful than they had been, say, fifteen years earlier. Politically, with the Democrats and Franklin D. Roosevelt in charge of the government, they had also lost much of their influence in Washington. Cárdenas considered nationalisation secretly, and taking into account the international situation and the proximity of war, he believed a US invasion of Mexico to be an unlikely response. He was the most popular Mexican president ever; amongst other things, he systematically applied Constitutional Art.27 distributing land to the peasantry. And this was actually the first time a confrontation with the companies had popular backing. The oil workers went on strike on 17 March 1938. Cárdenas seized the opportunity and, to everybody's surprise, decreed the nationalisation of the foreign oil companies on 18 March 1938 (Collado 1987: 200).[24] In his radio address to the Nation he made plain that the issue at stake was nothing less than Mexico's sovereignty.

The Nationalised Industry. Cárdenas' appreciation of the national and the international situation proved to be correct, though the international companies largely succeeded in depriving Mexican oil of its export markets. Even after the question of indemnity payments was settled (in 1941 with the American and in 1948 with the British companies), the national oil company Petróleos Mexicanos (Pemex) – founded in June 1938 – was never really accepted but just tolerated. In fact, Pemex concentrated on the rapidly increasing domestic demand, and did so successfully. Until 1966 there was always something left for exports.

Except during the Second World War, international financial institutions refused to grant any loan to the state-owned oil company (Philip 1982: 61–62). When Pemex, in 1947, applied to the Export-Import Bank for a loan in order to explore and to double reserves and production, it was turned down by the US State Department on the grounds that 'an unconditional

---

24. There were some minor exceptions such as Gulf Oil, a company that was not involved in the conflict.

petroleum loan would be interpreted in Mexico and throughout the world as United States government approval of a nationalistic approach to the problem of oil', which 'would weaken the position of the strategic Venezuelan industry' (quoted in Philip 1982: 77). The position of the State Department prevailed even against President Truman who wanted the loan to go ahead and, with it, the contracts Pemex was willing to sign with independent American companies. Finally, and exceptionally, in this case there was a diplomatic arrangement and a loan was made available, indirectly, to Pemex (Philip 1982: 76–77).

Theoretically, private investment in petroleum was still possible. In fact, between 1949 and 1951 sixteen exploration contracts were signed, precisely as a result of that loan. The exploring companies, if successful, were to be awarded a royalty of 15 to 18 per cent in compensation for the risk assumed (Meyer and Morales 1990: 83–112). Eventually, however, the door was closed completely. In 1960, the following lines were added to Constitutional Art.27:

> in the case of petroleum and carbons and hydrogen solid, liquid or gaseous, no concession or contract will be granted, nor will those subsist which may have been granted already. (Quoted in Burgoa Orihuela 1989: 147)

Basically, foreign markets were closed to Mexican oil, and Mexican oil was closed to foreign investment. This situation was to last until the international oil companies lost control over world markets to OPEC in the early 1970s.

Landowners. With the nationalisation of the foreign companies Mexican landowners were suddenly on their own. In 1941, their right to a 5 per cent 'indemnity' – actually a 5 per cent royalty – granted by the 1925 Petroleum Law, was cancelled, the government paying compensation. Royalty owners whose rights originated in leases prior to 1917 were asked to sell them to Pemex. The confirmatory or regular concessions still in force were dealt with similarly. This was a protracted procedure extending over more than two decades. The last concessions disappeared with the constitutional reform of 1960.

Something to Celebrate

According to Philip, public opinion played a very minor role in the nationalisation of the industry. 'There is no sign that there existed any general public opinion which played a real part in pressing Cárdenas to move against the oil companies' (Philip 1982: 226). He also claims that some union leaders kept secret the companies' last-minute offer to settle the labour dispute, as they feared that it might prove acceptable to the workers. This may have been the case, but the government was also sure of its ultimate support. The companies had become isolated up to the point where, once nationalisation was announced, 'no opponent of nationalisation within the country dared open his mouth' (Philip 1982: 224). One might suspect that amongst those opponents were Mexican royalty owners.

Indeed, this was essentially a question of governance. The companies had continued to rely only on their influence at the margin of, and in opposition to, the process of consolidation of the Mexican revolution, institutionally, economically, and politically, and they clung to their political enclave status in spite of the growth of the domestic market. For the Mexican government, by 1938, the problem was no longer one of taxing exports but of supplying the domestic market at reasonable prices. With revolution, and most notably with the Cárdenas government, export-oriented *latifundios* had been converted into small properties and *ejidos* producing for the domestic market. Similarly, the formerly oil-exporting enclave was converted into a national, domestic oil industry.[25] A Mexican public company was to produce Mexican oil for Mexican consumers, a policy which, not surprisingly, could count on overwhelming popular support. At present 18 March is still a day of celebrations.

2.4   Conclusions

The existence of a customary royalty is certainly the most significant single feature in both British coal and American oil leases. The different historical and political circumstances not withstanding, the outcome was in this regard, in qualitative

---

25. For a systematic elaboration on Mexican oil industry in its proper context see De La Vega (1999).

terms, basically the same. Once established, the inertia of a large and complex structure of long-term private leases embedding a customary ground rent – not only a royalty but also a surface rental and signature bonus – guaranteed a remarkably stable equilibrium. And both case studies confirm, beyond any doubt, the importance of the customary ground rent, thus proving Ricardian rent theory wrong.

To adapt private mineral property rights to the dynamics of coal production was certainly a much more difficult task than in oil, not only politically but also technically. With the benefit of hindsight it seems obvious that the British coal industry required significant reforms decades before the 1870s, when *productivity* began to decline. But there was very little discussion on reform until *output* started to fall forty years later. In oil, on the other hand, conservation legislation developed forty years ahead of the peak of production in 1970. It seems to me that this was due not only to political differences. In the case of oil, problems were obvious, immediate, general, and easy to observe by everybody on the surface. Nevertheless, it still took about seven decades – from the 1860s to the 1930s – to develop significant legislation on conservation. In coal, on the other hand, it was much more difficult to observe what was going on with increasing mine depths. Furthermore, reforms had a relatively immediate effect in oil but not in coal. Even after nationalisation of the mineral *and* the mining companies, it still took decades to modernise British coalmines. In fact, many were never completely modernised; they were simply closed down. And the modern ones were finally re-privatised.

Both cases make clear the advantage of public over private mineral ownership, at least for minerals which have to be extracted from the greater depths. Wherever private mineral ownership prevails society has to pay twice, ground rent as well as increased technical production costs. Indeed, according to our case studies the latter is more important than the former. This seems to be the case even in oil, conservation legislation notwithstanding, as comprehensive studies and estimates of unitisation *vs.* fragmentation prove. In the case of coal there are only isolated observations and no systematic study, although detailed records do exist of the problems the nationalised industry inherited from the era of private mineral property.

And there is also the experience of public ownership on the Continent, where coalmining was successful despite a much poorer natural endowment. The evidence suggests that fragmented landed property was finally much more of a problem in British coal than in American oil. The governance of British coal collapsed, whereas the governance of American oil was able to evolve and adapt. Ultimately adaptation consisted in not allowing the private mineral resource owners to interfere technically with production, though *in principle* their right to collect a ground rent was never questioned. As a matter of fact, this right was not questioned in British coal either. The government paid a full indemnity.

The case of Mexico brings in a host of very different aspects. Most importantly, the companies were foreign, producing basically for foreign markets. Given the economic importance of Mexican oil in the world economy and the underdevelopment of the national economy, a fundamental imbalance emerged. It was exacerbated by private mineral ownership and reform – taking back the reservoirs into public ownership – and was caught in the middle of a peasant revolution. The landed companies ended up in a counterrevolutionary alliance, which ultimately led to their nationalisation. However, if we look at British coal, the sequence was the same: the nationalisation of the mining companies followed the nationalisation of the natural resource. This seems to suggest that, in the case of Mexico, the importance of the political environment may be overestimated. Or, conversely, the difficulty of severing a complex structure from its root and grafting it on to a new structure without provoking its collapse may be underestimated. The nationalisation of the industry may be reversed, and has actually been reversed in the case of British coal. In Mexico this is also a possibility. Yet nobody has ever suggested, in Great Britain or in Mexico, re-privatising the natural resource.

As a matter of fact, with nationalisation of Mexican oil and British coal the issue of mineral ownership as such simply disappeared from public debate. The nationalisation of the oil industry became a powerful myth, an essential part of the revolutionary genesis of modern Mexico. The nationalisation of the natural resource, an issue that actually divided the nation, was suppressed from public consciousness and replaced by the nationalisation of the industry, which united the nation against divisive foreign powers. If we look at British coal, the situation is basically the same. The nationalisation of the natural resource by a Conservative government has simply been erased from the collective memory of the British people. Only the nationalisation of the mining companies is remembered, moreover as an act of a Labour government. This seems to suggest again that, in the case of Mexico, we can overestimate the importance of the political environment. The fact is that both cases are consistent with the way that modern economics deal with natural resources – that is, by not dealing with them.

3 PUBLIC GOVERNANCE OF MINERAL RESOURCES: FUNDAMENTALS

3.1 Non-proprietorial vs. Proprietorial Governance

The economic and technical advantage of public mineral owner-ship in hydrocarbons and in mining at great depth is proven beyond any shadow of doubt. The reservoirs and mineral deposits are managed by the state, which creates a Licensing Agency, and it is then the duty of this agency to facilitate and promote co-operation amongst investors according to the geology. However, there is still the question of ground rent to be considered. Should the state act as a proprietor and behave in the same way as a private landlord, charging a ground rent? Or should the state simply assume the role of an administrator of a public good, which is considered a free gift of nature to producers and, ultimately, to consumers? Mirabeau, as we have seen in Chapter 1, was very explicit on that point: the state should simply assume the role of an administrator. However, this was a *political* position, which does not follow necessarily from the public ownership that he justified only *economically* and *technically*. He never discussed explicitly the question of ground rent. But he had in mind the development of France: French mineral deposits, French companies, and French consumers. Under these circumstances – a 'closed economy' so to speak – special taxes on mining do not add to national income, though they affect, of course, the national distribution of income. Hence, in the (non-exporting) consuming countries, liberal, i.e. *non-proprietorial*, mineral governance makes sense. Yet *a priori* there is nothing to prevent the government from behaving differently, to act as a proprietor and to charge a ground rent. In mineral-exporting countries (or provinces), on the contrary, special taxes on mining add to national (regional) income, affecting the inter-national (interregional) distribution of income. Hence, it makes sense to act as a national (regional) proprietor and to charge an international (interregional) ground rent, though this is not compelling either. Anyway, regarding domestic markets, as already stated, even proprietorial governance generates nothing but normal taxes, which definitely do not add to national income.

Wherever private mineral governance has disappeared in the twentieth century, re-privatisation of the mineral deposits has never again even been mentioned as an option. Indeed, to the economic and technical advantage of public mineral ownership one has to add, from the perspective of the governments, the national and international political dimension which we already observed in the case of Mexico. This dimension, combined with private mineral property, reveals an obvious threat to sovereignty and national unity in all but the strongest mineral-producing countries, for instance the United States. From the perspective of the companies, on the other hand, even private mineral property would not protect them from sovereign eminent domain rights. Hence, once public mineral ownership prevails, *private vs. public mineral governance* is no longer an issue; instead, the issue is *non-proprietorial vs. proprietorial governance*. Governments, companies, and consumers agree on the principle of public mineral ownership; private mineral ownership in the United States is a relic, a quirk of history.

Non-proprietorial governance involves the concept of minerals being a free gift of nature. Hence, it is about facilitating a free and frictionless flow of investment into the reservoirs. Private and public proprietorial governance, on the contrary, erects obstacles to this flow by claiming ground rent. If one looks for one single indicator to measure the degree to which a governance structure is proprietorial or not, the most accurate is probably the relation between proven reserves and production, compared with the world average. For example, in the case of crude oil, in 1998 OPEC produced 42.5 per cent of the world's output, though it held 76 per cent of the proven reserves. This has to be compared with the most liberal oil-producing country of the world, the United Kingdom, with 0.5 per cent of the world's proven reserves producing 3.8 per cent of output. What we may call the intensity of exploitation is only 0.56 in OPEC, but 7.87 in the United Kingdom. The United States lies in between (Table 3.1).

3.2 Non-proprietorial Governance

In non-proprietorial governance the central criterion is the

Table 3.1:   Non-proprietorial vs. Proprietorial Governance in Crude Oil.
1998

	Proven Reserves (million b)	(%)	Production (thousand b/d)	(%)	Intensity of Exploitation
OPEC	809,044	76.0	27,739	42.5	0.56
USA	22,546	2.1	6,243	9.6	4.51
UK	5,191	0.5	2,506	3.8	7.87
World	1,064,128	100	65,273	100	1.00

Source: Republic of Venezuela, Ministry of Energy and Mines, *Petróleos y otros datos estadísticos*, 1998; pp. 203, 208.

profitability of investment. Licensing rounds open up new lands as soon as expectations of investors match the usual profit rate. The Licensing Agency has also to define the size and shape of the areas to be licensed, the length of the primary (exploration) and secondary (production) terms, the minimum level of activities required, the rules of relinquishment of idle areas, and the conditions for renewal. The latter can be taken for granted as long as the licensees are not in default and comply with the regulations. These definitions are all subject to *one* goal: to produce oil at the lowest possible price.

Excess Profit Taxation

The centrepiece of non-proprietorial governance is a fiscal regime based on excess profit taxation, such as the Petroleum Revenue Tax (PRT) in Great Britain or the Resource Rent Tax (RRT) in Australia.[1] In non-proprietorial governance there is no place for a customary ground rent set at zero by design. Hence, although consumers will still have to pay prices as determined by marginal investments, these prices will not include a surcharge for natural resource ownership. But Ricardian or differential rents – or excess profits generally – may still be very significant, and a fiscal regime may be set up to collect them, at least partially. The government may actually be obliged to set up such a regime, because otherwise it would be granting

---

1.   For an overview on petroleum fiscal regimes generally see Johnston (1994).

privileges to some investors that would be difficult to justify vis-à-vis ordinary taxpayers. Collecting those rents, taxpayers generally may benefit from lower-than-otherwise levels of taxation and/or higher public spending.

Excess profit taxation requires a benchmark for 'normal' profits. This may be, for example, an average profit rate over a given number of years, thus allowing for bad and good years. Let us suppose, for the sake of the argument, that the benchmark is an average of 15 per cent (before income tax) over 25 years. Moreover, let us assume that whenever investors evaluate an investment and expect this benchmark to be met, the investment will take place, but not otherwise. Then, apparently, a fiscal regime may safely target excess profits without restraining the flow of investment. Yet once such a fiscal regime is in place, it will be included in the model calculations of investors. To them, like all taxes, it is just a cost and, like all costs, a cost to be minimised. Hence, they will consider different options and reshape their projects. In particular, this will assuredly be the case if the fiscal regime attempts to collect 100 per cent of excess profits. In that case increasing expenditure is always the preferred option as long as it generates some profit. In other words, excess profit taxation generates incentive problems, distorting the flow of investment, a problem that becomes more serious the higher the percentage of excess profits to be collected. There is a built-in propensity towards over-investment and higher costs. Investments will take place although profit rates, on a stand-alone basis, may be far below the normal rate, and even negative.

Next, let us consider a non-proprietorial fiscal regime from the viewpoint of transaction economics. It requires special forms of bookkeeping, as profit rates play no role in normal corporate income taxation. Furthermore, there are two factors which mean that exploration and production has to be 'ring-fenced': to prevent, first, excess-profits from being siphoned off, through transfer pricing and outsourcing, to lower-taxed businesses elsewhere and, second, to prevent downstream costs – or even costs from completely unrelated businesses – from being brought in and offset against high-taxed excess profits.

Finally, let us consider a non-proprietorial fiscal regime from a public policy viewpoint. The fact is that even normal corporate income taxation has to face significant problems as soon as it deals with higher rates. In the United States, for example, federal corporate income tax rates soared during the Second World War to hitherto unknown levels, from less than 15 per cent pre-war, to about 50 per cent in the post-war period, and they remained at this level until 1985. Nevertheless, between 1950 and 1985 the corporate sector succeeded in bringing down the effective rate from about 43.5 per cent in 1950, to about 17.5 per cent in 1985. Investors lobbied successfully for all kinds of exceptions, allowances, and investment credits, threatening local and national politicians and authorities with withholding investments and/or moving elsewhere. In the end the Tax Reform Act 1986 brought down the nominal rate to 34 per cent, but at the same time it also largely eliminated those loopholes. It was argued that the new law would actually produce higher, not lower, fiscal revenues. To date, this has apparently been true. Federal corporate income taxes, compared with GDP, peaked in 1952 at 6.1 per cent. By 1985 this percentage was down to 1.5 per cent, but since then it has averaged 1.9 per cent. In contrast, the situation of wage and salary earners is very different. They are basically captives. Employers retain their income taxes; the law strictly regulates their allowances, and their individual threats not to work, or to move abroad, in order to achieve lower levels of taxation is rather ineffective. Hence, the post-war increase in personal income tax levels, which originally followed the same pattern as corporate income taxes, turned out to be sustainable and irreversible. In 1999, federal personal income taxes represented 9.6 per cent of GDP. (Figs. 3.1 and 3.2)

Excess profit taxation inevitably meets even stronger political opposition than normal corporate income taxation. Moreover, there are always good arguments against those taxes based on the disincentive to invest in marginal fields: there are indeed marginal lands everywhere, and even the most prolific oil field contains marginal barrels. Thus, it is easy to construct examples, and to find real ones, where an investment would have taken place had it not been for excess profit taxation. The claim for more 'flexibility' is endless. In conclusion, excess profit taxation is complicated. It is economically and politically costly to administer, potentially litigious, and requires strong political

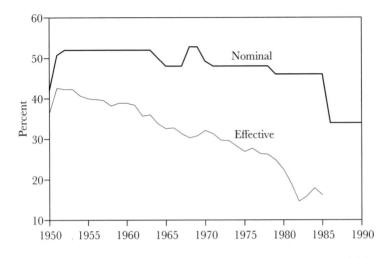

Source: Pechman 1987: Table 5.3

Figure 3.1: U.S. Corporate Income Tax: Nominal and Effective Rates
1950–1985

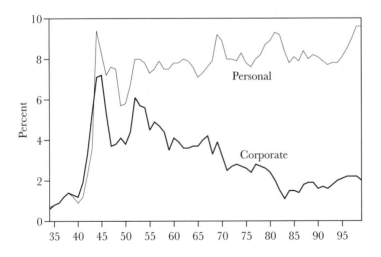

Source: US Government 2000: Historical Tables, Table 2.3

Figure 3.2: US Corporate and Personal Income Tax/GDP 1935–1999

institutions as well as highly specialised accountants, economists, and lawyers. Hence, in non-proprietorial governance it is not unreasonable to expect high excess profit tax rates to suffer the same fate as high income tax rates and to settle, in the long run, at relatively modest effective levels, and to expect that ultimately nominal rates will adjust accordingly.

Granting Licences

When lands are made available to investors, there is usually more than one applicant for each plot. However, some applicants may not be suitable, either for technical, economic or other reasons. Thus, the Licensing Agency has to shortlist them. Next, there must be a procedure in place to reach a final decision about who should receive the award. This may be a rather tricky question. Investment-related bidding parameters may be used, such as the length of seismic lines to be shot, the number and the depth of the wells to be drilled, or simply the total amount to be invested in the Primary Period (exploration). But, obviously, this may lead to distortions in the investment programme. One alternative is bonus bidding.[2] In a competitive market bonuses will reflect the net present value of expected excess profits net of tax. Hence, as long as excess profits are collected efficiently under this regime, one might be tempted to assume that bonuses would be relatively small. But in practice non-proprietorial fiscal regimes are not very efficient at collecting rents; they are designed to be elastic and, therefore, bonuses may actually be huge. Consequently, bonuses tend to diminish the real flow of investment. Finally, there is the fact that bonuses collect *expected* excess profits, which contradicts the general rule that income taxes are to be paid on real, and not on expected profits.

For these reasons bonuses have rarely been used in the United Kingdom, which, as we shall see, provides the model of non-proprietorial governance; and when they have been used, they have only played the role of tiebreakers. The sums involved were marginal. Basically, licences were awarded through a process of negotiation, related to the work programme of the

---

2·   For obvious reasons, this is the preferred option of American authors. See, for example, Mead (1994).

licensees and their general performance, the Licensing Agency – the Department of Trade and Industry (DTI) – taking the final decision at its discretion. But this demands a highly qualified bureaucracy as well as a political system with low levels of corruption and high levels of consensus. For this reason it would not be acceptable in many parts of the world, where bidding is the only acceptable option. Then it becomes a practical problem optimally to combine excess profit taxation with collective negotiation, and to define the bidding parameters in the least distortionary fashion.

3.3   Proprietorial Governance

Proprietorial governance grants access to lands only if expected profits and fiscal revenues are considered satisfactory by both investors and natural resource owners. In principle, then, what was said about private mineral governance obtains for public mineral ownership subject to proprietorial governance. However, as we have seen, transaction and surveillance costs play an important role, and these costs are much lower in the case of public ownership. On the one hand, one central and specialised Licensing Agency has an obvious advantage over a group of dispersed and diverse private landowners. Such an agency may employ a qualified team of experts, able to handle much more sophisticated rent-collecting devices. For example, the Licensing Agency may consider a fifty-fifty profit sharing and do without a royalty, which may cause relatively modest additional costs to the tax-collecting agencies; but these costs would be prohibitive to the individual private landlord. On the other hand, from the viewpoint of investors, it may be a waste of time and money to convince an individual landlord to introduce some change in the usual lease contract, even if such a change were to the advantage of both parties. It just may not be worth the trouble. But dealing with the state, the whole national territory is at stake, not a small piece of land, and the prize to be won is much bigger. Hence, the tenant companies may spend much more on negotiating and lobbying the landlord state. Therefore, public mineral ownership subject to proprietorial governance offers a greater variety of possibilities than private mineral governance; and one may also expect the former to be less stable than the latter.

Thus, for example, with fifty-fifty profit sharing no new or additional investment would be made if the expected rate of return of the investment, before profit sharing, were not at least 30 per cent. However, the marginal ground rent on production would be zero. Therefore tons of minerals or barrels of oil may be produced without making any profit; they may even be produced at a loss. The latter may happen because a discovery turns out to be poor, but still good enough to recover part of the investment; alternatively, in a depressed market there may be circumstantial commercial reasons to carry on producing, albeit at a loss; or there may be contractual commitments to be honoured. But, if there is no profit to share, why should the natural resource owner allow this to happen? The answer is that the state is not only a landlord, and so may have to, or may want to, adopt a more flexible stance towards investors. Nevertheless, the marginal unit of output relates to the customary ground rent in the same way as the marginal investment relates to the usual profit rate. The latter is undermined whenever investors accept a lower profit rate; the same obtains, *mutatis mutandis*, for the natural resource owners and their customary ground rent. Worse, while even at a lower profit rate investors still recover their investment, a barrel extracted is gone forever. This brings us back to the question of depletion and royalty. Furthermore, a flat royalty adds to operating costs and, hence, to the short-term price floor. It brings pressure on the mining companies to restrict output in order to maintain a higher price and prevents a unit of production being lifted without paying ground rent. Thus the natural resource owner shares only the risk regarding prices but not regarding profits. Therefore, there are good, though not necessarily compelling, reasons why one might expect a customary royalty to exist in proprietorial governance.

But there are also good reasons for abandoning the simplicity of royalty-based fiscal regimes when the fiscal take becomes very high. In that case the residual profit may become too small for it to function properly as the guiding criterion to produce or not produce an additional barrel. Other ground rent collecting devices may have to be brought in, on top of higher royalty rates, for example sliding-scale royalties, higher income taxes, and even excess-profit taxes. These devices, however, present all kinds of problems, which we have already mentioned. Most importantly, surveillance costs increase significantly and, at a certain point, the best option is to participate in the business – either through a public national oil company or as shareholder – so that the Licensing Agency is provided with a window on the industry. In Third World countries the principal arrangement of this kind is known as a Production Sharing Agreement (PSA), between private investors and the National Oil Company (NOC), which usually involves a sliding-scale royalty with the triggering event related to accumulated expenditure and gross revenue (Johnston 1994). Ultimately, if profits are still too high, the best option may be to nationalise, i.e. to invert the landlord–tenant relationship completely and to convert the private companies from tenants into service-providers to be paid, for example, a certain amount per lifted barrel. There is, however, a cost to be paid, such as the loss in efficiency and productivity that this kind of arrangements may entail. However, it may be worth the cost, since the Licensing Agency – together with its Agent, the National Oil Company (NOC) – is then in a position to take the fundamental decisions regarding the flow of investment, volumes and prices. It is thus able to focus on maximising ground rent.

With nationalisation proprietorial governance reaches its extreme. The State collects all profits, whether as natural resource owner or as investor; and the state is free to decide on volumes and prices. Yet the participation of the state in the industry entails new problems of governance. The surveillance of national public companies is very different from that of foreign private ones. The line dividing the Licensing and rent-collecting Agencies from the tenant companies may become blurred, and the evidence and arguments, which were so convincing against the foreign companies, may lose their persuasive power against the national oil company. Or, *vice-versa*, the so easily dismissed evidence and arguments of the foreign tenants, once they are taken over by the national oil companies, may be perceived as very convincing, and may have to be taken seriously. The same applies to foreign consumers. The national oil companies may act as intermediaries between both the foreign companies and consumers, on the one hand, and the government on the other, transmitting messages in both directions. The messages may be reinforced, toned down, filtered, or censored by the messengers. In other words, nationalisation is not the end of the story but only the beginning of a new chapter. New important players have entered the field of play, others have left, and the rules have changed. Yet the game goes on.

3.4   Sovereignty

In its most elementary form sovereignty comes down to the power and, hence, the right to grant or deny access to land. There is no way to own a piece of land except through the sovereign power. Once granted, access is still subject to the eminent domain right of the sovereign, even if this right is exercised in the form of private landed property. As already stated, this is defined as the right to tax, to police, and to condemn. Eminent domain rights are, of course, subject to rules defined by the sovereign community. Thus, the grantees will need to take note of the governance in place and to determine whether it will, or will not, allow them to defend their interests; and they will have greater concern the more isolated, the less mobile, and the more profitable the grant turns out to be. This is especially the case with mining rights and, above all, this is the case with oil.

In the history of oil the only example of stable governance is to be found in the United States, though it has certainly evolved over the century and a half of its existence. But the landlord–tenant relationship at its core and most notably the customary royalty rates have been very stable. Notwithstanding private mineral property rights, the states have the authority to impose severance taxes, i.e. production taxes economically identical to royalties but defined by law rather than by lease contracts. They have to be paid on top of royalties. Their rates are, therefore, subject to the sovereign power of state legislatures. The states have exercised this right, and a few increased the applicable rates significantly after the OPEC revolution of the 1970s. Excess profit taxation, on the other hand, is traditionally supposed to be settled once and for all through bonus bidding. Therefore the federal government has been extremely reluctant to fall back on it. Nevertheless, again under the extreme circumstances of the OPEC revolution and its aftermath, in the early 1980s a windfall profit tax was enacted. The right to police, to control and to regulate has been exercised in the major US oil producing states ever since the 1930s, subjecting production to prorationing on conservationist grounds and to condemn or to restrict private landed property rights whenever they became too obstructive. Nevertheless the political and economic system of checks-and-balances in place was strong enough to deliver reasonable results through the years of deep depression and external price shocks, accommodating the occasionally high tensions between consumers, the producing companies, and the natural resource owners.

In the oil-exporting countries such a complex political and economic equilibrium was not in place. Concessions were granted, especially in the Middle East, under colonial and imperial governance. The sovereign rights of the conceding countries were reduced to their absolute minimum. They were deemed to be sovereign enough to grant concessions but not to exercise their eminent domain rights. Most importantly, of course, they were stripped of their sovereign right to tax. In the Middle East it had 'been a deeply embedded principle for the companies to insist on complete exemption from taxation' (Lenczowski 1960: 70) in concession contracts which were to last up to 75 years – though these companies were subject to sovereign taxation in their home countries. Similarly, the international companies set production volumes, in (informal) co-operation with prorationing in the United States, in order to maintain prices at convenient levels (United States Senate 1952: *passim*), without taking into consideration the interests of local governments. More generally, in the Middle East – though not in Latin America – concessions were subject to 'international law of civilised nations' and international arbitration.

From the beginning the oil-exporting countries challenged this governance structure, which the international companies had set up after the First World War. Ultimately they did so successfully, for two reasons. Firstly, there was the general collapse of colonial and imperial governance after the Second World War. Secondly, the international tenant companies in the oil-exporting countries were far too successful and, hence, hopelessly isolated. They were also immobile as oil was scarce or, at the very least, unevenly distributed. Indeed, as it turned out reserves were concentrated in a dozen or so Third World countries. Hence, the international tenant companies could not resist the mounting pressure from the emerging landlord states because their threats to go somewhere else became less and less credible. In the end, with the OPEC revolution, the exporting countries succeeded in their demand for 'Permanent Sovereignty over Natural Resources'. They condemned the concessions, which were taken over by national oil companies, and the foreign tenants were basically transformed into production service providers. This process went hand in hand with an explosive growth of oil prices and fiscal revenues. Once the tenant companies had been removed as intermediaries, sovereign proprietorial interests of OPEC governments prevailed unrestrictedly over the interests of foreign consumers.

The oil-importing countries were taken by surprise. Until then, security of supply and the question of prices had been the responsibility of the international companies. But the governments of the large consuming countries were quick to react. They created the International Energy Agency (IEA), and began to work out a new governance of international oil in which their interests as consumers as well as the interests of the international oil companies as investors would recover most if not all of their former importance. To this end the developed countries have thrown their weight behind bilateral and multilateral trade and investment treaties, embedding oil in general governance in order to dilute the bargaining power of the resource-rich countries within the global economy. This network of international treaties is designed to replace the 'international law of civilised nations' of the old days. At the same time, the national oil companies have been targeted, in a strategy of 'agency capturing', in order to convert them from tax-collecting agents of the landlord states into promoters of private foreign investment. New forms of upstream contracts, which usually include the national oil companies as associates, are replacing the concession system of the past.

These new upstream contracts are designed as investment agreements, not concessions or other forms of access to the natural resource; and the new legal international framework only discusses the free flow of goods and investments. Not one word is said about natural resources. International arbitration is back on the agenda, but it now formally applies to both parties. Thus, on the basis of a bilateral investment treaty between Azerbaijan and the United States, for example, Azerbaijani investors in the United States have the right to sue the American government in international courts. Most importantly, this also applies to the sovereign right to tax, even if indirectly. When an investor considers that a tax increase is tantamount to expropriation, and its home country does not explicitly deny this viewpoint, then it has the right to sue the host government in an international arbitration court set up by the developed capital-exporting countries. Ultimately, the sovereign taxation of foreign investors in oil is thus being subjected to the consent of the governments of the consuming countries. To enforce these rules the national oil companies associated with private investors assume the role of hostages and, since they are exporting companies, there is always something to sequestrate.

The new governance of global oil, as this structure may be called, again reduces the sovereign rights of territorial states – but now formally for *all* of them, developed or underdeveloped, resource-rich or not – to its absolute minimum, to the granting of the rights of access. Once they have been granted, eminent domain rights are embedded in international treaties. At this level the consuming and capital-exporting countries are the most powerful, whereas the oil-exporting countries are simply equated to capital-importing countries. Should this trend continue to prevail, the natural resource will be a free gift of nature no longer to local peoples but to the global economy.

3.5 Ricardian Rent Theory and Taxation

Ricardian rent theory, when it comes to public landed property, can be a very useful political manifesto. No longer must it be considered a perfect model representing a real, yet imperfect, world; in its radical version it may now be promoted as a political programme for a real and perfect world. Governments can be advised and urged by professional economists turned consultants, to focus exclusively on differential rents, to be careful not to go beyond that even accidentally, and never to engage in any attempt to impose a customary ground rent. This is impossible anyway, governments can be told, as Ricardo has *scientifically* demonstrated ages ago. Who dares to doubt? Or, more modestly, who dares to question the validity of models based on 'perfect competition' for a world of public ownership?

In the international arena of the 1960s an important exemplar of this thinking was Professor Adelman of the Massachusetts Institute of Technology (MIT). At that time oil prices were falling, and OPEC was engaged in negotiations with their concessionaires to stop the falling prices from impinging on their ground rents, the prevailing arrangement being a fifty-fifty profit sharing. Adelman was ready to discuss the decisive question: '*Will Concession Revisions Put Up Prices?*'. First he insisted that rent always, and only, constitutes differential rent. Accordingly, the landlord's share of profit 'has no effect on the price because it has no effect on supply'. The reason was that 'so long as any profit expected after rent or royalty is less than enough to induce a private company to make the investment, it is to the landlord's benefit to take a lower royalty. For his alternatives are no operation, and no royalty. The landlord, as residual claimant, simply gets what is left, much or little.' His conclusion was that 'the whole problem of rents and royalties is superfluous to the determination of price' (Adelman 1964a: 104 ff. Italics as in the original).[3]

Adelman then went on to advise the negotiating parties that the new agreements should not specify any per-barrel amount. The formula should be more flexible, some kind of a percentage, but 'even a uniform percentage is probably too rigid' (Adelman 1964a: 107). If OPEC had followed his advice – which, as we shall see, it did not – marginal ground rent on investment would have been zero. Later, in the 1980s and 1990s, Alexander Kemp of the University of Aberdeen has played a similar role claiming 'an efficient tax system is one which is targeted on economic rents and collects a share of them' (Kemp, Stephen, and Masson 1997: 9). He considered royalty as outmoded, regressive and inefficient.

Thus the whole weight of modern economics is thrown behind worldwide non-proprietorial mineral governance. Ultimately,

---

3.   Similarly Bradley: 'The various types of rental payments will not be included in this study as part of the cost of crude because they are not causative elements in the establishment of price' (Bradley 1967: 10).

minerals are supposed to be a free gift of nature not to some local or national community but to humanity. It required a Frenchman to say so:

> The French idea admitted from the beginning that minerals, insofar as they are a natural resource, could only belong to the community as a whole and not to a particular individual .... It should also be noted that, from the philosophical point of view at least, the non-allocation of natural resources could also be extended to the states themselves by substituting the general interest of humanity for the interests of individuals comprising these states. (Montel 1970: 104; see also Madelin 1973: X)

Accordingly, only differential rents would accrue to local or national governments, which are supposed to open up their lands as soon as investors may be interested.

Playing Charades

Modern economics does not deal with land as such. Private landlords are considered non-actors, and the public landlord is supposed to behave accordingly. The idea that they might resurrect in the second half of the twentieth century and, worse, become reincarnated as sovereigns joining together in a cartel and playing a significant and most active role, was simply unimaginable. In the 1960s all energy economists forecasting oil prices agreed that OPEC was not worth their trouble. In their price equations it was supposed to be a constant and, what is more, a constant equal to zero. Yet OPEC turned out not to be a constant but a variable and, worse, by far the most important one.

Everyone was taken completely by surprise by the OPEC revolution of the early 1970s, including OPEC. Landlords – whether private individuals, or regional or national communities acting as such – have a similar theoretical understanding. As far as theory goes, they just take up whatever economics may offer them, picking out the pieces that may be useful to underpin their needs. Thus OPEC fell back on conciliatory Ricardian rent theory regarding royalties as a compensation for a 'wasting asset', claiming that their 'right to receive compensation for the intrinsic value of petroleum is uncontestable' (OPEC 1962: Res.

IV.33). In Britain, Marshall's conciliatory conception of royalties provided a simple and persuasive model for peaceful coexistence with landlords as 'sleeping partners'. Yet the same model provided OPEC member countries and their policy makers with a powerful motivation to *act*, convinced that they were not getting their due share. Similarly, in its *Declaratory Statement of Petroleum Policy in Member Countries*, OPEC defined excess profits as 'net profits after taxes which are significantly in excess, during any twelve-month period, of the level of net earnings the reasonable expectation of which would have been sufficient to induce the operator to take the entrepreneurial risks necessary' (OPEC 1968: Res. XVI.90). Once more, this was an invitation to *act*. In the early 1960s OPEC member countries were perfectly aware of the fact that they were not getting the best deal possible: after-tax profits were very high indeed. Yet nobody had any idea where their insistence on collecting all Ricardian rents would actually lead.

Anyway, the OPEC revolution would not and could not change the fact that in modern economics land was 'assimilated' to capital. To 'de-assimilate' land from capital – i.e. to re-admit land as a third factor of production – was out of the question. The only legitimate actors in a modern economy are entrepreneurs and workers. To ignore the issue of landed property is a matter of dogma. Hence, the sudden price increases of the 1970s had to be explained within the existing theoretical framework. This was done, on the one hand, by opportunely unearthing Hotelling's article published in 1931 (Hotelling 1931). Now widely publicised, it explained these increases as the consequence of the valorisation of a finite natural resource. What happened to oil prices in the 1970s would have happened anyway, with or without OPEC, due to scarcity (Gately 1984: 1100–14). On the other hand, little publicised but much more interesting, Johany in his book *The Myth of the OPEC Cartel* gave OPEC some credit, albeit only for the sudden price increase of 1973/4. He argued that the 'western oil companies were never one hundred per cent certain that their property rights on crude oil deposits would not be one day in jeopardy, consequently, they extracted more oil during the 1950s and 1960s than they otherwise would have; the result was lower-than-otherwise prices'. On the other hand, the oil-producing countries 'do not face ownership uncertainty, and thus have a longer time horizon which would dictate smaller amounts of output; the result is higher-than-otherwise-prices' (Johany 1980: VII).

Hence uncertain property rights were at the origin of the price explosion. This was, indeed, not an unknown problem to petroleum economics, as we have seen. In the history of American oil the 'rule of capture' had been, on the contrary, at the origin of many a price implosion. Johany, for his part, went on to conclude that though OPEC had been very useful in redefining these property rights, there was nothing else to do. He, a Saudi Arabian citizen, suggested that the now useless Organisation should be dissolved (Johany 1980: 71). The bottom line is always the same. Landlords, at best, might have been actors in the past, but they now belong to the past and cannot be tolerated, ideologically, as actors for the present. They may only be tolerated in disguise.

3.6 Politics and Natural Resource Ownership

The question of natural resource ownership and its relationship to prices is definitely a question of politics and not of economics. It is up to policy makers, whether they represent consumers, producing companies, or landed property owners, to choose the economic model that suits them best, and then go on to interpret it creatively. In private mineral governance Ricardian rent models are used to justify the underlying compromise. In the oil-exporting countries the policy may actually consist of maximising ground rent but, still, the same models are used. Though at certain moments the euphoric landlords may wave their hands and boast about having pushed prices up, as soon as they sober down, they step back in line and pretend that they have done nothing but make the market work, bashfully hiding their hands in their pockets. Finally, the policy of the consuming countries may consist, on the contrary, in sidelining the landlords in order to cut them out of the social fabric of the national or international economy. Yet this should not look like bloody surgery but the natural outcome of the invisible hand of the market. The transformation of proprietorial governance into a non-proprietorial one will modestly be attributed to 'competition'.

The same model may serve opposite policies, and different models may serve the same policy. The public debate on mineral governance, by its very nature, is of a political nature. Arguments must be effective and persuasive to serve the right cause. They need not be relevant from a strictly economic viewpoint; they may even be simply wrong, and still very useful; or they may be right, but politically counterproductive. The point is to be politically convincing in order to forge the alliance necessary to implement the desired changes.

Regarding landed property rights, the mining companies may be compared with nomads rather than settlers (Mitchell 1996). Their arrival in a new region stirs up problems related to their definition and creates all kind of frictions, controversies, and possibly confrontations. This is inevitably the case even in developed countries. The mineral riches underground attract them, not the people. The importance of the newcomers may be disproportionate to the regional economy. In this regard oil is unique in its incredible potential to generate rents. And, even if there is nationally well-established mineral governance, it may not have percolated to the region, where it still has to be assimilated economically, politically and socially. Obviously, this process is much more conflict-laden in Third World countries, where foreign companies are associated with colonial and imperial policies, an essential part of which was to implant a mineral governance of their liking. What is more, although in the developed countries land has long been associated to capital, in Third World countries capital had still to be associated with land. The companies were leading the way to capitalism.

Worldwide the nomadic international companies have to deal with, to co-operate with, to contain, to defeat, or to arrive at an understanding with an astonishing diversity of people and institutions, revolutionaries and counter-revolutionaries, environmentalists, guerrillas, landlords of feudal vintage and, last but not least, regional or national communities and their governments, democratically elected or not. They have only one thing in common: they happen to be the surface dwellers of mineral lands.

4 THE INTERNATIONAL OIL CONCESSION SYSTEM

In this chapter we present the international concession system, the first governance structure of international oil, as it evolved in the first half of the twentieth century culminating in fifty-fifty profit sharing. This structure began to evolve more or less simultaneously in different parts of the world. However, these parts were linked to each other from the very beginning through the international oil companies and their home governments. They also provided, therefore, the first links between the exporting countries. As a result a surprisingly homogenous governance structure emerged. To study its evolution, Venezuela, the most important exporting country in this period, provides the best starting point.

4.1 Venezuela

Venezuelan mining laws, a legacy of colonial times, were modernised in the second half of the nineteenth century following the liberal French patterns. Thus, the Exposition of Motives of the 1909 Mining Law stressed the 'security given to the operators in their concession', 'the freedom granted to them to work the mines, since the fewer obstacles, the better', and 'the facilities they are offered to acquire concessions'. Concessions were granted for a definite term, but with an option of renewal 'so that their owner, pressed by the ending of the term stated in the contract, does not attempt to destroy or misuse the remaining mineral resources with a view to extracting from the mine the greatest product in the least possible time' (quoted in Egaña 1979: 216–17). And, of course, the mines had to be worked; if not, the concession would expire.

Moreover, concessions were legally conceived as contracts 'so that the tax does not vary'. The principle was that the tax had to 'be moderate as well as equal for all contributors', taking into account that 'there is no property more risky than that of mines' (quoted in Egaña 1979: 216–17). However, contrary to this liberal spirit, on private lands the concessionaires had to pay the surface owners one third of their profits. Apparently Congress, not the government, introduced this legal requirement. The Ministry of Development objected to it on the grounds that:

> Such a precept constitutes an obvious restriction since nobody should provide the money, credit, intelligence, activity, perseverance, in short the whole material, intellectual and moral affluence required for success in undertakings of this sort only to find that subsequently, no less than a third of the profits has to be handed over to a partner who is forced upon the management and who neither works, contributes, nor risks anything. (Márquez 1977: 49)

On request from the government, the Supreme Court declared this stipulation unconstitutional. Regarding the reservoirs, the surface owners had no proprietary rights to claim.

The 1910 Mining Law, even more advantageous to the investors, offered the former concessionaires the opportunity to adapt their title deeds to the new Law, which they did. Hence, the seven important oil concessions granted between 1907 and 1912 were based, until 1943, on that Law. They were granted to Venezuelan citizens acting as intermediaries. They all ended up in the hands of Royal Dutch–Shell. Until its nationalisation in 1976, this company extracted from them the major part of its production in Venezuela.

The initial areas of these concessions varied between 50,000 and 27,000,000 ha. Yet at the end of the exploration period – the 'primary period' between two and eight years – the concessionaires had to select plots of 200 ha, which were then converted individually into exploitation concessions – the 'secondary period' to last for 30 to 50 years. They were subject to a surface tax of one *bolívar* per hectare per year. Much more important, however, was an *exploitation tax* of 2.00 Bs./t, or Bs. 1,000 per exploitation concession, whichever was higher. Thus, as a minimum, the concessionaires would have to pay Bs. 6.00 per hectare per year.[1] They were exempt from all other taxes, but they were subject to Venezuelan laws and courts, and the Calvo clause applied. The exploitation tax, at that time, was

---

1.   The gold parity of the *bolívar* was then Bs./US\$ 5.20.

simply a tax, and in its form – a fixed amount per unit – it was identical to what was then usual, either in agriculture, cattle breeding, or in mining generally.

National Mineral Ownership

The first successful well was drilled in 1912, though production was delayed because of the First World War. Yet the war also demonstrated the extraordinary importance of oil in modern warfare and industry, and the interest of foreign investors in Venezuelan oil intensified. Likewise, the Venezuelan government took a closer look at its oil policy. Last but not least, there was also the ongoing Mexican revolution and its oil policy.

Indeed, in 1917 – the first year of exports – the Minister of Development, Gumersindo Torres, decided temporarily to suspend the granting of new concessions to study the situation thoroughly. Otherwise future generations, he argued, would rightfully blame the present ones for 'not having been able to take care of our national wealth'. According to the Minister, 'until recently we rushed blindly into oil exploration and exploitation contracts and consequently the Nation received few, or no, advantages from them' (Torres 1918: XVI–XIX). In Venezuela, he concluded, the Treasury did not receive anything for the exploitation of oil reservoirs apart from the usual tax. 'However, the concept of a tax is different from that of a payment derived from contractual stipulation in return for the use of a national property'. Hence, 'the companies pay nothing for the right to exploit the reservoirs, as they do in all other countries, be it to the landowners buying or leasing oil lands, or be it to the State, if the lands are public' (Torres 1920: XVIII–XXII).

The 'other countries' the Minister referred to were, of course, the two biggest oil-producing countries at that time, Mexico and the United States. The liberal conception, according to which there was only a State/taxpayer relationship between the concession-granting state and the concessionaires, was abandoned. The new conception of public ownership was a *national* one, concession contracts establishing in the first place a business relationship.

Concession Dealers, Landowners, and the State

Torres did not question public mineral ownership, nor did he oppose the trade in concessions, with Venezuelan citizens acting as intermediaries. However, he believed that on private lands the landlords should have a preferential right, though he was also worried that they might sell their concessions at too low prices. Hence, he concluded, 'the urgent need to create in the Ministry of Development the Department of Oil' (Torres 1918: XVIII–XXII) to assist them and to strengthen their bargaining power. Obviously, Torres' reference was Mexico. He was thus somewhat at odds with the despotic ruler of the country, Juan Vicente Gómez, his relatives and political friends, all of whom were interested in the concession trade and unwilling to concede such a preference to any landlord.

On the other hand, Vicente Lecuna, a banker, was opposed to any concession trade. The state, he believed, should grant concessions directly to the producing companies and for the exclusive benefit of the Treasury. His reference was the new Mineral Land Leasing Law in the United States, which, according to his estimates, would on average result in a royalty of $15^1/_2$ per cent. He considered this percentage the minimum acceptable for Venezuela, as the country had no modern industry. As an oil-exporting country 'it only keeps the participation the law demands for the Republic' (Lecuna 1975: 8), he told Juan Vicente Gómez.

The first Hydrocarbons Law was passed in 1920. It incorporated elements from both references, Mexico and the United States. Landlords obtained a preferential right to concessions on their lands, though this right was limited to one year. As a matter of fact it only lasted nine months, as it was abandoned in the new 1921 Law of Hydrocarbons. Landlords then had to compete again with Gómez, his relatives and political friends. At the same time, however, the 1920 and 1921 Laws of Hydrocarbons established relatively high royalty rates. Not surprisingly, then, concession dealers and oil companies soon united in promoting a third Law of Hydrocarbons, in 1922, to reduce them. Once more it offered the former concessionaires the opportunity to adapt their title deeds. Those who had acquired concessions in recent years did so. Shell, with its older concessions, stuck to the more favourable 1910 Mining Law.

The 1922 Law of Hydrocarbons suffered only minor changes until 1943. Concessions were limited to ten thousand hectares. There was a signature bonus, according to geographical location, of Bs. 0.05 to Bs. 0.10 per hectare. The exploration period was three years. Thereafter, the area was divided into plots of 200 ha, and the concessionaires had the right to choose at their discretion half of the plots, which were converted into exploitation concessions to last forty years. There was another bonus to be paid, of Bs./ha 1.00 to Bs./ha 2.00. There was also an annual surface tax, starting at Bs./ha 1.00 to Bs./ha 2.00 increasing to Bs./ha 2.50 to Bs./ha 5.00 for the last ten years. Royalty rates were set at $7^{1}/_{2}$ to 10 per cent. Regarding the relinquished areas – so-called 'national reserves' – the government was supposed to negotiate the best possible deal for the Nation, i.e. higher rentals and royalty rates.

These concessions ended up mainly in the hands of American companies. Though they were latecomers and had to pay higher ground rents, they succeeded, as it turned out, in getting the better part of Venezuelan oil: the rich reservoirs beneath Lake Maracaibo. By the end of the 1930s Creole (Standard Oil of New Jersey; SONJ) controlled 50 per cent of Venezuelan production, Shell 35 per cent, and Mene Grande (Gulf Oil Company) 14 per cent. In 1936–37 the latter sold a 25 per cent share to SONJ, and another 25 per cent to Royal Dutch–Shell, which was related to the world-wide setting up of the international petroleum cartel. The monopoly of these companies, however, was not based on large concessions but on thousands of small ones. Up to the Second World War the government granted some 8,500 concessions and, as a rule, they were granted first to Venezuelan citizens or concession-trading companies. Gómez, his relatives and friends, somewhat illegally, were particularly active and successful in dealing with the 'national reserves'. From 1920 to 1938, concession dealers made Bs. 177 million in cash and Bs. 32 million in shares, apart from the royalty payments they would enjoy for many decades.[2] This was a significant amount of money. It possibly represented as

---

2. In earlier years the intermediaries got only a down payment. After 1926 a $2^{1}/_{2}$ per cent overriding royalty became customary. (Revista del Ministerio de Fomento 1939)

much as 30 per cent of the total of rents and royalties paid by the companies, with the remainder accruing to the government (Mommer 1991: 170).

The 1943 Petroleum Reform

In 1928 Venezuela, overtaking Mexico, became the biggest oil-exporting country in the world, and the second biggest producing country after the United States. This was the period of the Great Depression when the traditional export-oriented agrarian economy suffered a severe blow. But the oil sector was much less affected, and soon stabilised. Thus oil in its double role as an industry, on the one hand, and as a source of fiscal revenues, on the other, became of overwhelming importance. Venezuela became an oil country. Moreover, in 1934 the United States devalued the dollar but, thanks to its oil bonanza, Venezuela was one of the few countries in the world that did not follow suit. The gold parity of the *bolívar*, previously at Bs./US$ 5.20, was now Bs./US$ 3.09. Consequently, the companies had to significantly increase their spending in dollars to spend the same amount of *bolívares*. Accidentally, the gap between the fixed royalty as defined by the 1910 Mining Law, and the percentage royalty as defined by the 1922 Law of Hydrocarbons, was closed. Bs./t 2.00 no longer represented US$ 0.38 but US$ 0.65, whereas percentage royalties were unaffected. The country clearly benefited from not devaluing – though it was the death sentence for the traditional export-oriented agrarian economy.

The time had come to control and regulate. In 1929 Torres, again Minister of Development, founded a new Section within the Ministry, which specialised in oil, the *Servicio Técnico de Hidrocarburos*. Its personnel studied and trained in the United States. It was in charge of implementing and supervising the Regulations of the Law of Hydrocarbons, which were enacted that year. The Treasury was aware of the fact that fiscal revenues could increase significantly by just collecting existing taxes more efficiently. For example, the companies were now obliged to measure volumes at the wellhead so that subsequent losses through accident or seepage would not affect royalties. Of course, tensions and conflicts ensued. Moreover, the death of the despot Gómez in 1935 put a new complexion on the situation. The following year modern political parties emerged and discussed development policies, even though Generals continued to govern the country. It was in 1936 that Arturo Uslar Pietri coined the famous catch phrase *sembrar el petróleo* – 'sowing the oil'. Import taxes were no longer considered simply taxes but important policy instruments. However, the oil companies insisted on their contractual right of exemption from taxation, which was repeatedly acknowledged by the Supreme Court.

The government once more suspended the granting of concessions. Manuel R. Egaña, Minister of Development, declared 'the *right* of the State to the greatest possible share in the wealth of its subsoil' (Egaña 1939: XI. Italics in the original). The yield was to be used to attract a qualified immigration to the sparsely populated country and, generally, to encourage and to promote economic development. In one way or another, the legal, economic and political framework had to be adjusted. Though the companies were unwilling to co-operate, with the outbreak of the Second World War Venezuelan oil became of strategic importance to the Allies. In 1942 President Medina Angarita sent a personal letter to President Roosevelt informing him that the Venezuelan government had decided to go ahead with reform, with or without the co-operation of the companies. Still remembering vividly the Mexico debacle, the United States government asked the companies to co-operate.

Negotiations culminated in the 1943 Law of Hydrocarbons. The companies agreed to an immediate increase in royalties, from an average of about 9 to 16.67 per cent (one sixth). They also agreed to be subject to sovereign taxation. Hence, the issue of import taxes was settled. What is more, the government simultaneously passed an Income Tax Law setting the relevant rate at 12 per cent. This tax would ultimately affect not profits but fiscal revenues in the United States, the UK and the Netherlands. Moreover, as part of the deal, SONJ and Royal Dutch–Shell agreed to build two huge refineries in Venezuela after the war. In exchange, the old concessions were renewed for forty years.

The reform was a complete success. It may be summarised in a few words: the Venezuelan state, as sovereign and as natural resource owner, was put on the same level, in its rights and in its obligations, as the state on federal lands in the United States; the same was true *mutatis mutandis* for the companies.

Concession Dealers and Landowners. The 1943 Law of Hydrocarbons also put an end to the concession trade. Concessions were to be granted directly to the producing companies. Regarding the landlords, the Exposition of Motives condemned 'the vacillations that appeared in some of the first mining laws, which tended to ignore the constitutional principle of the country's uninterrupted tradition regarding State ownership of mineral resources', and reasserted 'the principle that the owner of the surface as such, has not the slightest right over the underlying mineral deposits' (quoted in González Berti 1967: 30). Yet acquired rights were never contested. With the renewal of the old concessions a few lucky concession dealers and their heirs continued to enjoy their overriding royalties until the nationalisation of the industry in 1976.

In Quest for Stability

Oil in Venezuela was thus on a par with the United States. The American Embassy in Caracas and American advisors had played a major role in the reform. Three of them deserve a mention: Max Thornburg, Petroleum Adviser to the US Department of State, and Herbert Hoover Jr. and A. A. Curtice, two private consultants. In a report to the government, Hoover and Curtice justified the customary royalty of one sixth on the grounds that, including the usual rental payments, it would result, on average and over the life span of a concession, in a fifty-fifty profit split, a point which was taken up by the government in the Exposition of Motives of the Law. The same American advisors also pointed out in their report that taking into account general taxation, most importantly income taxes, the profit split would be 60:40 in favour of the government. At pre-war prices, this was probably not too far from the truth. However, prices had increased with the Second World War, though the American government froze them during the War, and they were expected to increase further after the War. Accordingly, in new bidding rounds in 1944–45 the competing companies offered royalty rates up to one third, and paid Bs.

200 millions (US$ 60 millions) in bonuses.

Obviously, at higher prices the government's take would be relatively lower as Pérez Alfonzo, the spokesman of a small opposition party, Acción Democrática, pointed out in Congress. The government replied to his criticism with a reference to the aforementioned report, which stated that income taxation 'as applied in other countries, is used as a control over excess profits obtained by individuals and commercial enterprises. If used wisely this tax can become another guarantee for the Nation of its fair share in the profits of Venezuelan industry' (*El País* 28-12-1946). In October 1945, a coup d'état brought Acción Democrática to power, and Pérez Alfonzo became Minister of Development. In December, the Junta decreed a 20 per cent income surtax, which was transformed the following year, after a National Constituent Assembly had been elected, into a permanent reform to the Income Tax Law. The relevant rate was increased from 12 to 28.5 per cent. President Rómulo Betancourt in a message to the Assembly justified this increase quoting Hoover and Curtice. Without it, he argued, the government's share would have been far below 60 per cent. But he also promised stability:

> Without ignoring that the faculty of taxation constitutes one of the essential attributes of National Sovereignty, the Reform, which we present for consideration by the National Constituent Assembly, will be able to ensure for a long period the fair participation of the State and the Nation in the profits obtained by the extractive industries. (*El País* 28-12-1946)

However, the government's take in the profits of Creole and Shell was still below 60 per cent, and prices were soaring. In the most prolific concessions belonging to Creole and Shell, it was even slightly below 50 per cent. But Betancourt had promised stability and, most importantly, with the income tax rate at 28.5 per cent, any further increase would have been beyond US levels and, hence, strongly resisted by the companies.

But stability required some *customary ground rent*. A royalty rate of one sixth alone was definitely not a feasible option. Moreover, income tax had become an important part of ground rent and, worse, one that was set in a sovereign manner, which was of major concern to the companies. How to put the lid on it? Creole (SONJ) spotted the opportunity first: what could be better, more appealing and persuasive than a fifty-fifty profit split? The government accepted. The tax experts of the industry 'co-operated in drafting legislation requiring them to split the profit difference with the government in any year in which normal taxes and royalties leave the companies with a bigger take than the tax collector' (*Fortune* 1949: 177–78). This so-called *additional tax* of 50 per cent was introduced in the Income Tax Law in 1948. As a result, the profit split would always be at least fifty-fifty. Moreover, the companies agreed *voluntarily* to pay this tax retroactively for the years 1946–47, thus suggesting that there was some kind of business transaction, though a sovereign National Assembly had enacted the additional tax.

Next, history had to be re-written. The government now declared that the income tax increase of 1946 had failed to achieve 'the objective of a 50 per cent profit share for the country', whereas the additional tax, at last, would 'consecrate the principle that the Nation's share cannot be less than that of the companies' (Vallenilla 1973: 206). In their writings, the Acción Democrática party leaders, and most notably Pérez Alfonzo and Betancourt, from now on would insist that they never had asked for more than a fifty-fifty profit split. The international oil companies, on the other hand, played their part in the trade press. *Fortune*, in a remarkable article gave the new version of the events that led to the 'fifty-fifty agreement' in Venezuela. Regarding the 1943 Hydrocarbons Law, the article stated, the loudest opposition to the legislation came from Acción Democrática. Though this party 'asked for no more than a fifty-fifty share', it argued that, should the price of oil rise materially, 'the 16.67 per cent royalty formula would not give the government an even break' (*Fortune* 1949: 177–78). Hence the revolutionary government of Acción Democrática – the first democratically elected government in Venezuela – was supposed to have succeeded where the *ancien régime* had failed.

A new *customary ground rent* had been born. According to *Fortune*, Creole and Shell expressed themselves 'as reconciled to this deal'. In general, 'the oil industry – and Creole most emphatically – does not worry so much about the effects of the fifty-fifty tax law as it does about future politicians who may have sixty-forty or even seventy-thirty ideas' (*Fortune* 1949: 177–

78). Indeed, Creole, i.e. SONJ, was already involved, as we shall see, in consolidating the new reference internationally. But the new Venezuelan government – a military government since the government of Acción Democrática had been overthrown by another *coup d'état* in 1948 – would not be idle either.

In 1949, Middle East oil production overtook that of Venezuela. The fields in the Middle East were much more prolific, and rents and royalties were much lower. In Venezuela output was counted by the hundreds of barrels per well per day, but in the Middle East by the thousands. Middle East oil, beyond any doubt, could be a threat to Venezuela, a fact that the international companies were keen to point out. Joseph E. Pogue, a famous oil specialist closely linked to SONJ, took on this task in a well-publicised lecture in Caracas delivered in March 1949. Competitive pressure, he argued, might force the Venezuelan government to reduce costs in one way or another (Pogue 1949). Among his audience was Manuel R. Egaña, again Minister of Development. Deeply worried, he decided to act. He appointed a delegation to visit Saudi Arabia, Egypt, Iraq, Iran, and Kuwait, as he believed that – contrary to what Pogue was suggesting – it would be possible 'to achieve a balance of competing forces whereby benefits can be obtained for the peoples of the Middle East without detriment to the economic position of the people of Venezuela' (Egaña 1949a). The delegation was to hand over copies of all legal texts relevant to Venezuelan oil as well as invitations to the first Venezuelan Oil Congress, to be organised jointly by the government and the oil industry in the near future.

Conclusions

In the first half of the century Venezuelan oil policy was very successful. Landlords, even in their heyday, did not get more than concessions. Thus public ownership was a starting point for oil exploitation, which spared the country the Mexican turmoil. Venezuela also benefited from the debacle of the international oil companies in Mexico. Finally, there was the Second World War to complete a picture favourable to reform in Venezuela.

And there was the secular rise of income tax. US corporate income tax rates increased from nil at the beginning of the century to 38 per cent after the Second World War; discounting the effect of the depletion allowance in petroleum production, it was still a rise from nil to 27.55 per cent. These rates also applied to profits of American companies elsewhere in the world as far as there was no, or only a lower, national income tax. The situation in Europe was similar. Hence, there was a strong incentive for a country like Venezuela to collect income taxes at comparable rates.

Moreover, income taxation also entailed a very significant increase in the amount of information made available to the Venezuelan landlord state. Profit shares in any given year became public knowledge and, inevitably, would become the centre of attention. Thus, contrary to what happened in the United States, where historically a vague reference to a 50 per cent profit share, on average and over the lifetime of a lease, gave way to customary royalty rates, in Venezuela the one sixth royalty rate coupled with vague references to profit shares would give way to a usual yearly profit share of 50 per cent – or, at least, that was what the international companies intended.

4.2   Middle East

The concession system in the Middle East was of colonial and imperial origin. When Persia granted the D'Arcy concession, in 1901, the country was divided into spheres of British and Russian influence. In Iraq the tug of war for oil concessions began under Turkish rule; then the country was under a British mandate when the most important concession was granted to the Turkish Petroleum Company (TPC) in 1925. The sheikhdoms of Bahrain (1930), Kuwait (1934), and Qatar (1935) granted concessions under British rule. Only Saudi Arabia, which granted its most famous concession in 1933, was an independent kingdom. Every single concession covered a large part, if not all, of the national territory of these countries. The concession term varied between 55 years (Bahrain) and 75 years (Iraq, Kuwait and Qatar), and there were only vague provisions for relinquishment. Hence, the history of Middle East oil is largely the history of a few concessions. However, there is one of outstanding importance in the development of the governance of international oil: the TPC concession in Iraq.

The TPC Concession in Iraq

German, British, and Dutch interests struggled for oil concessions in Iraq at a time when it was still part of the Turkish Empire. Early in 1914 they overcame their differences and joined together in the Turkish Petroleum Company (TPC). Halfway through that year, with the help of an Armenian intermediary (C. S. Gulbenkian), TPC succeeded in extracting from the Turkish government a vague promise for a concession. Gulbenkian, in return for his services, was to be awarded a share in the company.

Then came the First World War. After the war, the situation was quite different. Germany had been defeated, the Turkish Empire had disintegrated, and Iraq was a British mandate. Britain considered the pre-war Turkish promise of a concession to be binding on the new post-war Iraqi government, and in the 1920 San Remo Agreement the German interests in TPC were transferred to France. This country, in return, guaranteed the free passage of Iraqi oil to the Mediterranean across its mandated territories, Syria and Lebanon. But the San Remo Agreement had left out one important victorious power, the United States, which at that time was anxiously looking abroad for new supplies. The US government demanded an 'open door policy', i.e. '(1) that the nationals of all nations be subject, in the mandated territories, to equal treatment in law, (2) that no economic concessions in any mandated region be so large as to be exclusive, and (3) that no monopolistic concession relating to any commodity be granted' (United States Senate 1952: 51). Moreover, the Americans 'proposed a plan for effecting the "open door" patterned along the lines followed by the United States Department of the Interior in the sale of Osage Indian lands. Under the plan TPC, within 2 years from the date of confirmation of a concession by the Iraq Government, would have selected for its own exploitation a total area not to exceed 12 blocks, the area of each block not to exceed 16 square miles' (United State Senate 1952: 55). The balance of the concession, supposed to cover the whole country, would then have been open for subleasing to any and all companies interested in oil concessions in this area.

The US scheme lapsed, but in 1922, American companies were granted in principle a share in TPC and, at last, in 1925 the company got a huge concession covering an area of 35 thousand square miles in the north. TPC was to start exploration within eight months and to build an export pipeline as soon as oil was discovered in commercial quantities. Royalty was set at four shillings (gold) per ton. It was to be adjusted twenty years after the commencement of production, and every ten years thereafter. If profits were increasing, the royalty would be raised accordingly up to a maximum of six shillings per ton; conversely, it could be lowered to a minimum of two shillings per ton if profits fell. The contract also established that 'no other or higher taxes, impositions, duties, fees or charges ... shall be imposed upon the Company' (Stocking 1971: 132), but only as far as special petroleum taxes were concerned. The company was subject to general taxes as far as they were 'ordinarily imposed from time to time upon other industrial undertakings' (Stocking 1971: 132). Last but not least, any doubt or controversy between the contracting parties was to be submitted to international arbitration. Both parties would appoint an arbitrator, and the two arbitrators would appoint a referee as a tiebreaker. Their decision was final. The contract was based on the 'international law of civilised nations' and no relevant national law was acknowledged.

There is no doubt that the Iraqi government had benefited from competition and rivalry between the European powers, the United States, and the companies. The fixed royalty was high compared with Mexico and Venezuela, and even more so compared with neighbouring Persia. This flat rate might have been, I believe, the equivalent of a royalty of one sixth of the then supposed value of Middle Eastern crude in the Persian Gulf.[3] However, transformed into a fixed royalty per barrel, the

---

3.   There is no piece of documentary evidence to sustain my belief, but it is based on the following facts: (1) One sixth was the customary royalty rate in Osage leases, used as reference by the American government. (2) In the case of Iran (see below), there is documentary evidence that 4 sh. (gold) per ton was justified as the equivalent of a royalty of one eighth. However, this was *after* the devaluation of the British shilling, which

information to be given to the Iraqi government was minimised. It only had the right to check volumes, not prices. The presence of US government officials also explains the favourable arrangement regarding general taxation, which has to be seen against the background of the 1901 D'Arcy concession, which granted complete exemption from taxation. However, things were about to change. Once the American companies got their share, their government retreated. The companies, not surprisingly, were keen to close the door. And in 1928 there was finally an agreement on the shares in TPC. Anglo-Persian Oil Company (APOC),[4] Royal Dutch–Shell, Compagnie Française des Pétroles (CFP) and Near East Development (US interests) got 23.75 per cent each. The remaining 5 per cent, without voting rights, went to Participations and Investments (Gulbenkian). At the time production started, in 1934, the Near East Development had been reduced to two shareholders of equal standing: SONJ and Socony Vacuum (Mobil).

The associates now asked for a review of the concession contract, which was granted in 1931. On the one hand, the contract was purged of all traces relating to the original American 'open door' policy such as sub-leasing blocks to competitors. On the other hand, 'general taxes' were fixed contractually at 3.6 to 4.8 pence per ton on top of the fixed royalty of four shillings and, with immediate effect, there was a shut-in royalty of £400,000 (gold).

Persia

Already in 1914, the participants in TPC agreed not to compete within the confines of the Turkish Empire but to apply together for concessions. This agreement was renewed by the associates in 1928 and became known as the 'Red Line Agreement' (the relevant area was demarcated by a red line on a map). Hence,

---

would be consistent with a one sixth royalty before devaluation. (3) In 1943, in the case of Venezuela, there *is* documentary evidence that the American government insisted on a royalty rate of one sixth, in opposition to the companies offering only one eighth. Mikdashi (1966: 62) claims that the reference was one eighth, but the only evidence he presents refers to the case of Iran.

4.   APOC acquired the D'Arcy concession in 1908.

TPC intended to set a standard within that area. But this new standard was at odds with the oldest concession in the Middle East, the D'Arcy concession, granted in 1901.[5] D'Arcy, a British citizen, transferred the concession in 1908 to APOC, and in 1914, on the eve of the First World War, the British government became a majority shareholder in the company. As it turned out, this was the most successful concession in the Middle East up to the 1950s. In the 1920s Persia became the fourth biggest oil producer after the United States, Venezuela, and the Soviet Union, and the third biggest oil-exporter after Venezuela and the United States. Output per well averaged 13,000 b/d. Costs were low enough to offset the disadvantage of its geographical location and even ensure extraordinary profits (Mikdashi 1966: 42).

The most important payment to the government was a 16 per cent profit share. In 1931, with the Great Depression and low oil prices, this percentage represented only £310,000. That year, in neighbouring Iraq IPC agreed to a shut-in royalty of £400,000 – whereas Persia was producing 5.7 million tons. After years of a very strained relationship, the Persian government decided to cancel the concession to force its renegotiation, and this resulted in the first major confrontation in international oil – apart from the Bolshevik Revolution – between an exporting country and its international tenant (United States Senate 1952: 55–56). The concession was renewed in 1933.[6] The new contract provided for a fixed royalty of four shillings (gold) per ton, a 20 per cent share in dividends, and a shut-in royalty of £750,000. In return, the new APOC concession was extended for another sixty years. Thus, the original D'Arcy concession, also granted for sixty years, was effectively extended for an additional 32 years.

Though there is no doubt that the country was now better off, the four shillings (gold) per ton royalty was agreed *after* the 29 per cent devaluation of the British Pound. This difference was barely compensated by the 20 per cent share in dividends. Moreover, this was a renegotiation of a most successful concession. Hence, Persia should have received a significantly

---

5.   For the original contract see Société des Nations (1932).
6.   This agreement was also published by the Société des Nations (1932).

higher ground rent than Iraq, but it did not. The country had a poor deal.

Other Early Concessions

In 1930 Bahrain granted a concession to the Bahrain Petroleum Company (BAPCO), a 100 per cent subsidiary of Standard Oil Company of California (Stancal). It provided for a fixed royalty and contractually fixed general taxes amounting roughly to four shillings and sixpence per ton. However, payments were established in Indian rupees, without a gold guarantee. In contrast, Saudi Arabia, an independent kingdom, was able to benefit from the discovery of oil in neighbouring Bahrain in 1932. Stancal, in this case, had to compete with IPC. Although in the end the concession was granted to Stancal in 1933 – founding California Arabian Standard Oil Company (Casoc) – the company had to agree to a fixed royalty defined not in Indian rupees but in British shillings. Moreover, there was a gold guarantee and – fortunately for Saudi Arabia – the 4 shillings per ton was agreed *before* the devaluation of the British pound.

Kuwait came close to benefiting from the competition between APOC and Gulf Oil Company. But these companies reached a prior agreement to form a joint venture, the Kuwait Oil Company (KOC), with a 50 per cent share each, and they also agreed on the terms to be offered to the Kuwait government (Mikdashi 1966: 82 ff). In Qatar the only applicant was IPC (TPC changed its name to Iraq Petroleum Company in 1929). The concession was granted in 1935 to its subsidiary, the Qatar Petroleum Company (QPC). In Qatar and Kuwait, rents and taxes were basically the same as in Bahrain. They were fixed in Indian rupees. Roughly equivalent to 4 shillings 6 pence per ton but without gold guarantee, they were exposed to inflation and depreciation of the Indian rupee. Anyway, though exploration in Qatar and Kuwait would soon be successful, production was delayed by the advent of the Second World War.

Conclusions

In the inter-war period the reference of four shillings emerged in Iraq, well ahead of real developments on the ground and as a reflection of the customary royalty rates of one sixth and one eighth in the United States. However, what endured was not the reference in the background but the number in the foreground written into the contracts. Its spill-over effect was strong enough even to penetrate Persia, the political and economic supremacy of the British Empire notwithstanding.

Those 4 shillings were watered down significantly in later contracts, either by the devaluation of Sterling or by being paid in Indian rupees without gold guarantee. What next? Though uncertainty was high, it was already becoming clear that some common pattern of oil concessions in the Middle East had to emerge. The governments of that region, inevitably, would compare their concessions with those of their neighbours. In other words, whereas in British coal and American oil convergence was the result of a continuous flow of investment into marginal lands, in the Middle East things were different. A handful of concessions granted by some governments to a few international companies turned a customary ground rent into a political necessity. This necessity was strengthened, of course, with the development of the international petroleum cartel. Only a few months after the 1928 agreement with TPC, the three largest oil companies in the world – Royal Dutch–Shell, APOC and SONJ – reached the so-called 'As Is Agreement', according to which everybody would be satisfied with its present share in the market. Gulf, Stancal, Socony and Texaco adhered to it later. Together the 'Seven Sisters' would control world petroleum markets, with the exception of the United States where the fragmentation of private landed property and anti-trust legislation made this impossible. The control of US production could only be achieved through the intervention of the supreme landlord, the state. The counterpart to the international petroleum cartel in the United States was prorationing, exemplified by the Texas Railroad Commission, which was implemented more or less at that same time.

The Seven Sisters strengthened their relationships by sharing facilities, from production to distribution. The crude-short and crude-long companies exchanged upstream and downstream assets. Thus Texaco bought 50 per cent of the Stancal concessions in Bahrain and Saudi Arabia, and a similar transaction took place in Indonesia. In Venezuela, in 1936–37,

SONJ and Royal-Dutch Shell acquired a 25 per cent share in Mene Grande, until then a 100 per cent Gulf Oil subsidiary. Last but not least, after the war SONJ and Standard Oil of New York (Socony) became partners in Aramco (Casoc was renamed Arabian-American Oil Company in 1944). Stancal, Texaco and SONJ held a 30 per cent share, and Socony the remaining 10 per cent.

4.3 Fifty-fifty Profit Sharing

After the Second World War, the political necessity of common standards soon extended beyond the region. Strong links developed between Venezuela and the Middle East. Firstly, the big international tenant companies in Venezuela were now also operating in the Middle East. Secondly, there was the growing involvement of the American government. Thirdly, there was the Venezuelan delegation visiting the region in 1949.

Ground rent had to increase given the doubling of oil prices after the Second World War. Within the Middle East, the obvious option was to move towards the upper limit of 6 shillings (gold) per ton, as established in the IPC concession, and fiddling, if necessary, with the different gold standards and currencies in use. But in Venezuela a much more generous reference had developed under the benevolent supervision of the US government. As it turned out, the American government was willing to concede the same deal to the Middle Eastern countries and, to start with, to Saudi Arabia, where all concessions were in American hands.

Saudi Arabia

In 1948, 4 shillings (gold) per ton amounted to about US$ 0.21 per barrel. At the request of the Saudi Arabian government, hinting at increasing prices, Aramco agreed to an immediate rise to US$ 0.32 per barrel. This was obviously in line with the expected increase in the royalty rate for the IPC concession, from four to six shillings. Nevertheless, in spite of the increase, Aramco, in 1949, paid US$ 38 million in ground rent to Saudi Arabia and US$ 43 million in income tax to the US Treasury. This was an odd situation, and it was getting worse as US corporate income tax rates were still rising, from 38 per cent in 1949 to 42 per cent in 1950, and finally to 52 per cent in 1952. In terms of crude oil production, taking into account the depletion allowance, the comparable rates were 27.55, 30.45 and 37.7 per cent. But by virtue of the generous legislation covering double taxation in the United States, there was a simple remedy at hand. Aramco negotiated with the Saudi Arabian government a new arrangement whereby, first of all, royalty payments for on-shore production were reduced again to US$ 0.21 per barrel, and to US$ 0.26 for offshore production. Next, with the help of US tax experts an income tax law with a 20 per cent rate was drawn up. A further law created a 50 per cent additional tax with the object of securing an overall profit split of fifty-fifty. Finally, this fifty-fifty profit sharing arrangement became part of the concession contract as a complementary agreement, coming into effect in 1950.

Ground rent per barrel in Saudi Arabia rose from US$ 0.32 to about US$ 0.68. But every cent above US$ 0.21 or US$ 0.26 per barrel could be credited against US income taxes that would otherwise have been payable. Indeed, in 1950 the company paid only US$ 199 thousand in US taxes, which were entirely due to profits made outside Saudi Arabia (Engler 1961: 223ff).

Iran

The unfortunate revision of the 1933 concession agreement in itself would certainly have been sufficient to create new conflicts in Iran.[7] But worse was to come with the Second World War. Oil became of strategic importance. The Allies, distrusting the germanophile Shah, occupied the country and forced him to abdicate in favour of his son. In the north, Soviet forces carried out the occupation, while the British took over in the south.

As early as 1943, representatives of Royal Dutch–Shell and some American companies visited Tehran asking for concessions outside the AIOC area.[8] The Iranian government engaged the two American advisors, Herbert Hoover Jr. and A. A. Curtice who, not surprisingly, drew its attention to the recent reform in

---

7.   The country changed its name from Persia to Iran in 1935.
8.   In 1935 APOC was renamed Anglo-Iranian Oil Company (AIOC).

Venezuela (Hamilton 1962: 39ff; Elwell-Sutton 1955: 108). In 1944, Soviet representatives joined in. The latter even succeeded in making the Iranian government promise to grant a fifty-year concession covering the northern part of the country, which would be run as a joint venture. For the first 25 years the Soviets would control 51 per cent of the shares, the Iranian government 49 per cent; thereafter, it would be 50 per cent each. Profits would be shared accordingly.

In the context of national and international political turmoil, however, the Iranian Parliament refused to grant any concessions, but this rush for concessions triggered an official inquiry into the existing AIOC concession. In 1947, the Ministry of Finance suggested that the country should follow the Venezuelan example. This was probably the consequence of the first direct contacts between the two countries earlier that year through their embassies in Washington. And in a Memorandum to AIOC in 1948, the Iranian Government complained that 4 shillings per ton no longer represented one eighth of the price of Iranian crude but less than one sixteenth. If it had applied Venezuelan standards, the government would have received, in 1947, £22 million instead of £7 million (Elwell-Sutton 1955: 163ff).

Negotiations followed in 1948–49. The Iranian government once more gave a retainer to Curtice, as well as Max Thornburg, another private consultant. The Iranian government insisted on a fifty-fifty profit sharing following the latest move in Venezuela. AIOC insisted on an adjustment to 6 shillings (gold) per ton, which was actually granted, somewhat ahead of schedule, by IPC to the Iraqi government in 1950. In 1947–48, taking into account all other payments, the AIOC proposal would have amounted to US$ 0.50 per barrel, and the Iranian proposal to US$ 0.80 (Longrigg 1968: 190).

The government reluctantly accepted the AIOC proposal. Legally, the deal had still to be approved by the Iranian Parliament. Then, on 17 October 1949, the Venezuelan delegation reached Tehran. Its members had been instructed to ask no questions, in order to avoid mistrust, but to answer all questions put to them. The Iranian officials showed an insatiable curiosity, and their questions covered just about everything concerning oil (Egaña 1949b). In December 1950, Parliament rejected the agreement, following the recommendation of a

Committee presided by Mosadeq. Then, in January 1951, the Saudi Arabian government and Aramco made public their fifty-fifty profit sharing agreement. In all haste, AIOC now wanted to subscribe to the same principle, but it was too late. In April Mosadeq was appointed Prime Minister. Nationalisation followed in May.

There is no doubt that the end of the British monopoly was welcomed by the United States (Longrigg 1968: 163). The US State Department, moreover, expected that a new concession would be granted not to AIOC but to a Consortium of British, US, Dutch, and French companies. However, the Iranian government wanted a break from its semi-colonial past, and, after all, there was a precedent: Mexico. But an international boycott of Iranian oil ensued and, eventually, in 1953 a coup d'état supported by the Central Intelligence Agency (CIA) brought down the Mosadeq government. The AIOC concession was renewed the following year. Even though nationalisation was formally maintained, it was abolished in substance, but the British monopoly in Iran was finally broken. An International Consortium would operate the concession. AIOC, now renamed British Petroleum (BP), retained only a 40 per cent share although, of course, it received compensation for the remaining 60 per cent. US companies also received a share of 40 per cent. SONJ, Texaco, Socal, Gulf and Socony received 7 per cent each, and 5 per cent went to a group of independent companies. Finally, Royal Dutch–Shell secured 14 per cent and CFP 6 per cent. The concession was to last for 25 years, with an option for renewal for 15 years. And the government received a 50 per cent profit share.

Conclusions

The fifty-fifty profit sharing agreement in Iran was the last to be concluded, as it had been introduced already in all the other important oil-exporting countries, including far away Indonesia. There were slight differences in form. Outside Saudi Arabia, the fixed tonnage royalty was generally transformed into a royalty of one eighth. The American reference had finally come to prevail everywhere. Yet even in the United States there was some irritation about the fact that the American companies had managed to set the total increase in ground rent against their tax liabilities to the Treasury.[9]

In Iran, the ageing colonial power, Britain, failed twice in her attempts to maintain her own much less advantageous position in that country. Revenues from Iranian oil were not only important to the British government, but also to the ailing British economy. It is noteworthy that the Venezuelan delegation visiting the Middle East played no role at all in Saudi Arabia, the first country to get a fifty-fifty profit sharing agreement in the region. By request of Aramco the Saudi government refused visas to the Venezuelan delegation. The Venezuelans would have presented a version of the fifty-fifty arrangement based on the exercise of sovereignty, whereas in the Middle East and Indonesia the fifty-fifty profit sharing agreements, including income tax, were part of the contractual relationship.

History was now re-written in the Middle East as it had been in Venezuela. To consolidate the fifty-fifty principle, it was alleged that it was deeply rooted in the past. Indeed, in 1960 a director of SONJ, H.W.Page, maintained that in the Middle East pre-war, 4 shillings (gold) per ton 'plus other payments to the governments came to an average of nearly 50% of the profit'. However, after the War, with inflation and the rapid increase in crude prices, along with higher United States and United Kingdom corporate income tax, the oil companies 'recognised that the fixed royalty payment no longer gave the equitable division originally intended, and that additional royalty payments were neither economically practical nor a permanent method of maintaining equity between the parties'. Hence, '50/50 was the result of this recognition of the need to restore the equity which had been frustrated by drastically changed conditions, beyond the control of either party and unforeseen at the time when the agreements were negotiated' (quoted in Penrose 1971: 168).

The fact is that throughout the term of fixed royalty (i.e. from 1925 to 1950), 'the Iraqi government received £40.0 million and the IPC collected a net profit of £76.1 million. The overall split of profits was 35:65 in favour of the IPC' (Mikdashi

---

9. The relevant Hearings in the US Senate are extensively reported in Engler (1961: chap. VIII).

1966: 106, 275). Moreover, the system in place to adjust the fixed royalty of 4 shillings after twenty years included no reference to any specific profit share. Moreover, in the case of Saudi Arabia, the government originally asked for a profit share of 30 per cent, but Stancal refused this proposal as being too onerous. The counterproposal was 4 shillings per ton, which the company, obviously enough, must have considered less onerous (Philby 1964: 80, 89). Equally hard to believe is the statement of the Chairman of the AIOC, shortly after its nationalisation, claiming that the tonnage royalty increase from 4 shillings to 6 shillings (gold) a ton was equivalent to a fifty-fifty profit sharing. The difference was 'that in years of high profit margins (e.g. 1950), the 50/50 system would yield higher revenues to the Persian Government; whereas in years of relatively low profit margins, the tonnage royalty would be better for the government' (quoted in Mikdashi 1966: 154).

Anyway, the international tenant companies were hailing fifty-fifty profit sharing as the ultimate compromise. According to the President of SONJ, then the biggest oil company in the world:

> Fifty-fifty relieves the country of any financial risk, and places that risk upon the company which is in a position to evaluate it and spread the risks of the search for oil over many areas. Any basis other than 50/50 could create an imbalance of interests which would reduce the attractiveness of the venture for one or the other of the parties. The 50/50 represents a tested principle for maintaining an equality of interests through all the aspects of an inevitably complex relationship intended to endure for many years. (Quoted in Mikdashi 1966: 141)

These words were said in March 1958. Only a few months later, in December, the fifty-fifty profit sharing arrangement came to an end in the country in which it was not embodied in the contracts: in sovereign Venezuela.

4.4   The Failure of Compromise

The international companies held the most productive oil lands in the world paying, with fifty-fifty profit sharing, the same ground rent and taxes as on marginal lands in the United States. Yet production from these marginal lands was determining prices on world markets (taking into account, of course, of transport costs). Thus, in the early 1950s, the posted price for a barrel of West Texas Sour (36° API) was US$ 2.44, and the price of a comparable barrel of Saudi Arabian crude was US$ 1.79. Still, differences in productivity were even greater. Tariki, once Oil Minister of Saudi Arabia, estimated the average after-tax profit rate of Aramco at 57.6 per cent. Mikdashi estimated that rate for IPC at 56.6 per cent for the years 1952 to 1961; at 69.3 per cent for the Consortium in Iran (1955–64); and higher than 150 per cent for KOC (1954–60) (Mikdashi 1966: 181, 221; and Mikdashi 1972: 141). In comparison, the average profit rate for companies in Venezuela, 22 per cent for the years 1947 to 1957, looked rather modest (Venezuela, Ministry for Mines and Hydrocarbons 1961: 115), though this was an average for a large number of companies. The figures for the big three, holding the most productive oil lands, were double this average.

Profits were very high indeed, and this was evident. New concessionaires in the Middle East always offered the host countries significantly higher ground rents and, additionally, a new feature – or a renewed feature, as it had already been present in the D'Arcy concession – a share in the companies running the concessions. Most spectacularly, in 1957 the Ente Nationale di Idrocarburi (ENI), the Italian state oil company, offered to the Iranian government on top of a 50 per cent profit share, a 50 per cent 'carried interest' in the joint venture to exploit the concession. As a 'carried interest' the government would take no risk. The costs of failure would be met exclusively by ENI. With this arrangement the profit share was 75:25 in favour of Iran. Neither the strong pressure exerted by the major oil companies on ENI, nor the intervention of the US Ambassador in Tehran calling on the Shah personally, could stop the signing of this contract. The following year Canadian and US companies signed another two contracts of that kind. Venezuela held a bidding round in 1956–57 where royalty rates of up to 25 per cent were offered, and bonus payments totalled $700 million.

The older concessions could clearly afford higher ground rents. Sooner rather than later they would also be asked to pay up. In January 1958, a coup d'état brought a new, provisional government to Venezuela, which would organise democratic elections. At that time, however, the state was in the middle of a financial crisis, high fiscal revenues of recent years notwithstanding. But the Venezuelan oil industry was booming in the aftermath of the 1956–57 Suez crisis. In 1957 profit levels had risen, on average, to 32 per cent. The easiest way out of the financial crisis was to make the oil companies pay. As there was no Congress, the provisional government legislated by decree, and it secretly worked out a reform of the Income Tax Law. President Sanabria enacted the reform in December, a few days after the general elections and just in time to apply it for the fiscal year that was about to end. The oil companies were taken completely by surprise. The maximum income tax rate was increased from 28.5 to 47.5 per cent. As a consequence fiscal oil revenues would amount to US$ 914 million in 1958, and net profits to only US$ 523 million. The distribution of profits was now 64:36 in favour of the government.

Outraged, the president of Creole, H.W.Haight, immediately sent a letter to the Minister of Mines and Hydrocarbons. He complained about the companies having not been consulted. He also claimed that the government had not taken into account 'the balance which has been sought between the government and the oil industry by means of the 50-50', and requested the government to reconsider its action. In the meantime the company would let it know 'the measures which gradually have to be taken to protect Company interests and to counter the effects of a tax increase which is out of line with the present situation of an enormous excess of world production capacity' (quoted in Mejía Alarcón 1972: 122ff). On the same day the President of Creole went away for Christmas holidays. In the airport he issued a statement:

> Venezuela has become the first country in the world to break so-called 50-50 principle of equal shares in fruits of industry completely disregarding acquired rights and ignoring the moral if not legal obligation to negotiate this break with the interested parties. Some oil-producing countries have recently concluded certain oil agreements which depart from 50-50 but in no case have existing concessions or fiscal agreements been modified. (*World Petroleum* 1959: 16)

The Minister for Mines and Hydrocarbons replied immediately that the tax reform 'does not injure any acquired right nor does it modify any existing agreement with the oil companies since the so-called 50-50 system emanates from the law itself and not from any formalised agreement'. Moreover, 'the reform maintains, in its entirety, the contractual arrangement regarding concessions'. All that had happened was simply a modification of the tax law, 'which affects all taxpayers equally and as it is a tax reform, comes exclusively within the sphere of national sovereignty' (quoted in Mejía Alarcón 1972: 22ff).

Haight did not return from his Christmas holidays. For the incoming government – once more headed by Betancourt – it was out of the question to reconsider the tax increase. Instead, the government would again send a delegation to visit the Middle East, in order to persuade all oil-exporting countries in the region to follow suit. The carefully elaborated conciliatory governance of international oil, with fifty-fifty profit sharing at its heart and the American reference as its backbone, was about to collapse.

5 THE SOVEREIGN LANDLORDS

5.1 Oil Prices and Production Control

The long-term floor to supply prices for domestic oil in the United States was given, historically, by marginal production costs *plus* the customary ground rent. World market prices, on the other hand, revolved around the US prices given the importance of that country as an oil producer. While the United States was an oil exporter – until 1947 – with the Gulf of Mexico being its principal centre of exports, the formula which the international petroleum cartel agreed on was to equate *cif* (cost, insurance, and freight) prices everywhere in the world to *fob* (free on board) prices in the Gulf of Mexico *plus* transport costs, regardless of where the oil was actually coming from. Hence, American oil was competitive everywhere. However, once the United States became an importer, a new formula was adopted according to which the *fob* prices of oil in the exporting countries were equal to domestic oil prices *cif* New York, the principal centre of imports, minus transport costs from New York to the exporting countries. Hence, imports from whatever source were competitively priced in relation to the US market. Thus, for example, in March 1959 the posted price of a barrel of West Texas Sour, 36° API, was US$ 2.83; the price formula in question produced a *fob* price for a barrel of Saudi Arabian Light of US$ 1.94 (Frank 1966).[1]

To hold this price structure together required control of production. In the United States this was achieved by the principal oil-producing states through prorationing, co-ordinated nationally after 1935 by the *Interstate Oil Compact Commission* (IOCC).[2] Officially, prorationing had no relevance to prices but only to conservation. This was a legal fiction but an important one; without it, prorationing would never have been legally upheld by the US Supreme Court. Since the early 1950s both the Canadian and the Venezuelan governments attended the IOCC meetings as observers, as these countries were the main

---

1. These kinds of price structures are known as 'basing point systems'. (Machlup 1949)
2. Later renamed *Interstate Oil and Gas Compact Commission* (IOGCC).

suppliers of imported oil. Canada was actually a net importer – importing in the east, exporting in the west – relying again on Venezuela as its principal source. Following the example of the United States, production in Canada was also subject to prorationing at provincial level. The international petroleum cartel controlled production in Venezuela and the other oil-exporting countries (United States Senate 1952: *passim*).

But the cartel weakened as competition intensified after the Second World War. In 1945, there were 28 US companies seriously involved in Middle East oil. In 1958, there were as many as 190 (Frank 1966: 91). In Venezuela some thirty companies, the majority of which were American independents (Vallenilla 1973: 220ff), were awarded important concessions in the 1956–57 bidding round. Venezuela was then still the biggest oil-exporting country in the world. At the same time US crude oil production was rapidly losing importance. In 1945, the share of US oil in the world's total was 61 per cent; in 1959, its share was down to 36 per cent. Moreover, US production was approaching its peak, and production costs of marginal wells were increasing whereas in the oil-exporting countries average costs were falling. In the Middle East, in 1959, this average was about US$ 0.20 per barrel; in Venezuela, it was twice as much. But US marginal wells produced at costs well above two dollars.

Hence, while the percentage of effectively controlled output was shrinking, the international price structure was exposed to increasing tensions due to the enormous differences in production costs and profitability. The market solution would have been, of course, lower prices. However, lower prices would have threatened the very existence of US marginal oil wells. Out of roughly 600 thousand oil wells, 400 thousand were so-called 'stripper wells', i.e. marginal wells exempt from pro-rationing. Though they represented two thirds of the wells, they contributed only one fifth to domestic output, but they were of enormous economic and political importance in the oil-producing states. Likewise, lower prices would have threatened the oil-exporting countries with substantial losses in fiscal revenues. Consequently, the governments of both the United States and the oil-exporting countries had strong reasons to intervene in the market.

In response to the weakening of the international petroleum cartel, the US government was already promoting in the mid-fifties a voluntary programme of import restrictions (Shaffer 1968; Bohi and Russell 1978). However, as the number of importing companies increased, a voluntary approach was bound to fail. In 1954 there were sixteen companies; in 1958 there were 61 (Shaffer 1968: 23). In particular, some of the newcomers to Venezuela openly disregarded the voluntary restrictions and, in order to enter the US market, they offered discounts of up to US$ 0.70 per barrel. Thus, whereas domestic crude oil production was cut back from 7.2 million barrels daily in 1957 to 6.7 million in 1958 in order to maintain prices, imports rose from one million barrels daily to 1.4 million. In an effort to contain the approaching crisis the governments of the United States and Canada sent a joint delegation to Caracas to explain to the provisional government the importance of voluntary import restrictions. The delegation also drew its attention to the discounts offered by the new concessionaires (Acosta Hermoso 1969, 1971a, 1971b; Tugwell 1975); to no avail, as it turned out, as the mind of the Venezuelan government was focused not on prices but on fiscal revenues. It was already busy preparing the important increase in income taxes, which put an end to fifty-fifty profit sharing in December of that year.

As prices continued to weaken, in March 1959 President Eisenhower introduced compulsory import quotas and, in reprisal to Sanabria's decree, Venezuela lost its traditionally privileged access to the US market. The international price structure of oil was breaking up. In the United States and Canada marginal oil wells would continue to set high price levels. In the rest of the world, Venezuela included, prices would continue to fall over the next decade. Given the low level of production costs in the oil-exporting countries, the fall was liable to be steep, and Venezuela was particularly exposed to the danger of becoming trapped between increased levels of ground rent and falling prices. In all haste the newly elected government – again headed by Betancourt – set up a *Comisión Coordinadora de la Conservación y el Comercio de Hidrocarburos* (CCCCH) in order to 'conserve oil and gas, which are non-renewable natural resources, and also to impose restrictions on trade and production with a view to securing a reasonable stability of prices and markets' (quoted in Pérez Alfonzo 1967: 175ff).

The haste was due to the forthcoming First Arab Petroleum Congress, to which Venezuela and Iran had been invited. The oil-exporting countries, including Saudi Arabia, had already met in 1951, on the occasion of the First National Petroleum Congress in Caracas. They met for a second time in April 1959, in Cairo, less than three years after the successful nationalisation of the Suez Canal in 1956. This was the propitious political background to the secret meeting of some of the heads of delegation – amongst them Pérez Alfonzo of Venezuela, Farmanfarmayan of Iran, Tariki of Saudi Arabia, Omar of Kuwait – which culminated in the so-called Gentlemen's Agreement. The heads of delegation 'agreed to take back to their respective governments the idea of setting up as soon as possible a *Consultative Petroleum Commission* which means common problems can be discussed so that common solutions can be reached'. More specifically, they agreed that 'an attempt ought to be made to maintain the price structure, since of necessity prices affect the level of participation of the oil producing countries', and that 'any change [of prices] should first be discussed and approved by all the interested parties'. Last but not least, the signatories also acknowledged the 'need to set up bodies in every country with the aim of co-ordinating from a national perspective the Conservation, Production and Exploitation of Oil' (quoted in Acosta Hermoso 1969: 17ff. Italics in the original).

Back home the Venezuelan government pressed ahead with the idea of controlling production. In a policy change with regard to the previous governments, Petroleum Minister Pérez Alfonzo declared his hostility towards the newcomers from 1956–57: 'If they were forced to close down or sell out because of growing pressure from Venezuelan taxes, labour and other costs, plus restricted sales opportunities in the markets, this would meet with the government's approval' (Pérez Alfonzo 1960: 143ff). As a matter of fact, the CCCCH repeatedly refused export permits for shipments at heavily discounted prices. Pérez Alfonzo also invited experts from the Texas Railroad Commission into the country to set up a system of prorationing. Nevertheless, his hope that the US government would reconsider its position regarding Venezuela's privileged access to the American market

– the slogan was *trato hemisférico* (*hemispheric treatment*) – did not materialise nor did the hope of the US government and the international companies that the Betancourt government would reconsider Sanabria's decree. Worse, in the Gentlemen's Agreement of Cairo, Venezuela was urging the other exporting countries to increase their profit shares, as a minimum, to 60 per cent in order 'to bring themselves into line with the recent position assumed by Venezuela and evidenced as a tendency in new contracts made in other countries' (quoted in Acosta Hermoso 1969: 17ff).

The Gentlemen's Agreement led to the foundation of OPEC in September 1960 after a further fall in world market prices, a fall which no longer affected the protected US domestic market. But in OPEC's founding resolution there was no great enthusiasm for regulating production, which was only mentioned 'among other means' to stabilise prices (OPEC Res. I.1).[3] Indeed, prorationing was an urgent issue only to Venezuela. In 1960 this country accounted for 30 per cent of world exports, it already enjoyed a relatively high ground rent per barrel, and it was approaching maturity as an oil producer. The ratio of annual production to proven reserves was 1:17. In the other oil-exporting countries this ratio was between 1:33 (Qatar) and 1:111 (Saudi Arabia). Thus, Venezuelan exports during the 1960s would increase, on average, only by 2.7 per cent annually while Middle East exports increased by 10.9 per cent. Consequently, in that region even falling fiscal revenues per barrel could still generate growing fiscal revenues and, what is more, there was even room for increasing fiscal revenues per barrel when prices were falling. In other words, though the Gentlemen's Agreement stated that 'of necessity prices affect the level of participation of the oil producing countries', under the circumstances this was not necessarily the case.

Moreover, there was also an important political difference. In sovereign Venezuela concessions were subject to national jurisdiction and legislation, whereas in the Middle East they were subject to international law and arbitration. Hence, OPEC production quotas would have required either the consent of

---

3.   The Roman numerals refer to the Conference; the Arabic numerals refer to the Resolution.

the companies – and, undoubtedly, also the consent of the consuming countries – or the willingness of the oil-producing countries to enforce them unilaterally. But when OPEC, at Venezuela's insistence, finally adopted production quotas for 1965–66 and 1966–67, the international companies threatened international arbitration and, as it turned out, these countries were still not in a position to enforce them unilaterally. This was hardly surprising, as quotas were the last thing oil companies and consuming countries would ever agree to. As a former Secretary General of OPEC has pointed out:

> The majors' ability to manipulate production in the Middle East has been, and still is, a potent weapon, which they have used and will no doubt continue to use to very good effect against individual countries in the area. Agreement on their part to operate in accordance with an OPEC Joint Production Program would effectively entail a relinquishment of the weapon that has enabled them to surmount many a storm in the past – for the production program is in essence an instrument whereby OPEC itself, rather than the oil companies, can assume the responsibility for deciding on the production level from the OPEC area as a whole, as well as the output from each member country. (Lutfi 1968: 68)[4]

Notwithstanding the fact that at that time all parties concerned would have been happy with maintaining the old price structure, the underlying conflict on natural resource ownership prevented them from co-operating in the control of production. The landlord states were firmly determined to increase their share, economically and politically, by putting an end to the old governance structure that tolerated, so to speak, private and public landlords only as 'sleeping partners'. The companies and the consuming countries were firmly determined to prevent them from becoming active participants. Prices inevitably continued to decline in the 1960s as competition between the companies in their capacity as producers intensified. Yet competition between the companies in their capacity as tenants actually strengthened the position of the oil-exporters. The newcomers, notwithstanding the fact that they had only obtained the left-overs from the huge concessions granted in the interwar period,

---

4. Lutfi was secretary general of OPEC in 1965/6.

once again demonstrated that they were able and willing to agree to economic and political conditions that were more favourable to the landlord states.

5.2 Fiscal Regimes and Oil Prices

The Gentlemen's Agreement of Cairo led to the founding of OPEC, the triggering event being the decision of the international tenant companies to cut posted prices. In August 1960, Aramco cut the posted price of Arabian Light from US$ 1.94 to US$ 1.80. Though this was not a dramatic reduction, it was an alarming one as the historical link with domestic oil prices in the United States had been severed. The oil countries feared that a much deeper cut could follow. A few weeks later the Petroleum Ministers of Saudi Arabia, Venezuela, Iraq, Iran, and Kuwait met in Baghdad, founding the Organisation of the Petroleum Exporting Countries (OPEC).

OPEC Membership

1960	Iran, Iraq, Kuwait, Saudi Arabia, Venezuela
1961	Qatar
1962	Indonesia, Libya
1967	United Arab Emirates[a]
1969	Algeria
1971	Nigeria
1973	Ecuador[b]
1975	Gabon[c]

a. Until 1974 Abu Dhabi.
b. Ecuador left OPEC in 1992.
c. Gabon left OPEC in 1995.

Market, Posted and Tax Reference Prices

Not surprisingly, OPEC's founding resolution dealt, above all, with prices. It urged member countries to 'endeavour, by all means available to them, to restore present prices to the levels prevailing before the reductions' (OPEC Res. I.1). Venezuela was already doing its best through its newly founded CCCCH. There is no doubt that Venezuela intended to restore market prices, but only in this country was income taxation based on these prices. In the Middle East, it was based on posted prices, i.e. on prices as published by the companies, applicable to third parties. (In fact, there were no posted prices in the Middle East prior to the introduction of fifty-fifty profit sharing). Hence, the four Gulf States simply notified the oil companies that in their opinion the recent reductions in posted prices were not justified, and for them the problem was to compel the companies, in one way or another, to restore earlier prices (Acosta Hermoso 1969: 18).

But the companies refused point-blank to co-operate with OPEC, or even to acknowledge its existence. However, as far as posted prices went, they did not adjust them downwards again, even though market prices continued falling. Yet OPEC deemed that this was not enough. In its IVth Conference, in April and June 1962, OPEC decided to act. As 'the Oil Companies have so far taken no steps to restore prices to the pre-August 1960 level', the Conference recommended that member countries should ensure that taxes would 'be paid for on the basis of posted prices not lower than those which applied prior to August, 1960'. If within a reasonable period no satisfactory arrangement could be reached, 'then Member Countries shall consult with each other with a view to taking such steps as they deem appropriate in order to restore crude-oil prices to the level which prevailed prior to August 9, 1960' (Res. IV.32). OPEC was now talking about *posted* prices to be transformed into *tax reference prices*, independently from falling market prices. Thus, falling market prices would not affect fiscal revenues.

Royalties

OPEC's IVth Conference also came back to the issue of a minimum profit share of 60 per cent. The way to achieve this aim had already been indicated in the Gentlemen's Agreement of Cairo. 'Taxes, especially in respect of income tax, should be treated as separate elements from royalties' (quoted in Acosta Hermoso 1969: 17ff). Indeed, fifty-fifty profit sharing was an oddity, in as much as it referred to the sum of royalty, the emblematic mineral ground rent, and income tax, properly a tax to be paid by any profit-making enterprise. Accordingly,

OPEC argued that petroleum being a 'wasting asset', 'in conformity with the principle recognised and the practice observed generally in the world' member countries were entitled to a compensation 'for the intrinsic value' of oil, 'altogether apart from their obligations falling under the heading of income tax'. However, under arrangements at present in force 'no compensation is paid for the intrinsic value of petroleum', insofar as a royalty was 'treated as credits against income tax liabilities'. Undeniably, the way the 50 per cent additional tax was structured, the payment of royalty was irrelevant; without royalty, the outcome would still have been a 50 per cent profit share. In conclusion, the companies should be approached 'with a view to working out a formula whereunder royalty payments shall be fixed at a uniform rate which Members consider equitable, and shall not be treated as a credit against income tax liabilities' (Res. IV.33).

A memorandum attached to this resolution aimed at further clarifying the conceptual differences between royalty and income tax:

> Royalty is payable by the lessee to the owner of the deposit on production .... It may variously be regarded as rent, as compensation for using up a wasting asset placed at the lessee's disposal, or as payment for the intrinsic value of the raw material produced .... Income tax, on the other hand, is a ... distinct item of liability to the government of the country in respect to the net profit earned .... Where the owner of deposits is not the government, the separation of royalty from income tax presents no problem, the payee being different in each case. Where, however, a government happens to be the owner of the deposit leased, the above mentioned fundamental distinction may become blurred because both royalty and income tax are in that case payable to the same person. (Quoted in Rouhani 1971: 222ff)

This is what was supposed to have happened in the Middle East. Although 'the companies are presumed to pay taxes on the basis of 50 per cent of their net income, their present practice of deducting royalties from amounts due under the provisions of income tax laws means that either they are not paying their full share of taxes on a 50 per cent basis, or else they are paying taxes correctly but evading payment of royalties completely'.

Moreover, the rate of one eighth provided in the concession agreements was deemed unsatisfactory:

> [In the United States] the royalties payable vary from 12.5 per cent to 25 per cent and are altogether distinct from income tax and other taxes. In Venezuela the lowest rate is 16.67 per cent whereas the highest is 25 per cent.[5] A 20 per cent rate applies in the case of recent agreements concluded in Saudi Arabia and Kuwait .... A consideration of outstanding importance is the fact that in the United States and in Canada the rate of royalty payable sometimes increases in proportion to the prospects of discovery of oil and to the actual production per well. In view of the fact that established reserves in the Middle East are abundant and actual production per well is overwhelmingly great, it would appear that a minimum of 20 per cent would be a just and equitable rate of royalty applicable in that region. (Quoted in Rouhani 1972: 222ff)

Obviously, a 20 per cent royalty plus a 50 per cent income tax would always guarantee a profit share, as a minimum, of 60 per cent. Sovereign Venezuela had put an end to fifty-fifty profit sharing by increasing income taxes. In the Middle East the exporting countries had to resort to negotiation, and these arguments about 'royalty expensing' and royalty rates provided them with a good starting point.

Negotiations

Negotiations got under way after the IVth Conference. Yet the oil companies continued to ignore OPEC, and insisted on negotiating individually with each country. Thus, the companies associated in the International Consortium in Iran talked with Fouad Rouhani, at the time OPEC's Secretary General, but dealt with him only in his capacity as a representative of the Iranian government (Acosta Hermoso 1971b: 91ff; Rouhani 1971: 217ff; Skeet 1988: 30ff). In these talks the companies showed themselves willing to compromise regarding special issues, which concerned only Iran, but not regarding OPEC Resolutions. *Mutatis mutandis*, the same happened with other

---

5.   In Venezuela the highest royalty rate was actually one third, paid by Sinclair in a concession acquired in 1944.

Member Countries. This strategy was quite successful. In the Vth Conference, in November 1962, the Organisation came close to breaking point. In the absence of agreement on a common strategy, the VIth Conference had to be postponed until December 1963, though according to the statutes, there were supposed to be two conferences annually. In the end, Saudi Arabia, Qatar, Kuwait, Iran, and Libya were prepared to accept the offer of the companies, whereas Iraq, Indonesia, and Venezuela rejected it. Of these three countries, however, only Iraq was directly affected. Indonesia, like Venezuela, had already ensured, on its own initiative, a minimum profit share of 60 per cent. In any case, there was no unanimity as required by OPEC statutes. Finally, there was no other way out but to agree to disagree. All Member Countries were authorised to proceed as they wished but, at the same time, they renewed their commitment to a common approach and procedure for the future (Res. VIII.49).

The final proposal of the companies was as follows: (1) Posted prices would be maintained at the present level, falling market prices notwithstanding, though they would not be restored to the level prior to August 1960; (2) The demand for a 50 per cent income tax on top of royalty was accepted in principle, but the royalty rate would remain at one eighth; (3) In 1964 – the first year the proposal would take effect – there would be an 8.5 per cent discount on those tax reference prices, to be reduced to 6.5 per cent by 1966; (4) Thereafter, if market prices rose, new negotiations would be opened.

The five aforementioned Member Countries accepted the proposal. A numerical example may help to clarify its practical consequences. Since 1960 the posted price of a barrel of Arabian Light was US$ 1.80. If we suppose that production costs were still at US$ 0.20, with fifty-fifty profit sharing, ground rent per barrel was US$ 0.80. With the new agreement, ground rent per barrel would increase to US$ 0.83 in 1964 and to US$ 0.85 in 1966. OPEC's original demand, on the other hand, was a tax reference price of US$ 1.94, and a 50 per cent income tax on top of a 20 per cent royalty. In this case the ground rent per barrel would have increased to US$ 1.064. From this perspective – comparing reality with wishful thinking – the result of the negotiations was not too impressive.

Nor was this result very impressive legally and politically, as the agreements were worded in a way suggesting that only formal corrections were taking place, without essentially altering the established contractual relationship. Thus, the transformation of the old posted prices into new tax reference prices was not acknowledged as such. They were still called 'posted prices'. By the same token, 'royalty expensing' was allegedly only an issue of good accountancy, not a fundamental questioning of fifty-fifty profit sharing. Last but not least, they were conceived as 'supplementary agreements' to the 'principal agreements' (the existing concession contracts) and, as such, also subject to international law and arbitration. It was on these political and legal grounds that Iraq rejected the proposal (Rouhani 1971: 232).

In 1966, OPEC asked the five Member Countries concerned to reopen negotiations with the international oil companies, with a view to further reducing those discounts (Res. XI.71). The companies, pointing to falling market prices, refused any deal. But then, in 1967, came the third Arab–Israeli war and the ensuing closure of the Suez Canal. The majority of OPEC Members being Arab countries, the war created a new political reality. The companies, in 1968, agreed to phase out the discounts completely by 1975. Ground rent per barrel, in our example, would thus increase to US$ 0.87 in 1970, and to US$ 0.91 in 1975.

To sum up, let us reconsider the results of these negotiations in the 1960s. The market price of Arabian Light, at the beginning of 1970, had fallen from US$ 1.80 to about US$ 1.30. Yet ground rent had increased, from US$ 0.80 to US$ 0.87. Production costs in the older concessions had fallen over the decade from US$ 0.20 to about US$ 0.12. As a result, the profits of the oil companies had fallen from US$ 0.80 to US$ 0.30 (Cf. Mikdashi 1972: 113). Thus, whereas ground rent had risen by seven cents, net profits of the tenant companies had fallen by fifty cents. Nevertheless, the profit rate of the major international oil companies in the Middle East was still close to 50 per cent, since with the increase in productivity the capital invested per barrel had fallen (Amuzegar 1975). In Venezuela, the figures for 1969 were as follows: the *average* market price of crude oil was US$ 1.79, and ground rent per barrel was US$

0.95. Production costs were US$ 0.39, and net profits also stood at US$ 0.39. Hence, profits per barrel were higher. Nevertheless, profit rates were lower, 29 per cent on average (Venezuela, Ministry for Mines and Hydrocarbons 1970: 140, 189). The government share had increased from 50 to 71 per cent in Venezuela, but to 75 per cent in the Middle East.

The Sovereign Landlords

From this more realistic perspective, the achievement of OPEC in the 1960s was impressive. OPEC succeeded not only in stabilising but also in increasing its ground rent per barrel against falling prices. Though the big international oil companies succeeded at first in dividing OPEC, later the Organisation succeeded in dividing the international oil companies. This was the case, most notably, in Libya, which granted its first concessions in 1955, subject to fifty-fifty profit sharing based on market prices. Independent companies controlled about 50 per cent of production. The Libyan government now imposed those agreements on posted or tax reference prices on the independent companies, though they had not taken part in the negotiations. Finally, Venezuela also adopted the system of tax reference prices. They were enacted in its Income Tax Law in 1966; at the same time the relevant income tax rate was increased to 52 per cent.

Worldwide a new price structure had evolved, with the Persian Gulf as an independent basing point, and with the fiscal take in that region as the principal component of *fob* prices. Everywhere else prices were higher, benefiting from lower transport costs, and everywhere else the fiscal floor to prices had been adjusted accordingly, taking into account, of course, differences in quality and production costs.

5.3   Declaratory Statement of Petroleum Policy

The mere foundation of OPEC entailed a significant shift in the bargaining power of its member countries. The ability of the international companies to play the oil-exporting countries off against one another was reduced. Wherever international tenant companies went to negotiate, whether in experienced

Venezuela or inexperienced Libya, their negotiating teams had to face a team of experts from the landlord states no less qualified and well informed.

In 1968 OPEC finally summed up its practical and theoretical knowledge and experience in a *Declaratory Statement of Petroleum Policy in Member Countries* (Res. XVI.90). Its most important principles referred to relinquishment, tax reference prices, equity participation and, last but not least, sovereignty.

Relinquishment

Neither the original concessions in Iran, Kuwait, Bahrain, Qatar, and Saudi Arabia, nor the revised IPC concession, provided for relinquishment of idle areas. Nor was there economic pressure to relinquish them, as there were no surface rentals. Thus, the international oil companies monopolised huge areas blocking the path for their competitors, at no cost, though they actually exploited only a small percentage. But when Iran renegotiated the D'Arcy concession in 1933, the original area of 500 thousand square miles was reduced to 100 thousand. Similarly in Saudi Arabia, Aramco agreed in 1948 to a schedule according to which it would reduce its concession from 500 thousand square miles to 230 thousand over the next 22 years; in exchange, the company was granted new offshore rights. Yet it was in 1961, in Iraq, where this issue came to a head, and where the original concession contract had considered relinquishment. After protracted but futile negotiations, the government decreed the relinquishment of 99.5 per cent of the concession area, leaving IPC only with those 750 square miles the company was actually working (Stocking 1971: 200ff). The IPC demanded international arbitration, which the government denied on sovereign grounds. Though this conflict was not solved over the next decade, and Iraqi oil production was punished with the lowest growth rate in the region, scarcely six months later the Kuwait Oil Company agreed to the relinquishment of 50 per cent of its area by 1962, and in 1963 Aramco agreed to an immediate reduction of its concession to 125 thousand square miles. Aramco also agreed to a schedule reducing this area further to 20 thousand square miles over the next thirty years (Cattan 1967: 11ff). Similar arrangements followed in all the other major concessions. Moreover, new upstream contracts in the 1950s and 1960s not only granted much smaller areas from the beginning but also stipulated the progressive relinquishment of acreage.

The relinquishment of idle areas, according to the *Policy Declaration*, was to become the general rule, for old and new upstream contracts alike. By the end of the 1960s, the international petroleum cartel had already lost most of its power to block its competitors from gaining access to the oil riches of the Middle East; this power had been recovered by the states.

Tax Reference Prices

Taxes or any other payments to the State would be based on 'posted or tax reference prices'.[6] Without further ado, OPEC claimed that these 'prices' were to be 'determined by the Government'. Still, the government could, 'at its discretion, give a guarantee of fiscal stability to the operators for a reasonable period of time'. Yet 'notwithstanding any guarantee of fiscal stability that may have been granted… the operator shall not have the right to obtain excessively high net earnings after tax. The financial provisions of contracts which actually result in such excessively high net earnings shall be open to renegotiation'. In the case of such renegotiation not being successful 'within a reasonable period of time', 'the Government shall make its own estimate of the amount by which the operator's net earnings after taxes are excessive, and such amount shall then be paid by the operator to the Government'. And the *Policy Declaration* gave a precise definition of 'excessively high net earnings': 'net profits after taxes which are significantly in excess, during any twelve-month period, of the level of net earnings the reasonable expectation of which would have been sufficient to induce the operator to take the entrepreneurial risks necessary'.

Equity Participation

In Middle East oil the presence of governments as shareholders has always been the rule rather than the exception. In the oldest

6.   Only Iran, until 1969, still offered new leases based on market and not posted or tax reference prices. But it did so in exchange for high equity participation as well as for other advantages.

concession in that region, the D'Arcy concession, the Iranian government was awarded shares worth £20,000, and in 1914 the British government became a majority shareholder of APOC. The French government became involved in oil throughout the region in the interwar period, through its national oil company, CFP. According to the original TPC concession contract, the Iraqi government was to be awarded a 20 per cent share in the company, though the international companies managed to make this clause ineffective: it would only apply if the company were to issue shares, which it did not intend. Still, this clause survived in some later concession contracts in the region.

It was only after the Second World War, however, that participation in equity of the concession-granting states became an important feature in new upstream contracts, and this was due to increasing competition amongst the tenant companies. In the Neutral Zone between Saudi Arabia and Kuwait, in 1948–49, the shares were 15 and 25 per cent. In 1957, ENI – the Italian national oil company – offered the Iranian government 50 per cent. Furthermore, although nationalisation had failed in Iran, this country had taken the lead amongst the oil-exporting countries in founding a national oil company. In 1959, creating national oil companies was one of the recommendations included in the Gentlemen's Agreement of Cairo. By the end of the 1960s, new upstream contracts in the Middle East normally included equity participation by the state of 50 per cent, to be managed by these companies (Schurr and Homan 1971: 127ff).

As agents of the landlord states the national oil companies (NOCs) did not share in the exploratory risk. Their share was established as 'carried interest', only to be effectively taken up if exploration was successful. Moreover, the equity participation was on top of a one eighth royalty and a 50 per cent income tax. Apart from a few exceptions, the legal status of these new upstream contracts was still the same as in the old concessions. They were based on international law and arbitration, and taxes were fixed contractually. Still, on the basis of equity participation the landlord states obtained a say in all entrepreneurial decisions of their tenants. Apart from being a rent-collecting device, this was an evolutionary approach to the question of sovereignty, an approach that was to be strengthened according to the *Policy Declaration*, as member governments would endeavour 'to explore and develop their hydrocarbon resources directly', although, if necessary, they would enter into contracts 'subject to the present principles, with outside operators for a reasonable remuneration'. However, 'in any event, the terms and conditions of such contracts shall be open to revision at predetermined intervals, as justified by changing circumstances'. Such revision should also apply to the older concessions. In other words, the standards would be set by the latest, and most advantageous, upstream contracts. Accordingly, regarding the old concessions, 'the Government may acquire a reasonable participation, on the grounds of the principle of changing circumstances'. In practice, 'reasonable' was defined as a participation in equity of 20 per cent – as had been promised by the San Remo Agreement in 1920 – though this was merely the starting point as the Saudi Arabian Oil Minister and principal proponent of this policy, Yamani, made plain (Yamani 1970).

Sovereignty

In 1965, Petromin, the Saudi Arabian national oil company, negotiated a contract with Auxirap, a French company with US participation, in which the 50 per cent income tax rate was not fixed by contract but was subject to Saudi Arabian tax laws. Moreover, the governing law was national law, and disputes had to be settled by national arbitration. In 1967, two similar contracts were signed with AGIP (Italy) and Sinclair–Natomas (US). Outside Venezuela these were the first three upstream contracts to be subject to national legislation and jurisdiction (El-Sayed 1967: 72ff). This should become the norm: 'except as otherwise provided for in the legal system of a Member Country, all disputes arising between the Government and operators shall fall exclusively within the jurisdiction of the competent national courts'. The *Policy Declaration* also considered the option that disputes may be subject to 'specialised regional courts, as and when established'.

Hence, though the *Policy Declaration* recognised, in principle, contractual obligations and rights, at the same time it also asserted the sovereign rights of the State. This stand, inspired by the doctrine of 'permanent sovereignty' – then espoused by the vast majority if not all Third World Countries – was restated in its Preamble, where the 'right of all countries to exercise permanent sovereignty over their natural resources, in the interest of national development' was considered 'inalienable', being 'a universally recognised principle of public law ... repeatedly reaffirmed by the General Assembly of the United Nations'.

Shifting Bargaining Power

There was no doubt that action would follow this Policy Declaration. On the one hand, worldwide exploration in the 1960s confirmed the virtual monopoly of the oil-exporting countries over the natural resource. In 1970, OPEC accounted for 73 per cent of proven world oil reserves, then 546.3 billion barrels. During that decade world production had increased very significantly – low prices had stimulated demand – from 20.9 million b/d to 45.7 million b/d, with OPEC increasing its share from 41.5 per cent in 1960 to 51 per cent in 1970. The USSR and the 'rest of the world' also slightly increased their share, the former from 14.1 to 15.4 per cent, and the latter from 10.8 to 12.5 per cent. But the United States had its share further reduced, from 33.6 to 21.1 per cent.

International political developments were also highly favourable to OPEC, as the struggle of the Third World countries for national independence and sovereignty experienced an extraordinary upswing. In addition, the Arab–Israeli conflict was of special importance to that organisation, with its majority of Arab member countries, given the fact that the parent countries of the most important international tenant companies – the United States, Great Britain, the Netherlands and, to a lesser degree, France – were strongly supportive of Israel. Nor was the outlook by the end of the decade peaceful, since the third Arab–Israeli war had ended with the occupation of more Arab territories.

5.4 The OPEC Revolution

By the end of the 1960s, Venezuela was still a lonely and somewhat distant example of a sovereign oil-exporting country (Cf. Lutfi 1968: 72). Yet a unique and surprising combination of geological facts, the level of economic activity and political events was about to trigger a rush of events, which would allow the other member countries to catch up within a few years.

There was, firstly, the fact that US crude oil production finally peaked in 1970 at 9.6 million b/d. (Despite huge price increases in the following years production has declined ever since.) Excess capacities in the United States disappeared, and net oil imports, which had increased from zero in 1947 to 2.8 million b/d in 1970, shot up to 5.7 million b/d in 1973. Concurrently, after a decade of falling prices and restrictive policies, excess capacities were also disappearing fast within OPEC. Finally, a booming world economy caused an extraordinary surge in demand. In 1973, OPEC production increased by a stunning 14.4 per cent.

In previous booms – during the years of the Second World War and the Korean War – the US government had frozen domestic prices and, with the support of the international companies, the price freeze actually extended to world markets. In 1973, the US government resorted again to freezing domestic prices but this time to no avail; in the end the United States was forced to adjust domestic oil prices to match world market prices.

Politically, the third Arab–Israeli war in 1967 led to a strengthening of nationalism in the Arab world. During that war there was a first attempt at a selective oil embargo against the United States, Great Britain, and Western Germany (Mikdashi 1972: 84ff). It failed, partially because there were still significant excess capacities outside the Arab oil-exporting countries, and even within the United States. It also failed because there were sufficient excess capacities in maritime transportation to prevent the closure of the Suez Canal – a consequence of the military conflict – from having an immediate dramatic effect. Oil exports from the Persian Gulf to Europe and to the US East Coast were simply re-directed *via* the much longer route around Africa. But, most importantly, it failed for political reasons. The Republics within the Arab League had promoted the embargo, whereas the monarchies – Saudi Arabia, Kuwait, and Libya – agreed to it reluctantly. Having faced the possibility of losing control over their oil policy because of a war in which they had no direct part, the latter founded the Organisation of Arab Oil Exporting Countries (OAPEC) in

1968. This organisation was supposed to keep in check the influence of republican forces by means of restricted membership. Algeria and Iraq attempted, unsuccessfully, to set up a parallel organisation. But in the following years both sides came closer, partly because of the coup d'état in Libya, which weakened the monarchist front, and partly because of political developments in republican Egypt, which led to a rapprochement with Saudi Arabia. As a result, in 1970 OAPEC relaxed its conditions of membership. Eight new members joined the Organisation during the next two years: Abu Dhabi, Algeria, Bahrain, Dubai, Qatar, Egypt, Iraq, and Syria. Thus the Arab countries created an institutional platform designed to use oil for economic development, but which was also to play an important role in a foreseeable fourth Arab–Israeli war.

Finally, the climax of this boom in autumn 1973 coincided – not accidentally – with that war. The outcome was the OPEC revolution. Against the background of an embargo of Arab oil-exporting countries and soaring prices, OPEC Member Countries switched from negotiations to sovereign decisions. There followed an explosive increase in tax reference prices and the nationalisation of the international tenant companies.

First Round (1970–71)

The geographical advantage of Mediterranean oil was enhanced by the closure of the Suez Canal. Accordingly, the oil companies agreed to abolish in the Mediterranean the discounts on posted prices, which had been negotiated with OPEC, with immediate effect and for as long as the Canal remained closed. In Libya, for example, this meant an additional ground rent per barrel of US¢ 8.5. The same benefits accrued to Saudi Arabian and Iraqi oil delivered through pipelines into the Mediterranean. But as the Suez Canal remained closed and OPEC had already managed to negotiate a general reduction of these discounts in 1968, the issue was bound to arise again soon. Moreover, the French refused any benefit to Algeria from the closure of the Canal, because they still considered the country their *chasse gardée* (Grimaud 1972). Before joining OPEC in 1969, Algeria had reacted in its own way to the 1967 Arab–Israeli war by taking an equity participation of 51 per cent in the US, British, and

Dutch companies, which were of lesser importance in this French-dominated country. By 1970, some of them had already been nationalised.

In 1969, Algeria (now an OPEC member), Iraq and Libya, agreed to renegotiate together tax reference or posted prices in the Mediterranean (Breton 1972), with the explicit support of OPEC (Res. XIII.80, XIII.81, XIX.105). The negotiations were led by Libya. The timing could not have been better. The bargaining power of these countries improved daily as a shortage of maritime transportation developed. By 1970, Mediterranean oil was already irreplaceable. Freight rates soared. With a closed Suez Canal but with freight rates at normal levels, the freight advantage of Libyan crude, compared with crude from the Persian Gulf, *cif* Rotterdam, amounted to US$ 0.83 per barrel. In September 1970, this had increased to US$ 2.09. This was not entirely due to the shipping market because in May an accident closed down the Trans-Arabian pipeline, withdrawing 500 thousand b/d of Saudi Arabian oil from the eastern Mediterranean. Syria denied Aramco authorisation to repair the pipeline. A transit country, it demanded higher wayleaves, the Suez Canal being closed. A few days later the Libyan government ordered a cut in production, on the basis of conservation legislation drawn up by OPEC experts. By September 1970, Libya reduced output by 800 thousand b/d. Thus about 1.3 million b/d had been withdrawn from the Mediterranean, and it could only be replaced from distant sources in the Persian Gulf, since elsewhere there was no spare capacity. Even so French companies in Algeria believed they could hold on to their colonial privileges.[7] In July, however, Algeria resorted to its sovereign rights to impose its claims. The French insisted on arbitration.

The Libyan government took advantage of divisions between the oil companies. An independent American company, Occidental, was the first to give in, at the beginning of September

---

7.   Algeria provides a late example of colonial governance. Constitutionally, in the IV. Republic, it was part of France. Hence, the country had a modern French concession system subject, of course, to a sovereign government – in Paris. But France, on the retreat, converted the existing concession contracts into colonial-type ones, stripping the government in Algiers of its sovereign rights.

1970. The others soon followed. The new agreement, following the pattern established by Algeria, stipulated an immediate increase in tax reference prices from US\$ 2.23 to US\$ 2.53, an additional two cents per year until 1975, and an increase of the income tax rate to 55 per cent. (A similar agreement was signed in Lagos, with Nigeria, not yet an OPEC member). The big international oil companies now announced an increase in posted prices in all oil-exporting ports east of Suez, from the Eastern Mediterranean to Nigeria. In November 1970, posted prices in the United States were also increasing by some US¢ 25 per barrel. The time had come for a general price increase. A few days later, under pressure of the Iranian government, the International Consortium increased the 'posted price' of Iranian Heavy, 31° API, by US¢ 9. It also accepted an increase in the income tax rate to 55 per cent. These benefits were passed on immediately to Kuwait and Saudi Arabia (Rouhani 1971: 3ff). OPEC, though completely surprised by these events, was well prepared. In its December 1970 Conference in Caracas, it agreed that (1) starting in January 1971, all discounts on tax reference prices would be scrapped; (2) income tax rates would be increased to 55 per cent as a minimum; and (3) tax reference prices would be raised uniformly in all member countries. The Gulf countries would take the lead in the negotiations, to be held in Tehran and to last no longer than one month. Within another two weeks, an Extraordinary Conference would be held to evaluate the results. Moreover, in case such negotiations were to fail to achieve their purpose, 'the Conference shall determine and set forth a procedure with a view to enforcing and achieving the objectives as outlined in this Resolution through a concerted and simultaneous action by all Member Countries' (Res. XX.120). The Conference in Caracas had not finished when the Venezuelan Congress reformed its Income Tax Law, raising the relevant rate from 52 to 60 per cent. At the same time the Executive was authorised to fix tax reference prices by decree.

Taken by surprise like everybody else, the international companies quickly joined forces, with the consent of the US government – necessary because of US anti-trust laws – and with diplomatic support from all OECD member countries (Duclos 1972). Finally, twenty-two oil companies faced OPEC's negotiating committee. This was the first time that the international companies had actually recognised OPEC. At the beginning of February 1971, in its Extraordinary Conference in Tehran, OPEC's threats became even more explicit. If necessary, the Gulf countries would implement the objectives agreed in Caracas through 'legal and/or legislative measures'. Moreover, 'in the event that any oil company concerned fails to comply with these legal and/or legislative measures within seven days from the date of their adoption in all the countries concerned', all Member Countries – with the exception of Indonesia – agreed to 'take appropriate measures including total embargo on the shipments of crude oil and petroleum products by such company' (Res. XX.131). The oil companies capitulated on 14 February. According to the new agreement, once again supposed to last five years, the tax reference price of a barrel of Arabian Light, *fob* Ras Tanura, was to increase within five years from US\$ 1.80 to US\$ 2.62. Ground rent would thus increase from US\$ 0.91 to US\$ 1.53. A new round of negotiations in Tripoli followed in March 1971, bringing the Mediterranean producers in line again, which included a formula to adjust posted prices every three months according to changing freight rates.

Equity Participation in the Old Concessions (1972–73)

In February 1971 the Algerian government announced that it was taking over a 51 per cent equity share in the French companies. At that time the 1970 boom was receding and France attempted an international boycott of Algerian oil, but the necessary international support was, at best, lukewarm. Six months later, the French agreed to the 51 per cent equity share, and also to an adjustment in prices and taxation in line with the Tehran and Tripoli agreements. Algeria now controlled 75 per cent of its production of one million b/d.

At the Caracas Conference, OPEC had also set up a Ministerial Committee to study the implementation of its policy of equity participation. At its Conference in July 1971, OPEC resorted again to threats of 'concerted action' (Res. XXV.139), if negotiations were to fail. The Arab Gulf countries – Abu Dhabi, Iraq, Kuwait, Qatar, and Saudi Arabia – appointed Yamani, Petroleum Minister of Saudi Arabia, as their representative. The companies, reluctantly, appointed a negotiating committee consisting of one representative each from Exxon (formerly Esso, SONJ), Texaco, and Shell. Meanwhile in December 1971 Libya nationalised the BP subsidiary in Libya (controlling 7 per cent of national production, then about 3.3 million b/d) in reprisal for British failure to support the United Arab Emirates (UAE) claim to the Tumb Islands against Iran.[8] In March 1972, Yamani announced that Aramco had accepted, in principle, 20 per cent equity participation. But Nigeria and Libya for their part were already demanding an immediate 51 per cent share. In June 1971, Iraq – after eleven years of continued conflicts – nationalised IPC, which then controlled two thirds of national production of about 1.5 million b/d. The international tenant companies, for the last time, tried to implement an international boycott, but now it was France which failed to agree. Iraq also enjoyed the backing of OPEC, which even set up a committee to prevent boycotted Iraqi oil from being replaced by other OPEC oil (Res. XXVIII.146). The boom in the world oil market, which resumed at the end of 1972, did the rest: the companies accepted the nationalisation of IPC in February 1973.

In December 1972, the negotiations led by Yamani ended successfully in New York. The Arab Gulf countries would acquire, from 1 January 1973, a 25 per cent equity participation in all concessions. This share would increase gradually to 51 per cent by 1 January 1983 (Al-Otaiba 1975: 169ff). With this agreement these countries would have a powerful voice on investment, volume of exports and their destination. 'As a corporate partner representing at the same time the sovereign, they possess all the power they need to control and direct the companies on all phases of the operations in the producing country and probably even on many phases of their operations abroad, holding their local interest in oil production as hostage' (Levy 1973: 169). Nevertheless the Kuwaiti Parliament rejected the deal and insisted on an immediate 60 per cent. The Shah of Iran announced in March 1973 the dissolution of the

---

8. In 1971, while negotiations for the creation of UAE were being completed, the claim by Iran for sovereignty over the Tumb Islands remained in dispute. Iran occupied the islands the day before the UAE came into existence, when technically Britain was still responsible.

International Consortium. The National Iranian Oil Company (NIOC) would take over its operation, and the associates of the Consortium would be demoted to service companies, with purchase contracts to last twenty years (Stobaugh 1978: 221). At the beginning of 1973 Libya, supported by OPEC (Res. XXXV.159), again started to single out the companies one by one, imposing on each of them 51 per cent equity participation. Meanwhile, in June 1973, Nigeria had taken an initial 35 per cent equity participation in all its concessions. And then, in October 1973, the fourth Arab–Israeli war broke out.

Second Round (1973)

After the Tehran, Tripoli and Lagos agreements, the international tenant companies were given no respite. Not only was equity participation progressing rapidly, but OPEC also responded with new demands after the devaluations of the US currency in December 1971 and February 1973. In both cases the oil-exporting countries negotiated an increase in tax reference prices, established in US dollars (Res. XXXI.122). Then, in 1973, a booming market went far beyond the expectations that supported the agreements on tax reference or posted prices. In September, OPEC demanded their revision (Res. XXXVI.160). Negotiations were scheduled for 8 October, but the fourth Arab–Israeli war began on 6 October. Nevertheless, negotiations began as scheduled. However, on 15 October, a number of Arab states decided upon a selective embargo against the United States and some other countries, together with a progressive reduction in oil production. On 16 October, OPEC's negotiating Committee announced the end of negotiations, and sovereignly increased the tax reference price of Arabian Light from $3.011 to $5.119. Ground rent per barrel increased, approximately, from $1.74 to $3.01. The international companies protested in vain. Consumers panicked, as cuts in Arab oil production over the following months amounted to 20 per cent.[9] In December, some cargoes of Iranian oil put up for auction by the government fetched a price as high as US$ 17.43.

---

9.   Iraq did not take part in these cuts. This country preferred, instead, to nationalise the rest of its oil industry. The selective embargo was eased after six months and ended completely in August 1974.

Following the Iranian auction, OPEC raised the tax reference price again, from \$5.119 to \$11.651; ground rent per barrel rose to \$7.00 (Rifaï 1974: 372ff).

Fiscal Revenues and Nationalisation

Though in 1974 tax reference prices basically remained stable, the time had come to fundamentally restructure the sector. Regarding the fiscal regime, Saudi Arabia increased its royalty rate from 12.5 to 20 per cent – in accordance with Res. IV.33 – and its income tax rate from 55 to 85 per cent. Thus fiscal revenues increased to US\$ 9.80 by the end of 1974, to be compared with production costs of only US\$ 0.12. Production costs compared with fiscal revenues fell from an already modest 25 per cent in 1960 to an insignificant 1.2 per cent by 1974.

Moreover, the landlord states had now also acquired a participation in equity. In Saudi Arabia, in 1973, this share was 25 per cent. In 1974 it was adjusted to 60 per cent. This arrangement went hand in hand with agreed 'buyback prices', i.e. prices the private partners would pay for equity oil they would market. By the end of the 1960s market prices had fallen to about 71 per cent, while buyback prices were set at 93 per cent, of tax reference prices. If we assume that the private companies sold their oil at that price, in 1973/4 they still enjoyed a handsome profit, though this was not to last. Increased royalty and income tax rates brought profits down to what they had been by the end of the 1960s, about US\$ 0.22 per lifted barrel. Back in 1960, it had been US\$ 0.80. Hence, whereas in 1960 net profits were equal to fiscal revenues, in 1974 they were equivalent to no more than 2.2 per cent of these revenues (see Table 5.1). Even in high-cost exporting countries such as Venezuela, fiscal revenues represented about 85 per cent of gross revenues. The business of oil in the exporting countries had without question become the business of landlords. Ground rents were far too high to allow tenants to set volumes and prices, which were now to be set by the exporting countries, with the tenants demoted to production service providers. Thus, Saudi Arabia, for example, increased its participation in equity to 100 per cent in 1980, and at the same time the former concession-holding companies set up a production services

Table 5.1   Fiscal Revenues, Costs, and Profits for a Barrel of Arabian
Light 1960–1974, US$

	1960 10/08	1970 01/09	1971 01/06	1973 01/10	1973 16/10	1974 01/01	1974 01/11
Tax Reference Price	1.80	1.80	2.29	3.01	5.12	11.65	11.25
Royalty Rate	*12.5%*	*12.5%*	*12.5%*	*12.5%*	*12.5%*	*12.5%*	*20.0%*
Royalty	0.23	0.23	0.29	0.38	0.64	1.46	2.25
Costs	0.20	0.12	0.12	0.12	0.12	0.12	0.12
Gross Profit	1.38	1.46	1.88	2.51	4.36	10.07	8.88
Income Tax Rate	*50:50*	*50%*	*55%*	*55%*	*55%*	*55%*	*85%*
Income Tax	0.58	0.73	1.03	1.38	2.40	5.54	7.55
Fiscal Revenues	0.80	0.95	1.32	1.76	3.04	7.00	9.80
Costs/Fisc. Revenues	25.0%	12.6%	9.1%	6.8%	4.0%	1.7%	1.2%
Participation in Equity	0%	0%	0%	25%	25%	60%	60%
Buyback Price	1.80	1.29	1.63	2.80	4.76	10.84	10.46
Net Profit	0.00	0.00	0.00	0.92	1.60	3.72	0.54
Gov. Take/Lifted Bl.	0.80	0.95	1.32	1.99	3.44	9.23	10.13
Priv. Profit/Lifted Bl.	0.80	0.21	0.19	0.69	1.20	1.49	0.22
Priv. Profit/Gov. Take	*100%*	*22.4%*	*14.6%*	*34.7%*	*35.0%*	*16.1%*	*2.2%*

Sources: See text.

company. That company continued to explore and produce,
but at a service fee of, roughly, US$ 0.21 per lifted barrel –
which was the same amount they obtained as concessionaires
at the end of the 1960s. The former concessionaires were also
entitled to buy a certain amount of the oil lifted at the official
price, thus removing any difference between reference, posted
and market prices.

De facto the international companies had been nationalised,
qua tenants, by the end of 1973, though the legal arrangements
would take time and differ from one country to the other. The
fiscal regime was tightened everywhere, but did not necessarily
follow the same patterns. Libya and Venezuela, for example,
maintained fiscal regimes based on tax reference prices. Libya
stuck to an equity participation of 51 per cent; Nigeria to 60
per cent. But everywhere, the formal differences notwithstanding, it was exclusively up to the sovereign governments to
set prices and volumes.

5.5 Conclusions

The control of access to the oil provinces of the world had been in the mind of international oil companies since the very beginning. On the eve of the First World War the participants in TPC pledged not to compete within the confines of the Turkish Empire but to apply together for concessions in order effectively to monopolise the whole area. A similar scheme was discussed at that time in Mexico where its effectiveness depended on overcoming the fragmentation of private mineral ownership. The Mexican Foreign Minister, in 1913, proposed to vest all existing interests into one state agency. Respecting acquired rights, Mexico's oil riches would thus be exploited under the control of this agency in co-operation with private investors (Knight 1986: 96–97). Similar propositions were discussed again after the First World War and the Revolution, though they never prospered. Later, the associates of IPC renewed the TPC agreement in 1928, which became known as the 'Red Line Agreement'. This agreement was the corner-stone of the international petroleum cartel. Its membership eventually extended to the seven biggest international oil companies. The 'Seven Sisters', as they were nicknamed, effectively extended their control to neighbouring Kuwait and Iran, as well as to distant Venezuela and Indonesia, through joint ownership of some major concessions, reinforced by joint ventures downstream. This set-up provided the links enabling them effectively to agree on, and to control, production worldwide. Concurrently, the obstruction of private mineral ownership in the United States was overcome through prorationing.

The international companies finally succeeded in controlling access, though in varying degrees, to all important oil provinces of the world outside the United States (and, of course, the Soviet Union). However, this was only possible because these oil provinces were subject to colonial governance or because they were located in weak, backward and dependent countries. No modern sovereign country would ever hand over to a few private companies the control of its natural resources. The cartel was weakest where the affected countries were strongest, and it would weaken continuously after the Second World War as the age of colonialism drew to an end. An early example of relative

independence was Venezuela, where the international companies did not get huge concessions nor were they able to prevent
the government from organising bidding rounds favouring their
competitors. A late example is Libya, already an independent
country when it granted its first concessions. But in all oil-
exporting countries, even where nation-wide concessions were
granted, some pieces of territory – and, most notably, waters –
were left out, for whatever reason, and were ultimately opened
up to competitors.

The development of the world economy and the growing
independence of Third World countries would inevitably entail
the development of a competitive world petroleum market.
Peculiar to oil, however, was the fact that this development also
entailed growing competition to gain access to the reservoirs,
which increased the cost of access. Oil riches – a whim of nature
– were largely concentrated in a few Third World oil-exporting
countries where OPEC replaced the companies' decaying cartel.
The latter concerned itself with profit, to be maximised within
a governance structure where the interests of consumers were
systematically represented – by maximising profits the companies
did their best to keep ground rent down – although consumers
complained frequently, and legitimately, about monopoly prices.
However, the international companies also kept the landlords
in check, while OPEC concerned itself with ground rent, to be
maximised by sovereign landlords. In the shadow of the later
prices, those earlier monopoly prices soon looked rather modest.

OPEC, on top of the long-term structural changes in its
favour, also enjoyed the advantage of having taken by surprise
both the international oil companies and the governments of the
consuming countries (and even itself). Although the international
companies, in the 1960s, responded to the growing pressure from
OPEC by exploring new and more expensive areas, most notably
in Alaska and the North Sea, they were also busy playing down
the importance of OPEC. Bluff, after all, was part of the business.
But the bluff also backfired, because politicians, the leadership
of the international companies, lawyers, and economists deceived
themselves. Thus, for example, politicians and the leadership of
the international companies had colluded to root fifty-fifty profit
sharing in the remote past, allegedly representing nothing but
an adjustment in line with the original contracts – a nodding in

the direction of sacrosanctity of contracts. Similarly, OPEC in the 1960s presented the end of fifty-fifty profit sharing and posted prices as nothing but a problem of good accountancy. Both parties and their lawyers presented the new agreements as simple interpretations of the previously existing one. Hence, everybody was always reassuring everybody that nothing had changed or was ever to change.

Energy economists, however, unanimously proclaimed that OPEC could never be a relevant actor. Ricardo *dixit*. As late as 1969, Edith Penrose's[10] assessment was that 'OPEC has never been as powerful in the international industry generally as were the major companies in their heyday'. Moreover, 'the companies failed effectively to contain the rate of supply in line with the rate of demand at existing prices for very long; OPEC has so far failed even more obviously in that task. But since it has at the same time succeeded brilliantly in its other task', i.e. increasing fiscal revenues, 'the contradiction likely before very long to bring an even more far reaching change in the structure of the industry is evident: increasing monopoly revenues are not consistent with decreasing monopoly power' (Penrose 1970: 235). According to her model, the increase of fiscal revenues from fifty to about seventy per cent of profits over the 1960s was an irrelevant fact. Market prices were falling, and that was her only criterion. In her one-dimensional conception of oil prices, it was not possible to think of them as the result of two different and independent forces. The same goes for Adelman,[11] already quoted in the first part of this book. In his major study he concluded that for 'at least 15 years we can count on, and must learn to live with, an abundance of oil that can be brought forth from fields now operated in the Persian Gulf at something between 10 and 20 cents per barrel' (Adelman 1972: 77). Competition would guarantee lower prices. Sticking dogmatically to his Ricardian rent model, he was quick to resort to conspiracy theories once things turned out differently (Adelman 1972: chap. VII). He was, of course, not alone. Baffled consumers everywhere in the world, inside and outside the United States, readily and as a matter of

---

10. Edith Penrose was arguably the most outstanding economist on our subject matter at that time in the United Kingdom.
11. Morris Adelman was arguably the most outstanding economist on our subject matter at that time in the United States.

routine, blamed the usual culprits of the past: the US government and the late international petroleum cartel.

Last but not least, OPEC member countries were also surprised. They had not the slightest idea that their penny-pinching tactics might culminate in a 'revolution'. In Venezuela, when President Rafael Caldera was told, on 27 December 1973, that nationalisation was on the agenda, he was completely surprised. Until that moment, as far as he knew, nobody in Venezuela had made such a suggestion. 'I have to admit, it never came to my mind that it could be possible or convenient to nationalise Creole, affiliate of Standard Oil, or Shell de Venezuela, affiliate of Shell Petroleum' (*El Nacional* 28-12-1973). The next day both the presidents of Creole (Exxon) and Shell de Venezuela, after an end-of-year courtesy visit to President Caldera, confirmed to the awaiting press that nationalisation was, indeed, imminent. Alluding to the international situation – the Arab oil embargo and the doubling of prices – they confirmed that radical changes were unavoidable. They also expressed their conviction that they would still play 'a very important role' in the future (*El Nacional*, 29-12-1973).

OPEC was confronted, unexpectedly, with the challenge to consolidate and to institutionalise its 'revolutionary' achievements. In its advance, it had crossed the old clear-cut front line between the member countries and the foreign oil companies. It had now to confront, or to deal with, the consuming countries. The issues at stake were prices and volumes. OPEC, after its 'revolution', would never agree, or disagree, on anything else. Member countries were no longer united in wresting their sovereign rights from the hands of a common opponent (a handful of international oil companies subjecting them to one and the same governance structure). From now on they were only united by the natural accident of oil, struggling with an opponent, which had invisible hands (the market), and subject to their own very different structures. Nor would their national companies provide any link between them. OPEC member countries would continue to agree or disagree on volumes and prices, but ultimately stick together against the consumers, even though over the next twenty years three of its member countries – Iraq, Iran, and Kuwait – were actually at war with each other.

Of course, the effect of surprise would soon fade away. Yet

many an energy economist now predicted steadily increasing prices. Ricardo had given way to Hotelling. Scarcity was supposed to be the driving principle behind oil prices in the long run. In the market place, however, the consequence of the 'OPEC revolution' – or the first 'oil shock' as the consuming countries named it – was an immediate sudden fall in the growth rate of demand for crude oil, and the call on OPEC oil actually stagnated. Libya after 1970, and Kuwait after 1973, cut their production on conservation grounds and in support of higher prices. In Venezuela, production from its ageing fields peaked in 1970, and production would have fallen anyway. Others increased their production, most notably Iraq, Iran, and Saudi Arabia. And then came the 'second oil shock', associated with the Iranian revolution and the subsequent war between Iraq and Iran. Consumers panicked, and some OPEC member countries decided again to take advantage of the situation; others followed their lead only reluctantly. The radical price increase generated, again and in the short run, large additional fiscal revenues. But now the demand for crude oil fell. OPEC, in order to maintain prices, cut production while the consuming countries were increasing their production by squeezing out of their reservoirs every possible barrel. In 1982, twenty-two years after its foundation, OPEC finally set up a quota system. Within the Organisation, Saudi Arabia assumed the role of a swing producer. But three years later, in 1985, OPEC production had fallen to 15.4 million b/d, i.e. half the level of 1974; its share in the world's total was down from 56 to 29 per cent. Fiscal revenues were falling. Adjusting for inflation, their revenue in 1985 was less than in 1974. Saudi Arabia, meanwhile, after cutting its production from 9.9 million b/d in 1980 to 3.2 million b/d in 1985, was no longer able or willing to maintain its role as swing producer. Then followed the price crisis of 1986, which brought prices down by some 50 per cent. OPEC abandoned its policy of official posted prices, and turned to production quotas that would be imposed on all member countries and imply much lower price levels (Skeet 1988: *passim)*. Demand for OPEC oil took off again. Though in recent years production levels have come close to those of 1979, they have not yet reached the 1979 level again. (Figs. 5.1, 5.2 and Table 5.2)

Energy economists switched back from Hotelling to Ricardo.

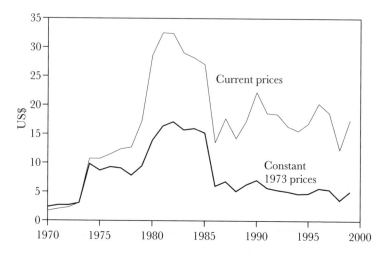

From 1970 to 1981, the Arab Light official price; as of 1982, the OPEC spot
Reference Basket price.

Source: OPEC, *Annual Statistical Bulletin.*

Figure 5.1: OPEC Oil Prices 1970–1999

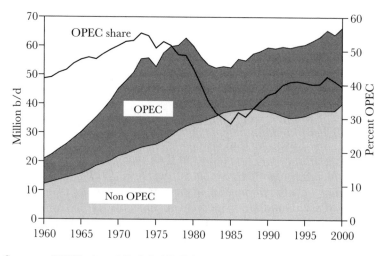

Source: OPEC, *Annual Statistical Bulletin.*

Figure 5.2: OPEC and Non-OPEC Crude Oil Production 1960–2000

Table 5.2: OPEC Fiscal Revenues, Selected Years, Billion of US$

	1970	*1974*	*1980*	*1985*	*1986*
Exports	14.4	110.3	282.6	128.9	76.6
Fiscal Revenues					
Current Dollars	7.6	91.8	274.9	121.2	68.9
1973 Dollars	10.7	84.0	133.6	68.1	30.7

Source: OPEC, *Annual Statistical Bulletin.*

Yet again, 'economics has nothing to say about the oil price other than pointing to a … low cost floor and a … high price-of-substitute ceiling. Price fluctuations are of the market, price *altitudes* are political variables' (Mabro 1991, italics in the original). Or, alternatively, thanks to quotas, OPEC could finally be thought of as a producers' cartel. As such it has not worked as well as the Texas Railroad Commission, or the international petroleum cartel in its heyday. Quotas had now to be agreed between, and implemented by, sovereign countries, but without any supra-national authority. However, these sovereign countries not only control production but also access to the natural resource, something that was beyond the reach of the Texas Railroad Commission, and something the international petroleum cartel had never wholly achieved. OPEC is thus able to restrict the flow of investment, which determines the long-term level of production. The power of OPEC is deeply rooted in its 'underground'. Quotas are only a kind of 'fine tuning'.

Although OPEC in the aftermath of its 'revolution' promoted the idea of a so-called consumer-producer dialogue, and some high-profile international meetings actually took place, nothing came of it. It was never more than a sideshow. OPEC was as unable as it was unwilling to compromise. All it could do was to cling to its natural monopoly. OPEC continues to be in control of three quarters of the world's oil reserves, but this is the only account with a favourable balance to OPEC. On any other account the balance is in favour of the consuming countries. Though technology may be the first thing that comes to mind, political and economic power, when it is a question of governance, is even more important. It was the turn of the governments of the big consuming countries to go on the offensive.

6. THE NEW ROLE OF
THE CONSUMING COUNTRIES

6.1 The International Energy Agency

The OPEC revolution was an event significant enough not only to cause a radical slow-down in the growth of demand for oil but also to dampen the growth of the world economy. The price increases from 1973 to 1974 cost OECD member countries the equivalent of 2.6 per cent of their GDP; the increases from 1978 to 1980 amounted to as much as 3.7 per cent (IMF 2000: 41), and these amounts had to be transferred through a costly structural adjustment. Moreover, to keep OPEC in check huge amounts of money were invested in expensive domestic oil and gas or alternative energy sources. There is no doubt that the two oil shocks played an important role in the sudden slow-down of the world economy in 1974–75 and 1980–83. And last but not least, there was the issue of security of supply.

The international tenant companies were no longer able to guarantee either security of supply or prevailing price levels. The governments of the consuming countries had to take these issues into their own hands. Yet in the short term there was very little they could effectively do. The defeat of the international tenant companies was also theirs, as demonstrated by the last act of the OPEC revolution, which took place in the midst of an Arab oil embargo. The developed consuming countries – the OECD countries – took the lead in confronting OPEC. In response to an initiative of the US government, in 1974 they founded the International Energy Agency (IEA).[1] Not surprisingly, it first adopted an International Energy Programme, with the status of an international treaty, to deal with emergencies. Member countries had to hold stocks for sixty – later ninety – days of consumption and prepare programmes of contingent demand restraint measures. An Emergency Sharing System was put in place, and the whole arrangement was supposed to operate in close liaison with the international oil companies.

---

1. However, the membership of OECD and IEA is not identical. France joined the IEA as late as 1992. Norway is only a conditional member. Mexico joined OECD in 1994, but not the IEA.

A Long-Term Programme followed in 1976. The objective
was to minimise dependency on imported oil. This was to be
achieved, on the one hand, by reducing demand – or, at least,
the growth of demand – through improved efficiency in
consumption, conservation, new technologies and, last but not
least, higher taxes on petroleum products. On the other hand,
the use of alternative sources of energy (domestic oil, coal,
natural gas, nuclear, etc.) was to be encouraged, and the
consumption of petroleum products restricted to those uses
where it was irreplaceable, i.e. basically to transportation. In
power generation coal was regarded as the most obvious
alternative to fuel oil when, after the second oil shock in 1979,
the IEA agreed to minimise the use of fuel oil for electricity
generation. National energy policy planning was to preclude
'new or replacement base load oil-fired capacity', and progressively confine oil 'to middle and peak loads', making
'maximum use of fuels other than oil in dual-fired capacity'
(Scott 1995: V.3, 224). By the 1990s, somewhat unexpectedly,
natural gas had largely taken over.

Towards the end of the decade the emphasis shifted towards
the increase of domestic supply. Member countries were
encouraged to exploit all economically appropriate opportunities
'to minimise declines in their own indigenous oil production'.
Accordingly, licensing and fiscal regimes should be revised 'so
as to encourage timely development' of the reservoirs (Scott
1995: V.2, 169). The same principle applied, of course, to
alternative sources of energy such as coal, relatively abundant
within OECD countries. Member countries should ensure 'that
fiscal regimes, e.g., government royalties and severance taxes,
... do not adversely affect the viability of coal mining
developments' (Scott 1995: V.3, 227).

It was now the turn of the consuming countries to question
the legacy of the American reference, albeit from a different
angle than the exporting countries. OPEC had done this by
transforming the US conciliatory fiscal regime into a radical
proprietorial one. The consuming countries went in the opposite
direction, developing a radical non-proprietorial fiscal regime
in order to maximise output. Until then, royalty had been
omnipresent and unquestioned, be it in private or public
governance of oil. On the rare occasions when American energy

economists addressed the issue of royalties, they maintained, against all the evidence, that this was actually a Ricardian rent-collecting device. But in Europe there were no vested interests regarding royalties. Hence energy economists were politically free to target royalties as non-Ricardian ground rent-collecting devices, and to condemn them as an obstruction to the free flow of investment. Most importantly, this happened in the United Kingdom where royalties, the emblematic ground rent, were scrapped in the early 1980s giving way to a more 'flexible' device, i.e. an excess profit-collecting device, in accordance with non-proprietorial governance.

Member countries were also urged, 'to promote diversified investments in world-wide production' (Scott 1995: V.2, 169). Indeed, by the end of the century non-OECD countries were already consuming more than half of world energy. Of special interest were, of course, the 'developing countries with significant potential for future hydrocarbon supply', where the IEA would 'support activities of international organisations to help improve investment regimes' (Scott 1995: V.2, 347).

National Oil Companies in the Consuming Countries

The governments of the European countries were the first to get involved as shareholders in the business of oil early in the twentieth century, and this reflected the concession system in the Middle East.[2] Most of the NOCs in the Latin American consuming countries were founded between the two World Wars. They were supposed to explore, to produce, and to refine domestically, within a general policy framework of import substitution and national economic development. The exporting countries began to set up their NOCs only in the 1950s. Conceived as agencies of the landlord state, they became active after the nationalisations of the 1970s. The last wave of NOCs in relatively resource-rich consuming countries was triggered by the OPEC revolution. Concerned about security of supply

---

2.   The British government became a majority shareholder of Anglo-Persian Oil Company (i.e. British Petroleum) in 1914. The French government promoted, and then became a shareholder of, the Compagnie Française des Pétroles in the 1920s to participate in Middle East oil according to the San Remo Agreement.

and the economic threat of high prices, Canada and the United Kingdom, for example, set up PetroCanada and the British National Oil Company (BNOC). By the end of the 1970s, amongst the consuming countries the United States was the only significant oil producer without a NOC.

This last wave of NOCs was short-lived. The issue of security of supply at reasonable prices was taken up collectively by IEA/ OECD within the context of a strong liberal environment. The new NOCs represented a limited national answer to the OPEC revolution. The liberal agenda was essentially a global one. Hence, these NOCs were dismantled and privatised during the late 1980s and early 1990s. At the same time the older European NOCs had also lost their *raison d'être* and they too were privatised. The UK took the lead in both cases. The Latin American NOCs suffered a similar fate. The old idea that the international oil companies were not interested in the development of national reservoirs but rather in importing from highly profitable concessions elsewhere, was now obsolete. Moreover, the model of protectionist, import-substituting economic development in Latin American countries was in deep crisis, and under increasing external pressure they too turned, in the 1990s, to privatisation and liberalisation. The Argentine Yacimientos Petrolíferos Fiscales (YPF), the oldest Latin American NOC, has already been privatised completely. However in Brazil, Petrobras, the youngest one in this group, has so far only been partially privatised. This leaves us with only one important set of NOCs: the NOCs of the exporting countries, the agencies of the landlord states.

A Global Agenda

Whatever could be done within the consuming countries was never going to be enough, since their natural resource base is insufficient: 76 per cent of the world's crude oil reserves are located within OPEC, with another 6 per cent in the former Soviet Union (a net oil-exporting area); and in the case of natural gas – an energy source of similar importance to crude oil with world-wide reserves equivalent to about one trillion barrels – OPEC holds 42 per cent of world reserves, and the former Soviet Union 39 per cent. Within the OECD, coal is the only abundant source of energy, but in a more and more environmentally conscious world it is stigmatised as the dirtiest; and nuclear energy has never lived up to expectations.

Thus, even with high prices, the possibility for OECD countries to limit their dependency on OPEC oil was constrained. With increasing demand and declining domestic production, these countries will have to import, by the year 2010, 70 per cent of their requirements, estimated at 45 million b/d. Demand in the 'rest of the world' is expected to grow even faster. This increase is likely 'to be met primarily by the major Middle East producers and Venezuela' (Scott 1995: V.2, 64), despite the widespread consumption of coal and, more recently, natural gas in power generation. Clearly, there had to be some arrangement with OPEC. But was it not worth trying to bring OPEC or, at least, some member countries into the new non-proprietorial governance of international oil? Since the OPEC revolution the performance of member countries had been very poor. Apart from wars between some member countries, military and civil unrest in others, and foreign indebtedness in most of them, not one had delivered the promised political and economic development. By 1989, some of them were internally very weak and divided, and they began to give in to the mounting pressure to re-open upstream oil to private investment. And then came the surprise of the century, the fall of the Berlin Wall and the collapse and disintegration of the Soviet Union, at that time the second most important oil-exporter. With the apparent victory of capitalism over communism and the end of the Cold War, new territories rich in hydrocarbons were suddenly and unexpectedly opening up to foreign investors. This new international political context provided a unique opportunity for the consuming countries to advance their agenda on a truly global scale. The nascent liberal, i.e. non-proprietorial, governance of international oil, still limited in its scope to the consuming countries, was suddenly upgraded to an integral part, and even to a model, for a new world of global capitalism.

6.2   Investment Treaties and Natural Resources

After the OPEC revolution, in order to contain and confront the policy of 'permanent sovereignty over natural resources', the developed consuming countries – first the Europeans, then the United States and other OECD members – started to negotiate a series of Bilateral Investment Treaties (BITs). Given the Third World majority in the United Nations, a multilateral approach was ruled out. Usually these BITs were concluded between one developed and one underdeveloped country. The flow of investment was predictably in one direction only, and the rules agreed upon, not surprisingly, were those to the liking of the capital-exporting developed countries. Traditional international law was thus revitalised with many Third World countries endorsing it.

After the demise of the Soviet Union the trickle of BITs turned into a torrent. The majority were concluded between OECD member countries and Russia, the Newly Independent Republics and the Eastern European countries. Then the European Union (EU) with its eyes on the hydrocarbon riches of the former Soviet Union grasped the opportunity to initiate multilateral negotiations. The first result in December 1991 was a non-binding European Energy Charter, the starting point for the subsequent negotiation of a binding Energy Charter Treaty (ECT), which was concluded in December 1994.

The 1989 USA-Canada Free Trade Agreement (USA-Canada FTA) deserves a mention in this context. In spite of its name, it also covers investment (Chap. XVI). In 1993 this treaty was extended to the North American Free Trade Agreement (NAFTA) to include Mexico. Last but not least, GATT's languishing Uruguay Round was also given a new boost leading to its successful conclusion in 1994 and the foundation of the World Trade Organisation (WTO). Though a treaty on trade, it has, as we shall see, some relevance to investment. Thus, in the five years from 1989 to 1994 the consuming countries achieved significant advances in setting up an international investment regime, and at its heart it contained the new non-proprietorial governance for international oil.

Defining 'Investment'

These investment treaties define 'investment' in an all-inclusive way. For instance, the US-Azerbaijan BIT defines contractual rights, such as 'production or revenue-sharing contracts, concessions, or other similar contracts', as well as 'rights conferred pursuant to law, such as licences and permits', simply as 'investments'. Hence, upstream contracts in oil are simply 'investment agreements' (USA-Azerbaijan 1997: Art. I). The same definition is found in the Canada-Venezuela BIT (1996), or in the ECT, though the latter only deals with investment in the energy sector (ECT 1994: Art.1.6). These treaties provide a legal framework for the exploitation of natural resources ignoring the possible existence of a landlord–tenant relationship. They only deal with the rights of 'investors'.

Trade-related Investment Measures. The USA-Azerbaijan BIT outlaws trade-related investment measures (TRIM) in a manner more radical than that of GATT/WTO. Neither party shall 'mandate or enforce, as a condition for the establishment, acquisition, expansion, management, conduct or operation of a covered investment', i.e. an investment of a US or Azerbaijan national or company, 'any requirement (including any commitment or undertaking in connection with the receipt of a governmental permission or authorisation)', in order to 'achieve a particular level or percentage of local content, or to purchase, use or otherwise give a preference to products or services of domestic origin or from any domestic source', or 'to transfer technology, a production process or other proprietary knowledge to a national or company in the Party's territory', or even 'to carry out a particular type, level or percentage of research and development in the Party's territory' (USA-Azerbaijan 1997: Art.II.1, VI). Each party shall also 'ensure that its state enterprises, in the provision of their goods or services, accord national and most favoured nation treatment to covered investments'. Finally, this treaty also insists that the governments, granting permits, licences, concessions – or whatever the form of granting access to the natural resource may be – shall not discriminate in favour of national citizens or companies. Furthermore, looking forward to the privatisation of state companies, the governments may not favour their nationals. In other words, the US government, for example, has the choice only to grant or not to grant leases on public lands, and to privatise or not to privatise its state companies, but it cannot discriminate against Azerbaijani investors in the United States.

The Canada-Venezuela BIT contains the same clauses, except that it does not outlaw a 'buy Venezuelan' policy of state enterprises, nor does it cover the making of an investment, the so-called pre-investment phase. Similarly, the ECT stipulates that 'a Contracting Party shall not apply any trade-related investment measure that is inconsistent with ... GATT' though, with the typical ambiguity of this multilateral agreement, it adds exceptions and clauses allowing signatories to opt out, and others designed to maintain the pressure on reluctant signatories to keep moving in the desired direction (ECT 1994: Art.10). Regarding the pre-investment phase, only 'soft-law' applies, as the ECT negotiations included countries less desperate than Azerbaijan to attract foreign investment. Each Contracting Party would only 'endeavour to accord' such a non-discriminatory treatment. Nevertheless, pressure was put on the reluctant signatories to agree to a firmer commitment on this point, through a 'Supplementary Treaty' still to be negotiated. (ECT 1994: Art.10.2, 3, 4)

Dispute Settlement. In the USA-Azerbaijan BIT private investors – *not* the governments – are given a menu of choices for the settlement of an 'investment dispute', from national courts to international arbitration, independently of whatever may have been written into the 'investment agreement' in question or into a foreign-investment law (USA-Azerbaijan, Art. IX.3). The same applies to the Canada-Venezuela BIT. The dispute settlement provisions in the ECT, heavily influenced by the precedents created with the USACFTA and NAFTA, were worded almost identically (ECT 1994: Art. 26). What is more, these provisions came into force immediately upon signing the Treaty, even before ratification by the member countries though, typically, there was the possibility of an opt-out from this clause.

Taxation

Regarding sovereign taxation, the USA-Azerbaijan BIT states, 'no provision of this Treaty shall impose obligations with respect to tax matters'. But there are some exceptions, the most important of which refers to 'investment disputes' based on 'an investment agreement or an investment authorisation' (USA-

Azerbaijan, Art. XIII). The latter, in plain English, are concessions or licences, while the former covers all kinds of upstream contracts, including those signed between NOCs and foreign investors – a most important point to which we will return later.

But where would 'investment disputes' originate? According to this Treaty, through a tax increase deemed to be the equivalent of an *indirect* expropriation or nationalisation. This is then simply called an 'expropriation'. Thus, if a national or a company asserts, 'that a tax matter involves an expropriation', it 'may submit that dispute to arbitration' subject to two conditions: one, that 'the national or company concerned has first referred to the competent tax authorities of both Parties the issue of whether the tax matter involves an expropriation'; second, that 'the competent tax authorities have not *both* determined, within nine months from the time the national or company referred the issue, that the matter does not involve an expropriation' (USA-Azerbaijan, Art. XIII.2; italics ours). Thus even investors without any contractual relationship are offered the option of international arbitration in tax matters as long as one of the parties – the US or Azerbaijan government – has not ruled, within nine months, that a tax increase or a new tax 'does not involve an expropriation'. The Canada-Venezuela BIT establishes the same procedure, though the two governments have only six months for their ruling. The ECT, while including its usual diplomatic caveats, has generally adopted the same procedure.

'Sovereignty over Energy Resources'

The only developed oil-exporting country, Norway, was party to the negotiation of the ECT.[3] Its presence probably explains why the question of sovereignty was taken up at all, though it was treated under the heading 'Sovereignty over Energy Resources' and no longer 'Permanent Sovereignty over Natural Resources' (United Nations 1962).

State sovereignty and sovereign rights over 'energy resources'

---

3.   The UK, as we shall see, though a significant exporter is firmly compromised with liberal governance.

were recognised, though only if they were 'exercised in accordance with and subject to the rules of international law'. In the same way, 'the rules in Contracting Parties governing the system of property ownership of energy resources' were not at stake, but they should not affect 'the objectives of promoting access to energy resources, and exploration and development thereof on a commercial basis'. It was also agreed that 'Contracting Parties undertake to facilitate access to energy resources, *inter alia*, by allocating in a non-discriminatory manner on the basis of published criteria authorisations, licences, concessions and contracts to prospect and explore for or to exploit or extract energy resources'. All this suggests that the next step could be to *oblige* the sovereign power, in one way or other, to put those 'energy resources' on the market. Remarkably enough, on the insistence of Norway, this was formally denied:

> Each state continues to hold ... the rights to decide the geographical areas ... to be made available for exploration and development of its energy resources, the optimalization of their recovery and the rate at which they may be depleted or otherwise exploited, to specify and enjoy any taxes, royalties or other financial payments payable by virtue of such exploration and exploitation, and to regulate the environmental and safety aspects of such exploration, development and reclamation within its Area, and to participate in such exploration and exploitation, *inter alia*, through direct participation by the government or through state enterprises. (ECT 1994: Art.18)

In this clause the desperate effort to avoid any suggestion of a link between energy and natural resources, especially non-renewable ones, is particularly striking. While the language may sound odd, there is nonetheless a recognition of the state's property rights: rights to deny investors access to particular 'geographical areas', to get a royalty for its 'energy resources', to set production levels, and to participate with its NOCs in exploration and production. This could hardly be more contrary to the spirit, and even the letter, of the rest of the Treaty. Its essential purpose, so systematically and carefully expressed, was to impress upon the resource-rich signatories the idea that there was no such thing as an international landlord–tenant business relationship but only a state–taxpayer one. This alien article had to be grafted onto the ECT since, without it, the complex multilateral negotiations would have failed. No such clause is to be found in the USA-Azerbaijan and Canada-Venezuela BITs. Nor is it to be found in the USACFTA. In NAFTA, however, Mexico succeeded in excluding its hydrocarbons from the relevant set of rules (NAFTA 1993: Chap. VI).

Present and Future of the New Regime

Non-proprietorial governance of international oil, which the developed consuming countries have been building in response to the OPEC revolution of the early 1970s, has evolved into a grandiose framework of international trade and investment treaties, an attempt to create one global economy united by free trade and free investment. In this global economy mineral resources would be subject to the global sovereign: consumers.

NAFTA and the ECT also promoted new rules between the developed countries. In both treaties the arbitration rules went far beyond whatever the European Union or the OECD had agreed to before. In the euphoria following the success of the ECT, the OECD launched the idea of a general Multilateral Agreement on Investment (MAI). This attempt failed, largely due to the resistance of France, and since then, ECT and WTO have moved more slowly.

The ECT became effective with its ratification by thirty signatories, which took place in 1998.[4] Yet not everything went smoothly. The United States had pressed hard to be part of the negotiations in order to prevent the ECT from becoming a 'European' treaty, but in the end it refused to sign. It regarded the approach to the pre-investment phase as too soft compared to the standards already established in BITs, and it was not willing to swallow the article on sovereignty. It believed that the ECT would create negative precedents regarding new BITs (for instance with Russia) and multilateral treaties (for instance with Latin American Countries).[5] It was nevertheless largely

---

4.   The only institutions created under the ECT are the Charter Conference and the Secretariat.
5.   In December 1994, at the same time as the ECT was signed in Lisbon, in Miami the Summit of the Americas was held, the largest ever meeting of Heads of States in the Western Hemisphere. The Summit agreed to create a 'Free Trade Area of the Americas', extending NAFTA all over

the US presence in the negotiations that produced, among other things, the far-reaching arbitration clauses.

Russia signed, but it has so far not ratified. This is, of course, a major failure of the ECT. After all, Russia controls 74 per cent of the proven reserves of crude oil of the former USSR, and 85 per cent of natural gas. 'Negotiations [were] largely led, on the Russian side, by the reformist groups, and the negotiations and their results [were] a strategy of the reformers aimed at imposing the Treaty's market economy model on the internal policy debate' (Wälde 1996b: 316). Yet back home, various national interest groups retained influence, not least in the oil and gas sector, in which over 60 per cent of Russian exports and fiscal revenues originate. From their perspective the ECT was difficult if not impossible to accept. From the viewpoint of the Newly Independent Republics things looked different. In the words of Kazakh President Nursultan Nazarbayev: 'I do not think that in today's world weapons can do anything to protect a country. Our main security guarantee (against Russia) will be a powerful Western business presence in Kazakhstan' (Ögütçü 1996: 78).

In practice, private foreign investors have not been successful in getting into Russian oil. By 1998 cumulative spending in the projects involving ARCO, BP, ENI, and Shell, was still minimal and the outlook is not promising (ECT/IEA 1998: 5). Yet the Russian government is under continuous pressure to ratify the ECT. Thus, at the G8 Energy Ministerial Meeting in Moscow,[6] in April 1998, the Energy Charter Secretariat and the IEA presented a Joint Paper on 'Energy Investment', largely based on 'valuable studies carried out by or under the auspices of the World Bank and the European Bank for Reconstruction and Development' (ECT/IEA 1998: 1). On the issue of equal pre-investment opportunities the Joint Paper asserts, 'national economic benefits arising from... an investment will not be determined by the nationality of the investing company'. Privatisation opportunities should 'be open to companies without discrimination on grounds of nationality. There should be no

---

the Americas. An integral part of this design is the 'Energy Initiative of the Americas' with its annual ministerial meetings.

6. i.e. the G7 plus the Russian Federation.

constraints on the subsequent resale and purchase of shareholdings or other assets after privatisation'. On energy trade, it recommends that WTO rules should be followed as closely as possible. Last but not least, it concludes that Russia 'should continue to pursue, as a matter of priority, ratification of the 1994 Energy Charter Treaty' (ECT/IEA 1998: 25–26).

In its Executive Summary the Joint Paper strongly argues against proprietorial and in favour of non-proprietorial fiscal regimes, that is against royalties and in favour of excess-profit taxation. 'Experience has shown that an unstable or unbalanced tax system can be the single most important factor in deterring investors. This has been particularly true where taxation is based on gross revenues rather than on profits, with allowance for incurred costs' (ECT/IEA 1998: ii). It is claimed that 'profit-based systems are more self-adjusting and give a better basis for investors to assess the fiscal impact over the life of their investment project.... Finding the right tax structure is of particular importance to Russia where the oil industry accounted for 70 per cent of federal government revenues in 1997' (ECT/IEA 1998: 21–22). In fact, the homeland of fiscal regimes based on royalties and severance taxes is the United States, and the United States is also the homeland of the largest, most prosperous and successful private petroleum industries in the world, and nowhere have fiscal regimes been more stable than in the United States.

The Joint Paper recommends implementing fiscal regimes in upstream oil based on excess profit taxation, on top of normal income taxes, but this is contrary to the worldwide trend over the last decades away from high taxation levels on profits in favour of gross revenue taxation such as value added taxes or, as we have argued in Chapter 3, personal income taxation (see Figs. 3.1 and 3.2).

The G8 also complained about the fact that 'high cost energy resources have been and are developed world wide, while cheaper resources are left in the ground. This is an unfortunate consequence of the geographical concentration of resources and monopolistic behaviour coupled with large political uncertainties. This waste of resources can be reduced through closer economic and political co-operation, underpinned by international treaties' (ECT/IEA 1998: 18). Indeed, both investors and consumers could save very significant amounts of money through lower costs and prices. Hence, the natural resource owners are urged to adopt profit-based fiscal regimes with the necessary downward-elasticity regarding prices, and upward-elasticity regarding costs. Yet under such regimes, there is no doubt that the oil-exporting countries would lose out.

Michael Klein, chief economist of Royal Dutch–Shell in London, has recently visualised this ideal Ricardian world of the twenty-first century in a scenario. He assumes declining real oil prices and, hence, he expects 'the fight over upstream rents continues to intensify'. As 'producer countries open up all parts of the oil and gas business for foreign investors', they 'revise tax regimes to attract investors. In particular, countries with marginal fields abolish royalties'. Thus, over time, 'auction design is streamlined and many contracts are awarded to the bidder of the highest marginal tax rate rather than an up-front signature bonus'. In the end, 'by 2040 all national oil companies are privatised and tax systems for upstream operations converge to regular corporate tax regimes as upstream rents diminish' (Klein 1999: 13–14).

In this scenario Klein assumes declining real oil prices, because the outcome is allegedly the result of competition, of market forces, not of those forces that actually create markets. But the assumption of declining prices is not essential to his scenario. Even assuming, perhaps more realistically, increasing scarcity of the natural resource and, consequently, increasing real production costs, fiscal regimes based on excess profit taxation, being elastic regarding increasing costs, would equally serve to minimise prices and fiscal revenues in the oil-exporting countries.

6.3 Targeting National Oil Companies in the Exporting Countries

Why should oil-exporting countries ever subscribe to such policies? These bilateral and multilateral 'investment' treaties represent the negation of 'permanent sovereignty of natural resources' and, more specifically, of OPEC's basic principles. As far as the Newly Independent Republics are concerned, desperate to keep Russia in check and, perhaps, ignorant of the international political economy of oil, it may not be surprising. OPEC, in the 1960s, would certainly have warned them and advised against acceptance, but in the 1990s it had lost most of its political clout. Worse, even some of its member countries – for example Venezuela, a very experienced and relatively developed oil country – subscribed to such liberal policies. The general explanation is to be found, of course, in the poor performance of the exporting countries since nationalisation. In most, if not all, of them there are 'reformist groups', keen to impose a 'market economy model on the internal policy debate'.[7]

Yet this is hardly a sufficient explanation, given the overwhelming importance of the oil sector in the majority of the exporting countries. Moreover, signing and ratifying this kind of international treaty is still not the end of the story, as effective implementation requires a powerful liberal agency, and while there are a number of candidates available for this task, the two obvious ones are the Petroleum Ministries and the NOCs. In practice, in the exporting countries the latter has been the preferred option. Wherever this is the case, the privatisation of the NOC is *not* on the top of the liberal agenda. Thus, typically, in the Joint Paper the Russian government was told that:

> Major studies have noted that the existing Joint Venture licensing arrangements are based on an administrative system that views the Subsoil Licence as the supreme document, while the agreement among parties to the Joint Venture is only secondary. This exposes the investor to several significant risks. The terms of the licence to use the subsoil are subject to unilateral change by new legislation and are terminable by the governments on various grounds. It is subject to all applicable taxes at all levels of government, and no protection is provided against adverse changes in tax laws or other laws .... Disputes are not subject to impartial adjudication because there is no contractual relationship between the Joint Venture partners and the government. (ECT/IEA 1998: 20)

As a matter of fact, all developed countries grant concessions or licences, in exactly the same way as intended by Russia, even if these countries had, or have, NOCs (for example Norway). Yet

---

7.   Regarding oil and WTO see Jiménez (2001).

in the exporting countries the problem, from the viewpoint of the consuming countries, is limiting their sovereign rights beyond the single sovereign act of granting access to the land. National investment treaties may do their part, but more could be achieved by combining these treaties with 'production sharing agreements' (ECT/IEA 1998: ii) or similar types of upstream contracts. This ensures that the NOC is directly involved in the business. The importance of this lies, of course, not in the NOCs' role as business partners but in their possible role as 'umbrellas' or 'hostages'. They may contractually guarantee that they will absorb detrimental changes in legislation, most importantly in taxation, whether by paying directly on behalf of the foreign 'partners', or through indemnities. Thus, indirectly, through so-called 'stabilisation clauses', the NOCs in these cases actually deliver the state as a hostage, and NOCs with their international sales have something the 'partners' can use to control them, something to sequestrate. It is in this context that international arbitration is of crucial importance.

Furthermore, and even more importantly, the NOCs can be transformed into the new liberal licensing and contracting agencies. Though in the past they had been the ground rent collecting agents of the landlord states, their role expanded enormously with nationalisation. They grew out of their role as mere operators, eventually becoming fully-fledged producing companies and, as such, ground rent paying tenants, resentful of their high tax bills and – in the case of OPEC members – resentful of quotas. In this new role they could be politically helpful by dressing non-proprietorial governance in a national costume, minimising adverse reaction and, thus, any danger that the liberal transplant might be rejected. Though privatisation is doubtless on the agenda further down the road, the priority is ensuring first that non-proprietorial governance is deeply rooted. The Joint Paper mentions Azerbaijan as the example Russia should follow.

7. CONSUMING VS. EXPORTING COUNTRIES: CASE STUDIES

The first case we present in this chapter is the United Kingdom, which emerged as an oil-producer in the 1970s and as an oil-exporter in the 1980s. It provides the textbook example of non-proprietorial governance. Not surprisingly, this new reference has met with strong resistance in the United States, the old reference and homeland of proprietorial governance, where royalty-related interests are widespread and deeply rooted. There, we will concentrate on the state of Alaska, a newcomer to the scene, where oil production took off with the completion of the Trans-Alaska-Pipeline in 1978. Alaska became an important oil-'exporting' state within the United States, 'exporting' almost all of its production to the lower 48 states. Finally, we look at the case of Venezuela, a traditional Third World oil-exporting country and founding member of OPEC. This country provides the best-documented example of changing governance in oil in the twentieth century.

7.1 United Kingdom

Fiscal Regime

The first licences in the British North Sea were granted in the mid-1960s.[1] The blocks covered about 250 km^2 each. There was a modest licence fee and a royalty of one eighth, which was in line with the American reference. But from the very beginning there was one important difference in the way the British government administered the – publicly owned – natural resource. Licences were granted through a discretionary process, a procedure that allowed the government to maximise the participation of national enterprise in the development of this new oil-producing province. It did so most successfully. Foreign companies had to pledge good behaviour, and there was a strong

---

1.   For the development of the British North Sea in general see Mabro *et al.* (1986).

incentive to comply, as their performance was taken into account in new licensing rounds. If it had not been for this policy, and a similar policy in Norway, the development of North Sea oil could have been handled from the Gulf of Mexico, at that time the only fully developed off-shore producing province in the world.

So far eighteen licensing rounds have been held and about one thousand licences were granted. They were granted through a bargaining process, the government negotiating investment levels and other conditions of the licence. Remarkably, bonuses were rarely used and, when they were, the sums involved were very modest, even after it had become clear that North Sea oil would be highly profitable. The first company to announce a big discovery, in December 1969, was British Petroleum (BP), soon followed by others in the early 1970s. Thus, many important discoveries preceded the OPEC revolution. By 1973 very large profits were to be expected. To collect them, the British government adopted a new approach, which was significantly different from OPEC as well as from the old US system.

To cope with excess profits, in 1975 the (Labour) government introduced a Petroleum Revenue Tax (PRT). This tax is triggered by the accumulated cash flow. Investments are treated as current costs. PRT has to be paid as soon as the accumulated cash flow becomes positive, by which time investors have already recovered their original investment. Moreover, there is an 'uplift' on investment expenditure; for every Pound of investment expenditure, investors are credited an additional 35 pence in order to compensate them for interest payments and the effect of inflation. And PRT will be paid only if the internal rate of return has exceeded 15 per cent. What is more, if PRT has been paid but the accumulated cash flow decreases in later years, PRT is paid back with interest. This applies for the lifetime of the licence (up to 40 years), which is extendable. In other words, excess profits are defined not on a yearly basis but over the lifetime of a reservoir.

PRT applies to the individual reservoir as the basic unit of production, which is ring-fenced to prevent excess profits being reduced, nationally or internationally, through the 'export' of profits through transfer pricing or outsourcing, or through the 'import' of costs from the downstream and other less profitable businesses. In other words, each reservoir is treated as an individual, separate business. Similarly, the whole of the United Kingdom Continental Shelf was also ring-fenced for the purpose of corporate income tax.

PRT was specifically designed to collect excess profits, or Ricardian rents, in the upstream. As a so-called 'resource rent tax' it is supposed not to obstruct the free flow of the marginal investment, or the extraction of the proverbial marginal barrel. Contrary to the American bidding system, which is designed to collect *expected* Ricardian rents or excess profits through bonuses, PRT collects them only *after* they have actually materialised. The licensees are given the option to spend the money first.

In 1975 the applicable rate of PRT was set at 45 per cent, but after the second price shock (1979) this rate was raised repeatedly, reaching 75 per cent in 1983. Moreover, with the persistence of extraordinarily high oil prices, in 1981 the government introduced a Supplementary Petroleum Duty (SPD), basically a severance tax of 20 per cent. But SPD, a levy on gross revenue, was abolished two years later. Simultaneously, royalty – a contractual levy – was also abolished, albeit only for new fields. Hence, by 1983 the fiscal regime in the British North Sea had been transformed into a purely non-proprietorial one, at least insofar as new fields and licences were concerned.

On the other hand, in 1975 the government created the British National Oil Company (BNOC), which, by law, was entitled to a 51 per cent participation in all new licences. Worried about security of supply, the company was also put in charge of marketing royalty oil. Obviously, BNOC could considerably enhance the power of the government to collect those excess profits effectively. But the government soon scaled down the role of BNOC. In 1982, its upstream assets were privatised. Though it continued as a major trading company, it finally disappeared in 1986. (Hoopes 1997)

By 1983, therefore, a decade after the OPEC revolution, the United Kingdom had developed a counter-example of liberal governance and a consistent non-proprietorial fiscal regime. Though it was already a net exporter of oil, it simply aimed at maximising output. Accordingly, the political debate on the fiscal regime centred exclusively on risks, profits and excess profits, on incentives and disincentives to production and investment.

The idea that something should be paid for the natural resource – i.e. a royalty – had disappeared. In the political culture that applies to UK oil policy today, royalties are simply 'outmoded' (Kemp, Stephen and Masson 1997: 11). At the same time, a first large gap was cut into the ring-fence: a cross-field exploration allowance was introduced as an incentive to exploration. In practice, this meant that the whole of the British North Sea could be explored using profits generated by the highly profitable fields, which were taxed at the PRT-rate of 75 per cent. Next in importance, in 1987, a cross-field development allowance was introduced. Finally, in 1993, those gaps in the ring-fence were sealed but as part of a deal to bring PRT down to 50 per cent, and to abolish PRT for all new fields (Rutledge and Wright 2000). The official argument was that the new fields were marginal anyway and, therefore, they were not worth the administrative costs of PRT. Thus, the development of the PRT rate followed a pattern we have already discussed in Chapter 3 in the case of corporate tax rates in the United States after the Second World War (see Figs. 3.1 and 3.2). In fact, the applicable corporate tax (CT) in the United Kingdom also followed the same pattern. The Finance Act 1984 reduced the Corporation Tax rate from 52 per cent (1982–83) to 35 per cent (1986–87), and it was further lowered during the following years. Finally, in 1999, the government brought the rate down to 30 per cent. Great Britain now has one of the lowest CT rates in the world.

Summing up, after 1983, in new fields the marginal fiscal take was 88 per cent of profits,[2] which created an obvious incentive problem. Every additional Pound spent actually cost only 12 pence to the investor. This was too high a rate to be sustainable, or not to create serious distortions. Hence, pressure built up to reduce this percentage. Fifteen years later it had come down to 65 per cent,[3] and to 30 per cent for fields developed after 1983. Today royalty is already being scrapped in the old fields (*Energy Exploration & Exploitation* 2001: 86–87). One can safely predict that PRT will also disappear soon, though this may involve a complex settlement as the companies will wish to reclaim part of it to underwrite decommissioning costs.

---

2. $88\% = 75\% + (1-75\%)*52\%$.
3. $65\% = 50\% + 50\%*30\%$.

Fiscal Revenue

Fig. 7.1 shows the development of oil and gas production from
FY77 to FY99,[4] and Figs. 7.2 and 7.3 show the evolution of
fiscal revenues and gross income. The effective percentage of
royalty, up to 1982, including (modest) licence fees and (rare
and modest) bonuses, averaged about 10 per cent,[5] but after
that date it declined as the new royalty-exempt fields came on-
stream. At present the average is about 3 per cent. PRT became
payable as early as FY78. It increased sharply, in absolute and
relative terms, with prices, volumes, applicable rates, and later
with the disappearance of SPD and royalty, and reached its
highest levels in the years 1983 to 1985. Not surprisingly, it
came down drastically in 1986 with falling prices. PRT was

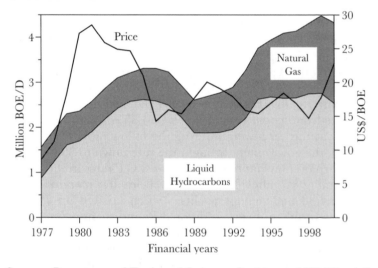

Source: Department of Trade and Industry: *Development of UK Oil and Gas
          Resources*, 2001.

Figure 7.1: UK Oil and Gas Production and Prices

---

4.   In the UK the fiscal year begins on 6 April, and ends on 5 April the
     following year.
5.   Royalty is paid at wellhead-prices. Gross petroleum income, however,
     is reported at landed prices. Therefore the legal 12.5 per cent royalty
     represents a lower percentage at the latter prices.

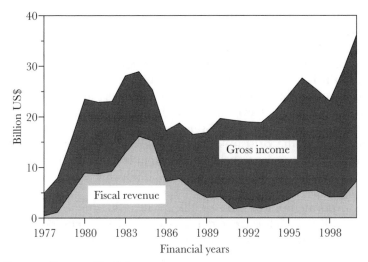

Source: Same as Fig. 7.1

Figure 7.2: UK Fiscal Revenue and Gross Income

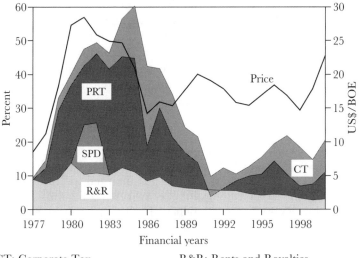

CT: Corporate Tax   R&R: Rents and Royalties
PRT: Petroleum Revenue Tax   SPD: Supplementary Petroleum Duty

Source: Same as Fig. 7.1

Figure 7.3: UK Fiscal Revenue as Percentage of Gross Income

designed to collect rents in the upswing, but also to be downwardly flexible regarding prices. In FY91, PRT in the whole of British North Sea production became negative. In other words, the government paid PRT back to the industry in that year. PRT was designed to be flexible regarding costs. The objective was that so long as the companies were able to produce an additional barrel, even at sharply increasing costs, they should be motivated to do so. And this, as we have seen, extended to the whole of the British North Sea regarding exploration and, partially at least, also to field development costs. Not surprisingly, then, even before the PRT reform of 1993, this tax was rapidly losing importance.

Corporate tax was most significant in 1986, due to the sharp fall of PRT, which is treated as a cost and, when refunded, as a negative cost. Thereafter corporate tax continued to fall until FY93, and then regained some of its former importance, probably due to the new PRT-exempt fields coming on-stream. In general, the picture that emerges from Figs. 7.2 and 7.3 is that, once a pure non-proprietorial fiscal regime is put in place, a fall in fiscal revenues follows during the next few years. The British North Sea is at present by far the lowest-taxed and most profitable oil province in the world.[6] It is not only consumer friendly, in the sense that it aims at maximising output by accepting that the natural resources are a free gift of nature, but it is also investor friendly, in the sense that it is very lenient in the collection of excess profits.

Incentivising Production

Production of liquid hydrocarbons in the UK peaked first in FY85, at 2.62 million b/d (Fig. 7.1). It then fell to 1.88 million b/d in 1988–89. A remarkable recovery to 2.82 million b/d followed in FY99 (generally believed to be the definitive peak). Since this recovery was obviously not due to prices, one may ask whether it had something to do with changes in the fiscal

---

6.   According to Barrows (1996: 13) the UK ranked sixth amongst the 144 fiscal systems that were analysed. However, the analysis of these systems is based on model calculation, and none of the first five countries offering even more advantageous conditions was actually producing oil. For a more focused and detailed study see Rutledge and Wright (1998).

regime introduced in 1983 and subsequent years. A detailed study on this subject concluded that, in 1995, out of a total production of 2.676 million b/d, about 355 thousand b/d would not have been produced without those changes. It should be noted that the fiscal revenue from this additional production, over the lifetime of the fields, was estimated at £2 billion, but the tax rebates granted to old fields were estimated at £5.3 billion. Consequently, there was a net loss in fiscal revenues of £3.3 billion. (Martin 1997: ii–iv)

There is no doubt that the lower level of taxation had a positive impact on production, although a property-conscious government would not have been very pleased by this overall result. But for liberal Britain the maximisation of output without regard for fiscal revenues was perfectly acceptable. From a proprietorial viewpoint the alternative course of action would have been to wait for technology to develop and/or prices to increase without the interim loss of tax revenues. In practice, had these additional 355 thousand daily barrels not been produced, this would have contributed to higher prices and encouraged a subsequent increase in production. In other words, the alternative is not simply 'to produce or not to produce', but 'to produce now or to produce later'. A non-proprietorial fiscal regime, however, prefers oil to be produced as soon as it is profitable for the private companies to produce it, that being considered the only relevant criterion.

A Textbook Example

The British fiscal regime ignores any claim of natural resource ownership. Consumers benefit from lower-than-otherwise prices due to the supply-side of the equation, whereas companies benefit from a low level of rent-collection. The losers are UK taxpayers generally who otherwise would benefit from lower taxation levels on income or expenditure.

Liberal governance of British oil is solid and robust. The way petroleum policy has been structured means that the oil-exporting feature of the UK economy – significant in terms of the volumes involved, close to one million barrels daily – is simply irrelevant. Indeed, it is so irrelevant that the British public at large is unaware of it; and the British government continues to consider the higher oil prices promoted by OPEC as a threat to the world, and therefore to the British, economy. Moreover, Britain boasts not only low up-stream but also high down-stream taxation. Nowhere in Europe is petrol more expensive than in the United Kingdom. In 1999, upstream taxation amounted to £2.6 billion compared with £29.7 billion downstream (Rutledge and Wright 2000: 3). From the viewpoint of the consuming countries in their tug-of-war with OPEC, increasing the fiscal take upstream sets a bad example, whereas increasing downstream taxation sets a good example. The United Kingdom is the textbook example for non-proprietorial governance.

7.2 Alaska

Fiscal Regime

In the United States oil fiscal regimes are based on lease contracts, which specify rents and royalties. In Alaska, where almost all the oil is produced on public lands, the law defines a minimum royalty rate of one eighth, the most common of the US customary rates. One eighth was the fixed royalty rate in the North Slope bidding round of 1969, which brought in US$ 900 million in bonuses.[7] However, beginning in 1973, the bidding rounds were based on a royalty rate of one sixth, and beginning in 1979 on one fifth, the bidding parameter being a bonus. Alaska also experimented at that time with a net profit share (NPS). The NPS amounts to a sliding-scale royalty, to be paid on top of the agreed royalty rate. It triggers in once the lessees have recovered their exploration and development costs.[8] Both royalty and NPS were used occasionally as bidding parameters, and royalty rate as high as 43 per cent and NPS as high as 93 per cent were offered in the days of extremely high prices and high expectations. But after 1983 the one-eighth royalty became once again the usual rate in new leases, with a bonus as the bidding parameter (State of Alaska 2000a: 105–6). The NPS device was abandoned because of its inherent incentive

---

7. At the time this huge amount came as a surprise and, with the benefit of hindsight, it heralded the forthcoming oil crisis in the USA.

8. Hence, these leases were very similar to production sharing agreements elsewhere, with the difference that they do not involve a NOC.

problems, which also entailed high surveillance and administrative costs. [9]

There is also a severance tax, which in Alaska is called a production tax. This is another kind of royalty, the difference being that it is indeed a tax, its rate being fixed by law and not by contract. It is therefore subject to the state legislator. In 1968, it was set at 3 per cent. With increasing oil prices this rate was raised. In 1977, it reached 10 per cent for natural gas and 12.25 per cent for crude oil. The rate for oil was raised again to 15 per cent in 1981, although the rate of 12.25 per cent still applied for the first five years of a new development. These increases went hand in hand with the development of a sliding scale, a so-called 'economic limit factor' (ELF), first introduced in 1977. For crude oil, for example, no production tax is paid if output per well is 300 b/d or less. For gas, the lower limit is 3,000 mcf per well and per day (about 535 boe/d). While the increasing rates were designed to capture higher fiscal revenues in response to higher prices, at the same time the scale became more flexible downwards regarding volumes. The minimum rate is now zero and no longer 3 per cent as it was before 1973. Thus, in the fiscal year 2000 (FY00),[10] Prudhoe Bay paid a 14 per cent production tax, Pt. McIntyre 9.6 per cent, and Kuparuk 9 per cent. These three fields accounted for over 99 per cent of all production tax revenues (State of Alaska 2000b: 42–43).

On top of royalties and production taxes, there is a state corporate tax, a net income tax, which was set at a maximum rate of 9.4 per cent in 1975. In 1978 the oil companies were 'ring-fenced' in order properly to quantify their profits originating within Alaska, i.e. to prevent them from diluting their profits nation-wide or internationally. Yet this arrangement met

---

9.   As a matter of fact, NPS was paid, for the first time, only in 2000. On the other hand, one should not underestimate the problems involved even in collecting royalties. Alaska, in 1977, engaged in a legal dispute over taxes and royalties. The point of discord was the way the companies calculated wellhead prices. The government won its case 17 years later, in 1994. The companies had to pay arrears totalling US$ 3.7 billion. (*Platt's Oilgram News* 21-11-1994: 3).

10. In Alaska the fiscal year 2000 (FY00), for example, begins 1 July 1999 and ends 30 June 2000.

with stiff resistance from the companies. Ring-fencing was finally repealed in 1981,[11] and worldwide combined profit reporting was now accepted. This was actually in line with what was happening at the same time at the federal level. The implicit loss of revenue was supposed to be compensated by the already mentioned increase of the production tax for crude oil from 12.25 per cent to 15 per cent. Finally, there is a federal corporate tax. Its rate evolved as discussed in Chapter 3 (Figs. 3.1 and 3.2).

Fiscal Revenue

Production of crude oil in Alaska took off in FY78, and peaked in FY88 at 2.05 million b/d. Oil prices, of course, followed the world market. Gross income – i.e. crude oil production multiplied by wellhead prices – peaked in FY82, and so did fiscal revenues. In relative terms, comparing fiscal revenues with gross income, they had peaked already in FY80, at 50 per cent (33 per cent state revenues plus 17 per cent federal corporate tax). In both cases there was a sharp fall after FY82. Since 1983, the fiscal take has averaged 26 per cent at state level, and at 34 per cent including the federal corporate tax (Figs. 7.4, 7.5 and 7.6).

Royalties, rents and bonuses – royalties representing about 98 per cent of that total – present a very stable percentage of gross income, on average about 12.9 per cent. Production tax had been increasing during the first five years (1978–82), and decreasing since FY93. This is consistent with the production profile and the operation of the safeguards mentioned earlier. At present those gross value levies average about 23 per cent of gross income.

The absolute and relative fall in fiscal revenue observed in the early 1980s is entirely due to the corporate tax. As Fig. 7.7 shows, it was certainly not due to falling prices. The political deal ending ring-fencing but increasing production tax by 2.75 percentage points (from 12.25 to 15 per cent) (State of Alaska 2000b: 30, 42–43) obviously fell short of compensating for the removal of the fence. The actual loss in fiscal revenue to the

---

11. For details on the confrontation about States' right regarding income taxation see Strohmeyer (1993: 209ff).

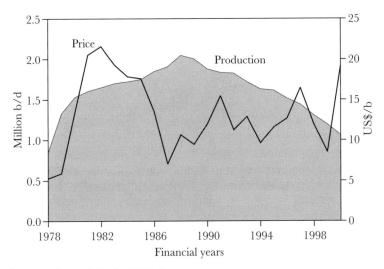

Source: State of Alaska (2000a).

Figure 7.4: Alaska Crude Oil Production and Prices

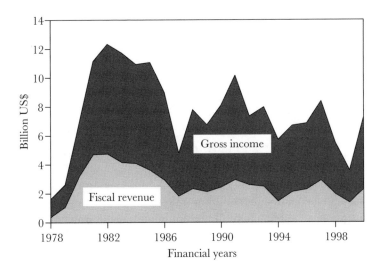

Source: State of Alaska (2000c: 91) and (2000d).

Figure 7.5: Alaska Fiscal Revenue and Gross Income

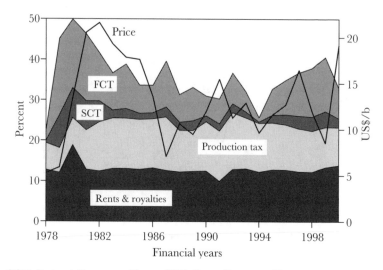

FCT: Federal Corporate Tax   SCT: State Corporate Tax

Source: Figure 7.5

Figure 7.6: Alaska: Fiscal Revenue as Percentage of Gross Income

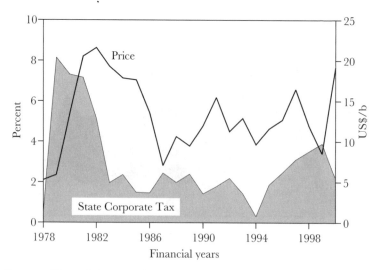

Source: Figure 7.5

Figure 7.7: Alaska State Corporate Tax as Percentage of Gross Income

state of Alaska was far higher. During the years of ring-fencing, FY79–FY81, state corporate income taxes averaged 7.5 per cent of gross revenues. Then they fell sharply, averaging about 2 per cent, and this happened before prices collapsed in 1986. Once in the realm of federal corporate income taxation and worldwide combined profit and loss reporting, the companies were in a strong position to minimise taxes, as pointed out in Chapter 3. Alaska also suffered the consequences of the sharp fall in effective federal corporate tax rates during these years, to which state corporate income taxes were now directly linked by a simple formula.[12]

Proprietorial vs. Non-proprietorial Governance

The governance of oil in Alaska has to be seen in the context of the proprietorial governance that exists in the United States generally. The latter is deeply rooted in a tradition of private mineral property. At present the number of royalty owners in the United States is estimated at 4.5 million, including private individuals, royalty trusts, local public bodies such as schools, and oil-producing companies (Rutledge 2001). Regarding the public domain, there is also a legal and constitutional tradition that links mineral royalties on public lands to education and other social programmes. Still, Alaska is outstanding in comparison with other oil-producing states on two counts. On the one hand, virtually all of its oil and gas comes from the public domain. On the other, it is sparsely populated – its resident population was 622,000 in 1999 – thus resembling the Emirates of the Persian Gulf. Every citizen in Alaska is aware of his or her share in public mineral ownership, an awareness that is strengthened by the existence of a *Permanent Fund*. This investment fund, to which over 25 per cent of rents and royalties accrue, was created by public vote and enshrined in the constitution in 1976. Last year it paid a dividend of US$ 2,000 to every Alaskan citizen.

Yet international companies and consultants have also aimed

---

12. We could not find any data on federal corporate income taxes paid on profits originating in Alaska. Hence, we used the data on state corporate tax to estimate federal income taxes.

at proprietorial governance in Alaska. In 1989, when the Legislator passed new legislation regarding the ELF with the effect of raising production tax on both Prudhoe Bay and Kuparuk (the largest fields) but reducing it for the small fields, the 'industry reacted angrily and suggested ... that by breaking the deal made in 1981, Alaska was sending the wrong message to any would-be investors' (Logsdon 1997: 179).[13] Giving way to the pressure, the government commissioned some international – mainly British – consultants to study Alaska's 'international competitiveness', the first of a series of studies that followed. Not surprisingly, they concluded that 'taxes which focus on profits rather than on gross production revenues are more efficient' (Logsdon 1997: 180). Accordingly, production tax and royalties should become more flexible (Cf. Kemp and Jones 1997). This was the beginning of a strategic debate. Today, even in government publications discussing 'Petroleum Fiscal Systems' gross revenue levies are qualified as 'regressive' and net revenue levies as 'progressive', very much in line with the British debate on the virtues of PRT (Cf. State of Alaska 2000c: 19–21).

The most important practical result of this campaign so far has been that the Legislature, in 1995, gave the Commissioner of Natural Resources broad authority to negotiate lower royalties for state leases, 'to allow for production that would not otherwise be economically feasible', and to introduce sliding-scale royalties related to prices (Alaska Statutes 38.05.180. Oil and Gas Leasing). This was a first step towards non-proprietorial governance, since traditionally in the United States, leases on public lands are state contracts and, having been awarded through public bidding, they cannot be renegotiated. The only way to change lease terms is to hand in the lease first, and then to acquire it again in a new auction. Thus, for example, if in a marginal lease – i.e. a lease paying only customary rentals and royalties – a non-commercial discovery is made, and this discovery is still non-commercial at the end of the primary period, the only option the lessee has is to hand the lease in. However, with the development of productivity and technology, the discovery in question may later become commercial, and the same company may acquire the lease again in a new auction.

---

13. Charles Logsdon is the Chief Oil Economist of the State of Alaska.

Or, to take another example, a lease, which may have been acquired at a time of high expectations, turns out to be unrealistic. But the lessee has only one choice: to hand in the lease and to acquire it again, possibly, under more favourable terms in a new auction. Though, obviously, the bonus that might have been paid is lost, royalty rates may come down closer to customary levels. Thus, there is a market mechanism that tends to adjust lease terms to accord with long-term expectations, which explains the extraordinary stability of customary ground rent combined with bonuses. By design, therefore, and in response to growing scarcity, there has been only a slow growth in royalty rates and severance taxes in the twentieth century, although the OPEC revolution gave them a push.

In 1995 Alaska, however, agreed to renegotiate individual leases, and this obviously undermined the integrity of the bidding process. A wave of renegotiations followed. Outstanding amongst them was British Petroleum renegotiating the Northstar lease, with a 93 per cent net profit share. Amerada Hess had originally acquired this lease in 1979, when expectations were skyrocketing. BP bought the lease in 1995 when expectations were low, with renegotiation in mind. The way this lease was structured gave BP an exceptional leverage: by not developing production beyond a certain low level, the NPS would never be triggered, and the government would be fobbed off with its 20 per cent royalty. In the negotiations that followed, the NPS was transformed into a 7.5 per cent sliding scale royalty – on top of the 20 per cent royalty – related to prices, partially adjusted for inflation (Logsdon 1997: 182).

Whatever the economics of a lease may be, there is no doubt that in these individual negotiations the government can only lose out and leaseholders can only win. They are not only much better informed after holding and exploring the lease for several years but they also make the final decision about whether to carry on or not. Hence, inherently, the government will concede incentives beyond those that would in practice be required (Berman 1997). Moreover, not only is bluff an important part of the business but also 'arm-twisting' such as the threat of international publicity campaigns about investment-hostile government policies. In other words, if there are good reasons in the first place to grant leases through public bidding, there are even better reasons to subject new lease terms to new public bidding.

The door was now open also for renegotiating customary royalty rates, since there are marginal barrels in every reservoir. Yet the first step in this direction was not taken in Alaska but in Washington. In 1995, the (federal) Minerals Management Service (MMS) was authorised to offer tracts in the deep waters (beyond 200m) of the Gulf of Mexico (US Outer Continental Shelf) with royalty suspensions for either a limited period of time, or a limited volume, or a specified threshold for the accumulated gross value of production, in 'order to make the new production economically viable' (US Government 1995). This legislation has been applied so far to four major fields. This was, too, a significant step towards non-proprietorial governance. Until then the established policy was to wait for more favourable economic circumstances and new technologies to develop. In particular technological advance, progressing metre by metre into deeper waters, was well publicised year after year. It was only a question of time before deep waters in the Gulf of Mexico would be able to pay a customary ground rent. However, the federal government decided not to wait, but to abandon its entitlement to a customary royalty. This may be explained, in part, by the fact that only a few international companies have the necessary technology to explore and to produce in these waters, and they were therefore in a strong position to ask for special conditions. In addition, in the outer continental shelf royalties are not shared with the bordering states. Hence, these companies were dealing exclusively with the federal government, a government of a consuming country.

What the deep waters of the Gulf of Mexico and Alaska have in common is that they are as far away from private mineral properties as possible in the United States. About 40 per cent of US oil is still produced on private lands, and one has also to keep in mind that royalty applies to all minerals, not just oil. Hence, implementing non-proprietorial governance in oil may be a difficult if not an impossible task, even in the offshore areas of 'exporting' states like Texas or Louisiana. Where public mineral ownership coexists closely with private mineral ownership, it is difficult to argue that natural resources should be considered a gift of nature in one case but not in the other.

But to question private mineral property rights is both politically and also economically out of the question. Economically, to work through the jumble of private property rights in order to nationalise royalties would exceed by far the possible benefits. Politically, in those oil and gas producing states, royalty owners constitute strong and widespread interest groups, and the federal nature of the US constitution extends their reach straight into Congress and the White House.[14]

Even today royalties and mineral incomes generally still enjoy the privilege, in the context of income taxation, of a 'depletion allowance'. This privilege is based on the recognition of an 'intrinsic value' of minerals, which is in complete contradiction to the liberal credo of mineral ownership as a gift of nature. True, the depletion allowance for oil was reduced from 27.5 to 22 per cent in 1969, and then lowered, gradually, to 15 per cent in 1984. Moreover, after 1975 the depletion allowance was limited to the first two thousand b/d, which in turn was lowered to one thousand b/d in 1985. Yet it is still a very important economic privilege for smaller producers, and there are thousands of them, and even more so for royalty owners, who are to be counted by the millions.

There is no doubt that some principles of liberal governance have made inroads into Alaska and the deep waters of the Gulf of Mexico, but there would be difficulties if they were to be extended, even if we cannot categorically exclude this possibility (which happened as we have seen in Chapter 2 in the case of British coal). But it can safely be predicted that, whatever may happen, each single step will take many years.

7.3 Venezuela

Venezuela[15] was the world's biggest oil exporter for 43 years, from 1928 – when it took over from Mexico – until 1970, when it was overtaken by Saudi Arabia, Iran and Iraq. In that year Venezuela's production peaked at 3.7 million b/d. The decline that followed was due both to the exhaustion of the ageing reservoirs and to a lack of investment. The most important

14. So far only the libertarian right has dared to question private mineral ownership. See Bradley (1996: 59–74).
15. This chapter relies heavily on Mommer (1998).

concessions were to revert to the country in 1983–84, and the government had made clear, in the early 1960s, that they would not be renewed. *No más concesiones* was the catch phrase. Hence, the fall of production was not the result of voluntary cutbacks in support of higher prices, as was then the case in Libya and Kuwait. Venezuela was lucky; her long-term oil policy came to fruition just in time. The implosion of volumes coincided with the explosion of prices (Fig. 7.8).

The national oil company, Petróleos de Venezuela, S.A. – PDVSA is its acronym in Venezuela, but PDV is the usual acronym internationally – took over on 1 January 1976. The company soon launched a massive investment programme to stop the decay of the ageing fields of conventional oil and to pioneer development of the Orinoco Belt with its gigantic accumulation of extra-heavy crude.[16] But production was cut according to OPEC quotas before the turn-around could be achieved. With declining demand, PDV's investment programme was scrapped. Production fell to 1.7 million b/d in

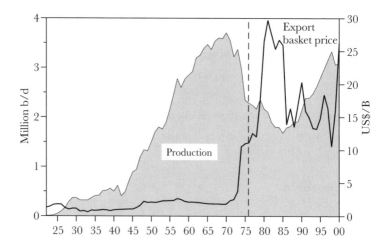

Source: Baptista (1997); Venezuela, Ministerio de Energía y Minas, *Petróleo y otros datos estadísticos.*

Figure 7.8:   Venezuela Liquid Hydrocarbon Production and Average Export Prices of Crude Oil and Products 1922–2000

16.   For a history of PDV see Boué (1993 and 1998).

1985. After the price collapse in 1986, production recovered and reached 3.3 million b/d in 1998. Following another price collapse that year, production was cut again to 3.1 million b/d in 2000.

Fig. 7.9 shows gross income and fiscal revenue (in Venezuela the fiscal year coincides with the calendar year). Gross income

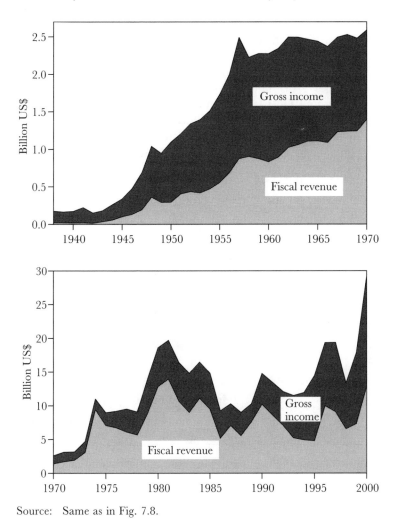

Source: Same as in Fig. 7.8.

Figure 7.9: Venezuela Fiscal Revenue and Gross Income 1938–2000

includes exports as well as sales to the domestic market of all hydrocarbons and refined products. Exports represented over 95 per cent of that total in the more distant past, and they still account for over 85 per cent. Fig. 7.9 is divided into two graphs to cope with the change in the order of magnitude after the OPEC revolution. At a glance, they reveal a long-term increasing trend in fiscal revenues from 1943 to 1981, and a falling trend thereafter until 1986. Since then, they have basically been stable, though with significant variations, whereas gross income has again been growing.

Fiscal revenues increased from 1938 to 1974 also in relative terms (Fig. 7.10). They averaged about 11 per cent of gross income from 1938 to 1942, but this percentage rose to 30 per cent following the petroleum reform of 1943 and remained at that level until 1957. Fig. 7.10 also reveals the quantitative insignificance of the additional tax, the famous fifty-fifty tax. Its significance was qualitative, suggesting that fifty-fifty profit sharing had been the result of a 'deal', of some binding agreement and not of sovereign taxation. Anyway, the

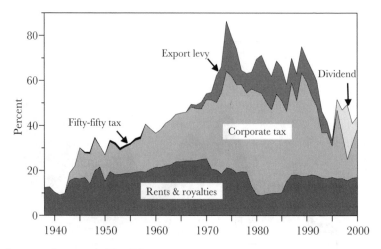

Source: Same as in Fig. 7.8.
For the fifty-fifty tax see Vallenilla (1973: 200–8).

Figure 7.10: Venezuela Fiscal Revenue as Percentage of Gross Income 1938–2000

government's share of gross income increased again after 1958 in spite of falling prices over the next twelve years; this was due to increasing income tax rates and, after 1967, to tax reference prices. (The latter, practically speaking, was the equivalent of an export levy). Fiscal revenues peaked at 86 per cent in 1974. With nationalisation the government's share was lowered, on average, to 66 per cent for the years 1976 to 1992. But then, in 1993, there was a sharp fall in the government's share in gross income.

In Fig. 7.11 we look at the same story in terms of profit shares. From 1938 to 1942, the government's profit share averaged, roughly, one third. From 1943 and until 1957, this share increased to one half, and from 1958 to 1966, it averaged two thirds. After 1967, a new increase in income tax rates and the introduction of tax reference prices paved the way to increase further the government's share, which reached a staggering 95 per cent during the two years prior to nationalisation. But the government's share was lowered to roughly 80 per cent after nationalisation. It remained stable at that level until 1992, but then fell to much lower levels, averaging less than 60 per cent from 1996 to 2000.

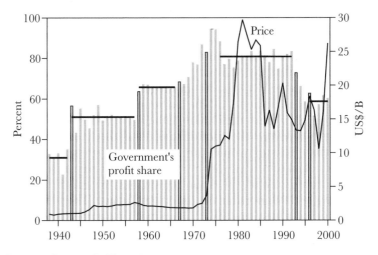

Source: Same as in Fig. 7.8.

Figure 7.11: Venezuela Fiscal Revenue as a Profit Share 1938–2000

Nationalisation

In December 1973, the international oil companies agreed to their nationalisation. In March 1974, President Carlos Andrés Pérez appointed an all-party Committee that included representatives of trade unions, the private sector, and professional associations of lawyers and economists. The Presidential Committee was not only in charge of drafting a Nationalisation Law but also of elaborating the organisational structure of the nationalised industry. A Petroleum Nationalisation Law (PNL)[17] was passed in 1975, and PDV was created the next day. The vesting day was 1 January 1976.

The national oil company was subject to the same fiscal structure as the concessionaires before them. However, royalty rates were levelled to one sixth. The income tax rate, which had gone up to 72 per cent in 1975, was lowered to 67.7 per cent, and 10 per cent of export profits were free from income tax to endow the company with the resources for the development of the national petroleum industry. Also taking into account an investment allowance of 2 per cent, this 67.7 per cent effectively came down to 59 per cent.[18] Income taxation continued to be based on fiscal export values, though these values were also lowered. As a result, the government's share, as compared with the years prior to nationalisation, fell significantly (Figs. 7.10 and 7.11). PDV was generously funded. By 1982 the company had already accumulated an investment fund of over five billion dollars.

However, the Venezuelan managers of the industry had opposed nationalisation until the last moment, and only accepted it because they had no choice. They then began intensive lobbying to prevent the 'politicisation' of the industry. They argued that disaster would threaten if the high standards of efficiency of private enterprise could not be maintained. This, and the continuity of operation, could best be guaranteed by preserving as far as possible the existing structure. The Petroleum Nationalisation Law and its implementation responded to their

---

17. Its official name was *Ley Orgánica que Reserva al Estado la Industria y el Comercio de los Hidrocarburos.*
18. We can safely ignore the domestic market as virtually all profits stem from exports.

claims. The government would only control PDV, the holding company, the President of the country appointing the eleven members of the directorate. The Minister of Energy and Mines has no say in these appointments, though he presides over the shareholder meeting. But they all are peers, equally appointed by the President. PDV was conceived as a public limited company with the state as its sole shareholder. Its affiliates maintained the original structure of the concessionaires, operating the same areas, exercising the same activities, and with the same personnel apart from the foreigners at the highest levels of management, who were replaced by their Venezuelan deputies. Only the smallest companies were dissolved and absorbed by others. This resulted in fourteen affiliates. Furthermore, *Corporación Venezolana de Petróleo* (CVP), the national oil company founded in 1960, directly controlled by the Ministry and once supposed to play a crucial role with the reversion of the concessions, was also dissolved and absorbed by one of these successor companies of the former concessionaires.

The formal set up of nationalisation weakened the Ministry of Energy and Mines (MEM) institutionally. Perhaps more importantly, nationalisation also weakened the Ministry politically. MEM no longer had to deal with foreign con-cessionaires but with a national oil company. Until then the cause of the natural resource owner had been the national cause, whereas the cause of the producing companies and consumers had been a foreign one. This difference became blurred with nationalisation. The nationalised industry had won privileged access to *Miraflores*[19] and, by the same token, to the political parties and the media. It was thus enabled to make its case, and it was no longer a foreign case. Discounts on market prices could now be seen in a different light, a strategy to conquer markets for truly Venezuelan oil. Similarly, whatever hampered the free flow of investment could be seen as an obstruction to the development of the national oil company and, ultimately, to national development generally. No longer were foreign companies and consumers to be blamed for submitting Venezuelan oil to their strategies of prices and volumes; instead, OPEC could be blamed.

---

19. *Miraflores* is the Presidential Palace.

Nationalisation in Venezuela weakened the landlord state. How much so, remained to be seen. On the one hand, there was the political leadership of the country, from the two parties on which the political system was based, Acción Democrática (AD) and Christian Democrats (Copei). They were committed to use the abundant flow of fiscal oil revenues to speed up the development of the country. On the other hand, there was the question of loyalty of the old and new management of the industry. The latter, a handful of PDV directors, came from the ranks of that political leadership.

The governance of nationalisation was to be tested soon. In February 1983, the country had gone from boom to bust, from an abundance of foreign exchange to a currency and foreign debt crisis. Months earlier, in a last minute effort to contain the developing crisis, the government fell back on PDV's investment fund, which until then was deposited in American banks. The company was ordered to transfer the money to the Central Bank, where it subsequently fell prey to devaluation. At the same time, extremely high prices led to sharply falling demand and ever more restrictive OPEC quotas. The management of PDV was faced with a worst-case scenario: the crippling of the national oil industry in order to maximise fiscal revenues, which ultimately were simply squandered. At that point the PDV leadership took the fateful decision never to hold cash again and to spend the money before the government could levy taxes on it. Though the company would always claim that by doing so it was maximising profits, this was never the case. The problem with profits was that they would still end up in the coffers of the government. PDV only maximised activities, expanding in real terms, maximising volume, turnover and sales in all phases of the industry both at a national and an international level. In practice, the company engaged in a long-term fiscal revenue minimising strategy.

PDV developed its own agenda. Though it was initially a hidden one, it became more open and more daring the more the country weakened and fell apart during the next fifteen years. During these years the company integrated slowly but steadily into one enterprise with a strong *esprit de corps*. The affiliates disappeared, the company being restructured according to its activities (exploration and production, refining, transportation, etc). By 1998, PDV came close to fully implementing its agenda, taking over the administration of the natural resource, displacing MEM and defying the OPEC quota. But then world petroleum markets broke down again, and this time PDV was to blame, not the Ministry or OPEC.

Fiscal Export Values and Prices. The system of fiscal export values in place at the time of nationalisation had evolved out of tax reference prices. With rising market prices, the 'tax reference prices' were no longer applied to the domestic market but to exports. In 1970, they were renamed accordingly. At the same time Congress enabled the government to set them at whatever level it deemed appropriate. After 1974, they were set at a level consistent with market prices as determined by OPEC, plus a mark-up, which, at the time of nationalisation, was over 25 per cent. Its level was set with a residual profit in mind, a profit of, say, US\$ 1.25 per barrel. Moreover, one has to keep in mind that royalty payments were also based on conventional prices. Hence, the leeway the company had in order to compete in the market was limited to its costs and its profit margin. The fiscal take was for all practical purposes a fixed ground rent per barrel.

The government loosened its grip after nationalisation. In 1977, it roughly halved the mark-up. But with the second price shock it was restored to former levels though, at the same time, the conventional price for royalty oil was frozen (see Fig. 7.10). But then, in 1981, with demand flagging due to high prices, PDV argued that it needed more commercial freedom in order to be able to defend its market share. PDV also lobbied Congress to cap the discretionary power of the government regarding fiscal export values. Congress indeed limited the mark-up to a maximum of 30 per cent for the year 1982, 25 per cent for the years 1983 to 1985, and to 20 per cent for 1986 and thereafter. What is more, these maximum rates were to be based on 'the income for sales as declared by the taxpayer' (*Gaceta Oficial*, No. 2894 Extraordinaria, 23-12-1981), i.e. by PDV. Since the government continued to stick to these maxima, the national oil company was effectively enabled to grant discounts which, in the first place, would entail lower fiscal revenues (about 80 per cent), and only in the second place lower profits (about 20 per cent). MEM was losing its fiscal control over prices. In 1984, it abandoned the system of fiscal export values, according to which it had set reference prices for every single crude and product. Fiscal export values came down to one 'fiscal export value': a percentage, the mark-up on prices set by PDV. The same applied to royalty oil, as in 1986 – after the price collapse – the conventional price was equated to market price, as declared by the national oil company.

But there was no reason for mistrust: PDV was not an integrated company which could manipulate transfer prices in order to minimise its fiscal liabilities. This, however, was about to change, once the company had decided never to hold cash again. Where could the money be spent at a time when production was cut? As it could not be spent inside the country, it had to be spent outside. The answer was PDV's internationalisation policy. In 1983 the company bought its first participation in a foreign refinery, from Veba Oel in Germany. At the time the company argued that this refinery would provide a market for Venezuela's heavy crude, which was otherwise difficult to place. As a matter of fact Veba Oel never processed Venezuelan heavy crude; instead, PDV used this refinery to place its lighter crude, which was easy to market anyway. But the point was that it sold this crude to itself, at a discount averaging over two dollars per barrel (Guevara 1983).

Celestino Armas and Rafael Guevara from Acción Democrática, then in opposition, became aware of PDV's transfer pricing, and raised the alarm in Congress. As a consequence the following AD government brought PDV's internationalisation policy effectively to a halt. But in 1986, in the midst of the breakdown of world petroleum markets the panicking government again allowed PDV to go ahead in order to conquer and secure markets. Though OPEC no longer pretended to set prices, it restored quotas soon after the debacle. PDV now carried on with its internationalisation policy concentrating mainly on the US market, where the company operates under the name of Citgo. It bought systematically into refineries signing long-term supply contracts, granting substantial discounts to its affiliates, and thus effectively transferring significant portions of its profits abroad.

In 1989, another AD government followed, headed again by Carlos Andrés Pérez. He appointed Celestino Armas Minister of Energy and Mines and Rafael Guevara Vice-minister. Together they tried again to bring PDV's internationalisation policy to a halt. As it turned out, PDV was by then strong enough openly to defy even President Pérez. It bought the remaining half of Citgo's Lake Charles refinery, having bought the first half in 1986. President Pérez opposed the deal. But PDV had its way by claiming the exceptional circumstances that Southland was about to sell its share to an unsatisfactory partner, and promising it would retain the second half only for the time necessary to find a satisfactory buyer. After two years President Pérez personally, as a last resort, ordered the company to sell. PDV dragged its feet. Even if Pérez had not been impeached in 1993, he would have been out of office long before the refinery could have been sold. In fact, in order to fend off any future intention of the government in that direction and to circumvent its financial restrictions, PDV began to use its long-term supply contracts as collateral for foreign loans. Thus, the transferred profits were conclusively put out of the reach of the government in Caracas, since to cancel the long-term supply contracts even with 100 per cent owned subsidiaries of PDV would still first require cancellation of all the foreign debts of the company. Currently these debts are approaching ten billion dollars. This set-up explains the unchecked growth of PDV's international refinery network, at present about two million b/d, and its expansion into the retail business, with over 14,000 gasoline stations in the United States. In the second half of the 1990s, PDV was transferring on average about half a billion dollars annually from PDV Caracas to its foreign affiliates (Boué 2002).[20] Nor had the foreign affiliates ever paid dividends to the holding company in Caracas, but that, of course, was not the point of the exercise; payment of dividends was, anyway, legally linked to paying the debts first.

Oil Opening (Apertura)

On the brink of insolvency, the incoming Pérez government had to submit to an IMF adjustment-programme and World Bank-ordained reforms in 1989. Part of this was an increase in

---

20. The graphs presented above do not capture the effect of transfer pricing.

taxation on the downstream in the domestic market, a first tactical step in preparing the country for a decrease in taxation in the upstream. Opening the economy involved also, and most importantly, the privatisation of state enterprises. In the oil sector, however, outright privatisation was not the top priority, though the return of private investors certainly was. The international companies and the consuming countries were primarily concerned to dismantle the political and institutional framework that had led to nationalisation in the first place.

In 1990, President Pérez appointed Andrés Sosa Pietri President of PDV. Belonging to one of the most distinguished families in Caracas, an entrepreneur and ex-Senator, he soon told the whole world about his convictions – a radical break with the traditional discretion of PDV executives – which happened to be in line with non-proprietorial governance, even in its idiomatic expressions. Sosa did not believe that MEM and OPEC had ever been important players in world petroleum. He believed that the price increases in the 1970s had been coincidental, as had been all past achievements of Venezuelan oil politics. The role of the Minister in the shareholders' meeting was to do 'nothing but to moderate its sessions' (Sosa Pietri 1993: 65). OPEC was nothing but a myth (Sosa Pietri 1993: 90). If the Organisation were to be maintained, it should be converted into a research centre co-operating with IEA. Anyway, his preference was for Venezuela leaving OPEC and joining IEA (Sosa Pietri 1994). To shake off state intervention, Sosa wanted to bring in private investors, transforming PDV into a private company by placing shares on national and, preferably, international stock exchanges. Thus 'the company would regain its autonomy, and the state would be obliged to apply to the company a tax rate more appropriate to an industrial concern that wants to attract private investors' (Sosa Pietri 1993: 79). He drew up an ambitious plan to transform PDV from a *national oil* company into a *global energy* company.

Under his leadership the company came out into the open, defying the political leadership and assuming a high-profile public presence. This profile was decisively enhanced, nationally and internationally, by the fact that the government put the company in charge of dealing with private investors, which were about to be allowed in again. According to Art. 5 of the

Petroleum Nationalisation Law, there were two options, namely operating agreements or associations. The first form was supposed to be quite modest in its reach, purely technical in nature 'without affecting the essence of the reserved activities'. The second form was much more far reaching though limited to 'special cases' (PNL 1975: Art. 5). Associations were subject to the approval by Congress, but operating agreements were not.

In 1990, PDV affiliate Lagoven was negotiating an association agreement to produce and export liquefied natural gas. It agreed with its associates – Exxon, Shell, and Mitsubishi – that it would consult the Supreme Court in order to obtain a 'pronouncement with respect to the supremacy of the 1975 Nationalisation Law' (Lagoven 1993: F-3). Lagoven further requested the Supreme Court to repeal Art. 3 of the 1967 Hydrocarbon Law, which was the only new article in the otherwise unmodified 1943 Hydrocarbon Law. It dealt with the different kinds of agreements which CVP, the first national oil company founded in 1960, would be allowed to enter into with private investors.[21] It was very clear on one point: the fact that the state-owned company that entered into a contractual relationship with private parties would not impinge upon the sovereign rights of the state. Such contracts would still be subject to sovereign taxation and the Calvo clause, and even disputes between the associates had to be settled in Venezuelan courts. The basic outlines of any agreement had to be approved by Congress, and the final agreement had to be published in the Official Gazette. In economic terms, these new kinds of agreements had to be more advantageous to the Nation than a concession, and their term was shortened from 40 to 30 years maximum. It was up to CVP to negotiate the actual contracts.[22]

The Supreme Court in its 1990 Ruling answered positively to Lagoven's request, arguing that with nationalisation and Art. 5 of the 1975 Petroleum Nationalisation Law 'a totally new general norm' (Corte Suprema de Justicia, 23 April 1991) had

---

21. This article was actually an important precedent for OPEC Res. XVII.90. The Secretary General of OPEC at the time the latter was drawn up was Francisco Parra, a Venezuelan. About the role of Parra see Skeet (1988: 49 ff).

22. Five so-called Service Contracts were awarded in 1971.

been created, an entirely fresh start that invalidated previous laws and regulations that had departed from the concession system. Thus, with one stroke of the pen, the ground under the old proprietorial governance was cut away. The only specific legal basis for a contractual development of association agreements was now Art. 5 of the Petroleum Nationalisation Law, which had been the only controversial article in this law. President Pérez introduced it into the PNL by request of the private sector, and against the vote of all other members of the Presidential Committee. Its text now had to be read on a stand-alone basis: it simply authorised PDV to enter into association agreements with private entities, in all the reserved activities, for a definite term and maintaining a participation that guaranteed the control of the state.

As a next move, in 1991 PDV submitted to MEM and to the Committee of Energy and Mines of Congress a draft for operating agreements, which would be used for marginal fields. The draft of this so-called operating services agreement was accompanied by expert opinions from outstanding Venezuelan lawyers and law firms. They unanimously agreed that this was, indeed, an operating agreement in line with Art. 5 of the PNL. Their verdicts were essentially based on the criterion that the private companies would be paid for their services, the oil produced remaining at any time the property of PDV. But what is the difference between paying a service fee for a barrel of oil or buying one? As these contracts were to last for twenty years – an extension may be granted at any time – there had to be a deflator. In a service contract one would expect the deflator to relate to costs and to input, not to output. In the PDV draft the deflator was the Special Index for Energy of the Consumer Price Index for all Urban Consumers in the United States, which obviously correlates closely to oil prices, i.e. to output and not to input.[23] The draft agreement was essentially an arrangement whereby oil was produced and sold to PDV at a discount, out of which PDV – not the private investors – would have to pay rents and royalties. Indeed, the private investors were classified as service providers and not as oil producers and, therefore, operating services agreements were only subject to non-oil

---

23. For a detailed legal analysis see Vallenilla (1995).

taxation. Basically, this meant an income tax of 34 per cent. PDV assumed the role of an umbrella protecting the private producers from hydrocarbon taxation, which was the object of the exercise.

PDV was given the go-ahead. Thus, on legal grounds at least non-proprietorial governance had advanced fast without meeting resistance. All expert opinions and law firms were paid by PDV. Indeed, the legal department of the Ministry had been dismantled after nationalisation. It never crossed the mind of the political leadership at the time that the national property rights over the natural resource could be put in jeopardy by the national oil company. Hence, PDV's strategy to subvert the legal and institutional framework through reinterpretation, appealing to Venezuelan courts, was bound to be a success. There was simply nobody representing the cause of the natural resource owner. For this very reason, however, nobody ever objected to the judge of the Supreme Court in charge of writing the Ruling quoted above, Román J. Duque Corredor, who was for many years a lawyer employed by PDV. As such he had already claimed, in 1978, not only that Art. 3 but the entire 1967 Law of Hydrocarbon had been repealed by the PNL (Duque Corredor 1978: 11). He left the Supreme Court just in time also to be amongst those experts who supported PDV's draft of an Operating Services Agreement.

Outline of Contractual Development. The first upstream contracts were operating services agreements. In 2000, there were 36 of them, covering an area of no less than 48 thousand km^2, producing about 500 thousand b/d. In different bidding rounds the pretence of dealing with operating services agreements was gradually given up. In the first contracts, in 1992, the reservoirs were still defined in three dimensions. In 1993, they were being defined in two dimensions, i.e. by the surface covering them, thus authorising the companies to explore deeper strata. Finally, in 1997, large surrounding areas were incorporated and full-scale concessions were granted. Similarly, the private companies were progressively allowed to market their oil, even though the contracts were still labelled operating services agreements and PDV continued to play its role as an umbrella in the context of the fiscal regime.

However, the legal basis of operating services agreements was relatively weak since only the Committee of Energy and Mines had approved them, not Congress. Association agreements approved by Congress would provide for a more solid legal underpinning. As a first step, in 1993 PDV asked Congress to approve guidelines or principles regarding three associations; one was the liquefied natural gas project and the other two were projects to produce and upgrade extra-heavy crude. It was proposed that these kinds of associations were to be moved from the hydrocarbon section of the Income Tax Law to the non-hydrocarbon section. Hence, they too would benefit from an income tax rate of 34 per cent, and they would not be subject to the fiscal export value. As it happened, at that time President Pérez had just been impeached, and PDV seized the opportunity to ask for more: to phase out the fiscal export value over the next three years.

PDV also wanted Congress to endorse its role as a hostage in these association agreements, which would include a so-called stabilisation clause permitting the national oil company to compensate the foreign shareholders for losses in its patrimony 'caused by decisions taken by national, provincial or local administrative authorities, or by changes in legislation implying an unjust discriminatory treatment of the Company or of those shareholders' (*Gaceta Oficial* 9-9-1993). This clause was intended to emasculate the taxing authority. According to Johnston, an international American consultant, it was still 'hard to imagine that a government body such as a parliament or a congress would effectively cede its authority to the national oil company'. Aware of recent pressure in international oil, he expressed his belief that it was 'unlikely that such clauses will flourish' (Johnston 1994: 171). Venezuela proved him wrong.

Regarding the legal mandate of a controlling interest for the state, PDV suggested that a minority share would be enough, provided that PDV retained a veto-right regarding certain decisions, while the possibility that PDV would ever acquire a majority share was explicitly ruled out. Last but not least, though disputes would be settled according to Venezuelan law, the private companies – not PDV – would be free to choose the court of their preference, either Venezuelan courts or international arbitration tribunals. PDV would also give up its privilege as a public company. Its international downstream assets and, most importantly, the oil exported – royalty oil included – would therefore be open to sequestration.

International arbitration was the most disputed point in this process. Shell took the lead. The first operating services agreements were subject to national arbitration, which Shell did not consider satisfactory. At that time the trade press still accepted that in Venezuela international arbitration would be 'totally unconstitutional'. If the government succumbed to Shell's demands 'there will be a nationalistic uproar in Congress that could cut short the Pérez presidency' (Kielmas 1992: 16). Similarly, Johnston in his book expressed the opinion that 'the Venezuelan Constitution required that any contract disputes involving the public interest be resolved exclusively in Venezuelan courts. With that in mind, it would be difficult or foolish to draft an arbitration clause in a petroleum contract that places the venue for arbitration outside of Venezuela' (Johnston 1994: 153). Anyway, in early 1993, the government 'succumbed' to Shell's demands and, indeed, Pérez's presidency was cut short one month later, albeit for very different reasons. Congress agreed to PDV's guidelines and demands after a debate lasting a few weeks.

Still, this did not make international arbitration constitutional. To strengthen further the new non-proprietorial governance structure, international treaties followed. Since 1996, upstream contracts of whatever kind – operating services agreements or association agreements – included a clause acknowledging 'the applicability of any international treaty relating to the mutual protection of investments, to which both Venezuela and any country of which the Investor is a national, may now be or hereafter become parties' (Profit Sharing Agreements 1996: Art. 25.5). At that time the Venezuelan government was negotiating BITs with Canada and the United States. The Venezuelan-Canadian BIT was ratified by the Caldera government and signed into law by President Chávez. Yet the even more far-reaching US-Venezuelan BIT met with strong resistance, and the Caldera government suspended the negotiations.

Fiscal Regime. For some marginal fields handed over to private investors PDV negotiated a 1 per cent royalty rate with MEM, though the majority were subject to the usual rate of one sixth. PDV argued that those marginal fields would otherwise not be profitable. The company advanced the same argument regarding the associations in liquefying natural gas and in processing extra-heavy oil. Regarding the latter, Congress approved one association in Orimulsión, and four in syncrude. Orimulsión is a mixture of extra-heavy crude with water, in a proportion of 70:30, plus an emulsifier. This mixture can be burned as a kind of 'liquid coal' in power stations, replacing fuel oil in response to the IEA programme quoted above. The extra-heavy crude pays formally a royalty of one sixth, but on the basis of a net-back price related to coal which, over the last years, has been more or less constant at US$/b 0.68. Thus, the royalty per barrel has been about US$ 0.11. Syncrude is a partially refined and upgraded extra-heavy oil, which is then exported to be refined further, just like conventional crude. In this case the barrel of extra-heavy oil is priced more or less in line with crude oil, but for the first nine years there is only a 1 per cent royalty, which will increase to one sixth thereafter.

Hostility to royalty, however, was a matter of principle. In 1996 ten promising areas of conventional oil, totalling 18 thousand km^2, were auctioned off under the contractual framework of so-called profit-sharing agreements. Not only were they subject to an income tax rate of 67.7 per cent but they were also subject to a profit-sharing scheme of up to 50 per cent. The combined marginal income tax rate was thus as high as 84 per cent. The royalty rate was set at 1 per cent, to increase to one sixth as a function of the internal rate of return.[24] At that time PDV's chief economist was already campaigning to scrap royalty completely, and to rely exclusively on excess profit taxation through higher income tax rates (Espinasa 1999).

The proprietorial fiscal regime was on the verge of being completely replaced by a non-proprietorial one. Moreover, in 1989 PDV switched to worldwide accounting, which allowed

---

24. This bidding round was designed with a long-term strategy in mind. The first step was to transform a flat royalty in an excess profit levy, combined with very high excess profit tax rates. Later the government will be convinced that these rates are far too high and, therefore, have to be renegotiated. Regarding 'tactical overbidding' see Hawley, Bramley and Castellani (1994).

the company to charge all kinds of costs related to its internationalisation policy against its income tax liabilities in Caracas. Most importantly, amongst them were the financial costs of that policy, i.e. the service of its multi-billion foreign debts. As already mentioned, in 1993 Congress phased out the fiscal export value. However, equally important but less visible, PDV also succeeded in introducing into the new Income Tax Law very generous adjustments and allowances for inflation.

Fiscal Revenue. We can now have a new look at Fig. 7.10. Fiscal revenue, from 1976 to 1992, averaged 66 per cent of PDV's gross income, but only 37 per cent – excluding dividends – from 1996, the first year the fiscal export value had disappeared completely, up to 2000. This fall of 29 percentage points was caused by three factors. First and most evidently, it was due to the disappearance of the fiscal export value, which, other things being equal, represented a fall of eleven percentage points. Increasing costs explain nine percentage points. Outstanding amongst the cost increases were the operating services agreements and the financial costs of internationalisation. Regarding operating services agreements, the real average cost to the producing companies was probably not higher than the average cost of PDV, but the price PDV paid for that oil was, and this price appeared in its accounts as a cost.[25] The remaining nine percentage points are to be explained by the generous adjustments and allowances granted by the 1993 Income Tax Law. Indeed, the effective tax rate of PDV fell from an average of 59 per cent between 1976 and 1992, to 37 per cent from 1993 to 2000.

Not surprisingly, as soon as the fiscal export value had disappeared, desperate governments tried to claw back part of their losses through dividends, a mechanism they had never used before. They only managed to recover some nine

---

25. In one case at least detailed data is available. Benton Oil & Gas Company produced between 1993 and 1999, on average, 26 thousand b/d at an operating cost per barrel of US$ 2.42, which is virtually the same as for PDV's own production. However, PDV paid on average US$ 9.23 per barrel to Benton Oil & Gas, and profits of this company are only subject to non-oil taxation. (Benton Oil & Gas Company 10K Report to the Security Exchange Commission, 2000)

percentage points, increasing the average from 37 per cent to 46 per cent, but still losing twenty percentage points compared with the average prior to 1993. There is an important difference between the fiscal export value and dividend. The first was paid monthly, based on estimated prices and subject to subsequent minor correction. Dividend is paid more than one year later, only after net profits have been assessed. Thus PDV obtained leeway to spend first and to leverage its future income streams.

Private investors in association with PDV have again become major producers in Venezuela. At present, about 25 per cent of the total is produced in these kinds of associations. Operating services agreements are accounted for by PDV and thus included in Fig. 7.10. The first associations in producing and upgrading extra-heavy oil only started production in 2001. Their fiscal regime will reinforce the trend of falling fiscal revenues. The profit-sharing agreements will make no difference. On the one hand, their exploratory success has so far been disappointing and, on the other, their fiscal regime grants maximum opportunity to bring effective tax rates down and, ultimately, to force renegotiation upon the government.

OPEC Quota

Part of PDV's agenda, no longer a hidden one, was to produce at full capacity and expand fast. Accordingly, output grew from 1.9 million b/d in 1990 to 3.3 million b/d in 1997. Though Minister Armas ordered PDV to stick to the OPEC quota, things began to change in August 1990 with the Iraqi invasion of Kuwait. For the first time since its foundation OPEC was not in a position to exploit an emergency in world petroleum markets. The Arab Gulf states, and Saudi Arabia in particular, were willing to supply whatever they were able. Venezuela, too, began to produce at full capacity. PDV continued to do so even when the emergency was over. Indeed, PDV seized the opportunity of President Pérez' impeachment to take over national oil policy. In 1997 the country exceeded its quota by some 900 thousand b/d, and PDV boasted publicly about never again cutting a single barrel, even though since 1995 all operating services agreements and association agreements, with one exception, have included a clause that allows for curtailment of production, subject to international treaty commitments of the country and limited to the national average.

The exception was the only association agreement in Orimulsión. Since the 1980s PDV has focused on the Orinoco Oil Belt, the huge reservoir of extra-heavy crude, to get around OPEC quotas. The company argued that the extra-heavy crude was not crude at all; this is technically correct, as it is not a liquid at normal temperatures and, therefore, it could be classified as bitumen. Thus, it should not be subject to OPEC quotas, which apply only to crude oil. The government accepted this argument regarding Orimulsión. At present PDV transforms about 70 thousand b/d of extra-heavy crude into 100 thousand b/d of Orimulsión, which is not included in its OPEC quota. It is expected that the production of Orimulsión will soon increase sharply. Yet the government did not accept the same argument regarding the production of syncrude, which is formally subject to OPEC quota. In practice, however, this is irrelevant since the volumes of syncrude are tied to the financing of these multi-billion dollar projects. By the end of the year 2001, about 240 thousand b/d of extra-heavy crude will be upgraded to 208 thousand b/d of syncrude. By 2005, the four projects will have been completed, producing about 570 thousand b/d of syncrude from 650 thousand b/d of extra-heavy crude. These volumes, too, are expected to increase again after 2005.

Extra-heavy oil production, therefore, began to be important, too important to be ignored by OPEC. Pressure against the OPEC quota was building up, since including extra-heavy oil in Venezuela's OPEC quota would mean displacing highly taxed conventional crude from PDV's own production. The loss in fiscal revenues, at present price levels, could be as high as ten dollars per barrel. The rush into the Orinoco Oil Belt, which started from the argument that it was not subject to OPEC quota, could be interpreted as a mechanism to force Venezuela into leaving the organisation.

Outlook

The year 1997 was the heyday of the *Oil Opening*. Internationally, Luis Giusti, President of PDV, was honoured with the 'Petroleum Executive of the Year Award', which was handed over to him in London by the previous recipient, John Browne, chief executive of British Petroleum. Nationally, the company was playing a high-profile political role, and its leadership was convinced that the time had come fully to implement its liberal – i.e. non-proprietorial – agenda, which ultimately would involve the privatisation of the PDV affiliates. To clear the way, in 1997 the association agreement in syncrude, *Cerro Negro* (Lagoven, Mobil, and Veba), included a clause that specified the conditions under which the PDV affiliate could be released from its role as a hostage: *if* Lagoven reduced its initial participation of 41.67 per cent to less than 12.5 per cent, *or* if at least 50.1 per cent of Lagoven itself was privatised.

In 1998, however, came the most serious breakdown of the world petroleum markets in over fifty years, made worse by PDV's performance and provocative public declarations. Even the formidable and all-pervasive public relations machinery of PDV could not convince the country that falling prices were good news. The outgoing Caldera government, in a sudden *volte-face*, agreed with OPEC to institute substantial cuts in production.

In February 1998, a year of general elections, it seemed likely that the independent candidate Irene Saenz would win the elections, and that PDV would play a central role in her government. The military coup-leader from February 1992, Hugo Chávez, was also a candidate, although opinion polls gave him only a few percentage points. But Chávez moved as inexorably upwards in the opinion polls as world petroleum prices moved downwards. Supported by the small political groups which had opposed PDV's liberal oil policy, his victory in December that year brought the implementation of the new non-proprietorial governance at least temporarily to a halt.

Chávez put MEM in the hands of Alí Rodríguez Araque and Álvaro Silva Calderón, who had both opposed PDV's liberal policy for many years. Venezuela became again an active member of OPEC. In 2000 the country hosted the second OPEC head-of-states meeting. Prices recovered beyond expectations. However, prices were only one aspect of the problem. The other was much more difficult: to arrest and to reverse the trend towards non-proprietorial governance. A first test was the new Constitution (known as the Bolivarian Constitution). It establishes in Art. 303 that PDV, the *holding* company, cannot be privatised, but PDV *affiliates* can. PDV, the holding company, does not produce a single barrel of oil. Thus, another piece of the jigsaw has been put in place, at the completion of which – if the trend continues – PDV will have been transformed into the new licensing agency, replacing MEM.

MEM, however, no longer accepted transfer prices for royalty payments, and PDV was obliged to pay according to open market prices. But MEM has failed so far to stop the pricing of extra-heavy oil in line with coal in the case of Orimulsión, as President Chávez gave his personal and widely publicised backing to its production. Moreover, the Ministry of Finance continues to accept the discounts regarding income taxes. MEM, however, succeeded in stopping a bidding round for natural gas that was being prepared by PDV. It went ahead, under the control of the Ministry, but only after the enactment of a new Natural Gas Law, which established a minimum royalty rate of 20 per cent. Royalty rates were used as bidding parameters and in the auction, held in June 2001, rates as high as 32.5 per cent were offered. Moreover, in November 2000 the National Assembly enabled the government to reform by decree the existing legal framework for hydrocarbons over the next twelve months. The new Hydrocarbon Law, promulgated in November 2001, establishes a minimum royalty rate of 30 per cent for liquid hydrocarbons, though this rate may be lowered, at the discretion of the government, to 20 per cent, and even to one sixth in the case of extra-heavy crude used to produce Orimulsión; but the rate of 30 per cent can also be restored at any time. The Law also reserves to the state a majority shareholding in any upstream contract. Last but not least, the new Hydrocarbon Law requires a separate accounting for upstream and downstream activities. Though the 30 per cent royalty rate will only apply to new licences, concessions or contracts, and not to the existing ones, it will apply to PDV. On the other hand, however, PDV continues to stick to its traditional policy that, whenever OPEC quota limits the possibilities for spending money within Venezuela, it increases its spending outside. The company continues to expand internationally into the refining and retail business.

There is one politically important aspect of liberal governance we have not mentioned: PDV's aversion towards private national entrepreneurship, whose participation in PDV's bidding rounds was deliberately restricted. Participants, in order to qualify, had to be experienced oil producers. Though the Venezuelan private companies had for many years provided inputs and services to the oil industry which, taken together, covered everything an oil company does, by virtue of the Petroleum Nationalisation Law there was no Venezuelan oil company. But Congress obliged PDV, in the third bidding round for marginal fields in 1997, to reserve the smallest five fields, out of twenty on offer, to private national companies; and MEM designed the recent licensing round in natural gas to encourage and to promote the participation of private national enterprise. At the same time, however, PDV successfully lobbied the Chávez government to resume negotiations for a bilateral investment treaty with the United States. According to the last draft of this treaty, it will reduce the possibility for nationalist oil policies, since it covers not only investment but also procurement and the pre-investment phase. In other words, the draft outlaws any 'buy-Venezuelan' policy by public companies, and the government would no longer be able to give priority to nationals in the granting of concessions or other forms of access to the oil reservoirs. The only trace of nationalism still to be found in the draft is that if PDV (or any other public company) is privatised, Venezuelan nationals may enjoy preferential rights in the purchasing of shares.

7.4 Conclusions

In Fig. 7.12 we compare fiscal revenues as a percentage of gross income in the United Kingdom, Alaska and Venezuela. In the United Kingdom, excess profit taxation was highly effective in the early years with sharply increasing prices, and for a few years afterwards, but the non-proprietorial fiscal regime placed the companies in a strong strategic position, economically and politically, to minimise fiscal liabilities thereafter. Since 1993 new fields are no longer subject to any specific petroleum taxation. The United Kingdom set up non-proprietorial governance at a time when it was an oil-importing country, but it remained unchanged when the United Kingdom became an exporting country.

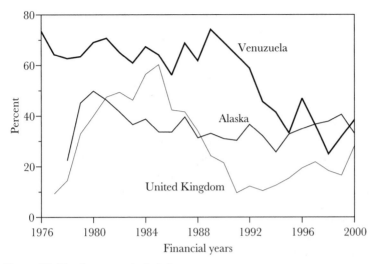

Note: Dividends are not included.

Source: Figs. 7.3, 7.6, 7.10.

Figure 7.12: The UK, Alaska and Venezuela: Fiscal Revenues as Percentage of Gross Income

It is in Alaska that the perception of a business relationship between the natural resource owner and the producing companies is the most deeply rooted. Alaska managed, with the background of the OPEC revolution, to increase its production tax significantly, from 3 to 15 per cent, but the fiscal regime settled down at that point. More recently it has been subject to international pressures to liberalise, but so far the institutional framework has proven to be strong enough to prevent significant change.

For the United States, the governance structure in oil is rooted in private property, and the fact that a state, or the country, is an importer or an exporter is simply irrelevant. This may change as public lands and waters supply an increasing percentage of American oil. Though the United States is still the second biggest oil producer in the world, it became a net importer in 1947, and at present it imports about 60 per cent of its needs. It is thus the biggest oil importer in the world. Due to the development of offshore fields, about 60 per cent of its production now comes from public lands. However, non-proprietorial governance has so far progressed very little.

Finally, in the case of Venezuela, Fig. 7.12 shows the collapse of proprietorial governance in this traditional oil-exporting country, an extraordinary event. The surprising fact is not that the national oil company embraced the liberal, non-proprietorial ideal. This also goes, for example, for Statoil, the Norwegian national oil company, which was partially privatised in 2001. But when Statoil adopted a policy of internationalisation, the government demanded completely separate accounts. Similarly, the Norwegian government followed the British example by scrapping royalties in 1986. At the same time, however, it removed from Statoil a large part of its revenues as the 'State's Direct Financial Interests'. The State's Direct Financial Interests is similar to royalty with the difference that the government proportionally contributes to the costs of production, which are thus tightly controlled. Moreover, the money goes directly to the government, reducing the otherwise disproportionate cash flow of Statoil as the rent-collecting agency. It thus also prevented Statoil from becoming a state within the state. The government firmly controls prices, and has been able efficiently to maintain high income tax rates. The national oil company, of course, has to assist the government technically (Rodríguez 2000; Jiménez 2002). Statoil may finally be privatised completely, but this will not mean the end of proprietorial governance in Norway.

The failure of the Venezuelan government can only be explained by the general breakdown of the country. It failed in its non-oil economic policy and, simultaneously, it failed to set up any reasonable governance structure in oil after nationalisation. Thus it was too weak to hold the line against the well-designed strategy of the developed consuming countries, their international organisations, companies and consultants. The country has literally been torn apart. A similar development is taking place at present in Algeria (Aïssaoui 2001).

Wherever the governments of the exporting countries have managed to keep control of their country, non-proprietorial governance has made little advance, even though they may have readmitted private investors. This is the case, for example, in Iran. Other exporting countries, however, have shown a surprising resistance to re-admit private investors at all, most notably Saudi Arabia[26] and, so far, Mexico.

Wherever non-proprietorial governance prospers in oil-exporting countries, it is a symptom of decay, of a deepening political and economic crisis: political, because of the divisive effect of the foreign intervention; and economic, because the country is impoverished.

---

26. 'The only Gulf country that is not likely to invite companies into upstream oil imminently is Saudi Arabia'. (Mitchell 2001: 57)

8   THE GOVERNANCE OF OIL

8.1   Private Governance

Our study of the governance of oil began with British coal for one fundamental reason: it provides on the one hand a complete, and in many ways unique, example of private mineral governance, and on the other of the transition from private to public governance. It was the best, perhaps only suitable, historical example of private mineral governance that could be compared with US oil. In both cases a customary ground rent emerged from the market for leases, a minimum to be paid on marginal land and on marginal output. At the core of this arrangement we found a customary royalty. Whatever the historical reasons which led to the establishment of any particular customary royalty rate in a mining or petroleum producing region, once in place it proved stable in spite of variations in the economic environment. Hence, economics only defined a broad range of possibilities for the royalty rate, out of which one happened to be taken up in each region. Thereafter a widespread web of contractual, economic and political relations developed and assured its stability.

Private mineral governance in British coal finally collapsed and the deposits were nationalised. It was too rigid. It failed to adapt to technological change and the growing depth of coal mines and, therefore, became increasingly obstructive. Ground rent as such, which remained stable, was not the problem. In any case, the landlords were paid full compensation for their reservoirs. But private governance in US oil was flexible enough to survive. Property rights of natural resource owners were redefined in time to prevent them from becoming too obstructive, but without questioning their right to a ground rent. We concluded that there were basically three reasons why reform succeeded in US oil and failed in British coal. Firstly, there was the technical fact that oil reservoirs are exploited by the sinking of wells, taking advantage of the liquid or even gaseous nature of oil, whereas coal had to be mined underground. Thus, the need for reform in oil, unlike coal, was observable on the surface. As a consequence of the 'rule of capture', wells were drilled on both sides along the boundaries of surface properties, and it was not necessary to be a petroleum engineer or a geologist to understand that this was the absurd consequence of the lack of coincidence between surface and subsoil property rights. In coal the system of tunnels followed an equally absurd pattern, defined by surface property divisions, but this was not obvious to the people on the surface. Secondly, modernising existing infrastructure was much more difficult and costly for coal than for oil. Finally, there was the political fact that in Great Britain the landowners were a distinctive and powerful class, powerful enough to prevent reform for centuries, whereas US landowners in oil were only one pressure group amongst others.

Through comparing British coal with Mexican oil we highlighted the importance of the social and political dimension in mineral governance. In Great Britain the issue was not the governance of all natural resources; coal was a separate and isolated case, and a strictly national one. However, in Mexico the governance of oil developed in the midst of an agrarian revolution and involved international companies: this led to a tangle of social, economic, and political relations – both national and international – far more complicated than those surrounding British coal. Private mineral governance in Mexico threatened, above all, the success of the Revolution. However, out of revolutionary turmoil and international confrontation the sequence of events that developed in Mexico was the same as for British coal: more precisely, the nationalisation of the industry followed that of the natural resource. In both cases, under private mineral governance, an intricate relationship between natural resource and capital ownership had developed, forming a kind of joint organism (like Siamese twins). The hope that at least one of them – private enterprise – would survive their surgical separation was disappointed.

8.2 Public Governance

The stability of private mineral governance is due to the high cost of changes. It is even more costly, economically and politically, to switch from private to public mineral governance. Therefore, in spite of the theoretical advantages of public over private mineral governance, the switch only happens under extraordinary economic and political circumstances. Yet once we move into the realm of public governance of the natural resource, the question of moving back to private governance never arises. Privatisation, when it is promoted, only applies to the industry. It is one of those changes that vested interests may oppose strongly, but, once they happen, the interests completely disappear. Hence, the controversy that may surround public mineral governance is not about *public vs. private* but *non-proprietorial vs. proprietorial* governance and fiscal regimes.

Regarding fiscal regimes public governance is much less stable than its private counterpart as the costs of change are much lower. Thus, for example, in private mineral governance the costs of changing a customary royalty rate is simply prohibitive, as it would require negotiation amongst thousands of lessees and tens of thousands of lessors. Even renegotiating one single contract may be too expensive, and generally there are several royalty owners. Thus, the normal procedure in US oil in place of renegotiation is to abandon the lease and, possibly, to acquire it again under new conditions later. In public mineral governance, however, a customary ground-rent is a legally defined parameter, and though it may be embodied in the concessions or licences granted, there is only one royalty owner, namely the state. Given its eminent domain rights, the cost of raising the general level of ground rent, once the decision has been taken, is almost negligible. But, conversely, from the viewpoint of investors and consumers, it may be worth spending very significant amounts of resource in convincing a government to lower those levels, as the prize to be won may be very large. Hence, the stability of public mineral governance depends not so much on the economy but on the political, legal, and institutional structure of the country.

The United States in this respect provides a borderline case, as its public mineral governance is rooted in private mineral governance. As the latter is losing importance in oil, because so much of it is now produced on public lands (especially offshore), this link is weakening. In Mexico, on the contrary, a stable governance structure in oil only developed after the nationalisation of the industry, which neutralised the political weight of private ownership. Mexico withdrew from world petroleum markets for several decades, but by isolating itself the country was able successfully to focus on its national problems, supplying the domestic market with cheap oil. The experience that led to this result is deeply imprinted in Mexico's memory though, of course, it is encoded, as is usual with collective memory. Thus, 35 years later, after the huge discoveries in the early 1970s and against the background of the 'OPEC revolution', a unique public debate developed around the question of whether Mexico should really become an oil exporter again. Economically, there was no doubt that the benefits would be huge. But politically doubts arose. Would the country not become entangled yet again in international power politics, where its role was likely to be that of the match ball rather than a player?[1] And though Mexico did again become a large oil-exporter, it kept its natural resource closed to private investment, even more radically than other exporting countries which nationalised their oil industries in the 1970s.

8.3 International Governance

Mexico was an exception. In the other oil-exporting countries private mineral ownership never played a significant role. Therefore, from the beginning the oil industry in these countries was based on concessions, and an evolutionary process took place. *National* public mineral ownership on the one hand, and *foreign* companies and consumers on the other, defined the international political and macro-economic dimensions. The international companies and consumers had their own ideas about the role of public mineral ownership, reflecting their experience at home and elsewhere in the world. The most appropriate and acceptable to the exporting countries were those ideas conforming to what we called the 'American reference', which culminated in the fifty-fifty profit-sharing agreements after the Second World War. But whatever the contract terms or the levels of ground-rent and taxes the parties agreed in existing concessions, better terms were always offered in subsequent agreements. The latter were always more favourable to the exporting countries, an unmistakable indicator that the market

---

1.   See Morales, Escalante and Vargas (1988). This debate was important
     enough to attract the attention of a famous Mexican novelist: Carlos
     Fuentes. (Fuentes 1978)

was not in equilibrium. The systematic efforts of the big international oil companies to restrict competition certainly slowed down the upward trend of ground rent, but it failed to curb it. The same applied to their policy to punish collectively countries that took the lead in revising the existing contracts. Nor was the strong economic power of the consuming countries sufficient to deter the governments of the exporting countries from maximising fiscal revenues: the exporting nations had far more to win in oil revenues than to lose through their stance in the rest of their economy. Last but not least, in the context of global decolonisation, the consuming countries were also unable to prevent the exporting countries from becoming independent and sovereign.

Maximising international ground rent in oil culminated with the nationalisation of the concessions of the international companies. This meant that the ties that so far had bound national natural resource owners to international consumers were severed. The international governance of oil broke into two extreme models. In the exporting countries, a sovereign proprietorial governance structure was established. In the consuming countries, the international oil companies were free to join consumers in their effort to develop an – equally sovereign – non-proprietorial governance structure. The only remaining link between national natural resource ownership and international consumers was the world petroleum market, a link far too weak to prevent the abyss between the two parts from deepening.

A strong and committing landlord–tenant relationship was broken up, a relationship that embodied a landlord–consumer relationship by defining the ground rent to be paid. It was replaced with a weak and evasive producer-consumer dialogue.

8.4   Global Oil and Nation States

For the large consuming countries, non-proprietorial governance in oil made a perfect match, nationally and internationally, with the neo-liberal crusade of the 1980s. This was no longer only about natural resource ownership but also about private enterprise. The involvement of the governments of some European consuming countries in some international oil companies as shareholders had lost its *raison d'être* and, accordingly, they sold their shares to private investors. State intervention in oil could now be condemned wholesale. The political and economic environment was nowhere more propitious for liberal governance than in Great Britain. In this new oil-producing country the role of natural resource ownership was completely suppressed. The structure in place guarantees that wherever the issue of natural resource ownership might show signs of returning, the industry will nip it in the bud. In the international oil industry the 'British reference' replaced what we had referred to as the 'American reference'. The latter – a nuisance in a world where natural resource ownership is supposed to play no role at all – has been suppressed from the collective memory.[2] It was now the British reference that laid claim to global validity, and there is no doubt that this claim received a strong backing with the demise of the Soviet Union (a backing similar in strength, but opposite in direction to that which the oil-exporting countries once enjoyed with the demise of colonialism).

The exporting countries also consider the natural resource to be a free gift of nature but only to domestic and not to foreign consumers. The latter have to pay an international ground rent. Furthermore, according to the spirit of the age, these oil revenues are supposed to serve the economic development of the country. However, the economic and political performance of the Third World oil-exporting countries after the OPEC revolution has been rather poor. Having absorbed their high fiscal revenues, most of them ended up incurring foreign debts. They thus became vulnerable to external pressure to re-open the natural resource to private (foreign) investors. Moreover, private investors were to return not only in oil but also as a part of a global package, which also aimed at the non-oil sector. This package was easier to impose on, and also to sell to, the countries with the worst political and economic performance. Moreover, because of the attraction of 'one global economy', this package was appealing to the professional classes

2. An astonishing example amongst academic writers is Susan Strange. In her overview on American oil, in the context of international oil, she replaces – a Freudian slip? – 'leases', 'lessors' and 'lessees' with 'concessions', 'governments' and 'concessionaires'. (Strange 1998: 198)

everywhere, not only in desperate countries. But what about natural resource ownership and territorial states? Modern economic science argues that natural resource ownership has never been important. Similarly, it is now argued that in a global economy territorial states are no longer important (Strange 1998: 238–39).

In the exporting countries, the liberal – i.e. non-proprietorial – agenda is concentrating on the NOCs in its strategy of 'agency capturing'. They have been chosen to become the new non-proprietorial licensing and contracting agencies and to substitute for the traditionally proprietorial Ministries of Petroleum, although they are not the only option since new agencies may be created from scratch. However, since the grafting of non-proprietorial governance onto the oil-exporting countries requires the neutralisation of their defences, this makes NOCs a particularly suitable target. They emerged from the OPEC revolution, which heralded the victory of the landlord states over their international tenants. They are symbols of national pride. But the role that the liberal agenda wants to assign to NOCs does not make sense, either politically or economically, to the exporting countries. In order to ensure the stability of such new arrangements, therefore, requires nothing less than the severing of a significant part of the ruling bureaucracies and political classes from their countries and from their peoples. They will have to be co-opted into the world of international institutions. But this policy creates dangerous and threatening situations for weak oil-exporting countries; it heralds disaster.

L'argent n'a pas de maître is an old saying. With an eye to globalisation, it could easily be rephrased with *Le capital n'a pas de patrie*. But one may even more easily rephrase the old saying *Nulle terre sans seigneur* with *Nulle terre sans souverain*. Peoples, communities of all kinds and of all sizes, are essentially rooted locally, living in a geographical area to which they feel strongly attached, a habitat to which they belong. And peoples, through history, have always claimed sovereign rights on their habitat. Without doubt, others may also claim certain rights to the same territory, even sovereign rights, on the ground that there is one mankind sharing one globe; for instance, nobody has the right to refuse the thirsty access to water. One may also argue that the resource-rich countries have no right to refuse resource-poor countries access to their riches. The modern concern about the environment, global warming and contamination, reminds us in no uncertain terms that mankind is indeed sharing one globe. However, the resource-rich countries have the right to impose conditions on access to their resources and to safeguard their sovereign rights. Short of war, negotiation is the only avenue open to sorting out conflicts over sovereign rights. The conditions that may be agreed will vary widely. We have noted differences even in the oil-importing countries in their attitudes to non-proprietorial governance. Similarly, not all oil-exporting countries subscribe to proprietorial governance. These variations can be accommodated. However, the liberal agenda for oil now goes further. It is a policy according to which the sovereign rights of resource-rich but otherwise poor and weak countries are acknowledged only for their ability to grant access rights to their oil reservoirs, since only sovereigns can grant this kind of rights and from that there is no escape. But, once granted, they are to be stripped of their eminent domain rights, as previously happened in colonial times, even if the legal and institutional backing of today is a much more sophisticated structure than that of the imperial era.

There remains a possibility that non-proprietorial governance will not prosper beyond the early advances it has already made in some exporting countries. A few years will probably be enough to show the heavy losses in fiscal revenues that non-proprietorial governance will entail for the exporting countries. Lessons may be learned in the future, but at what price?

This book is dedicated to local peoples sovereignly living together on one globe.

REFERENCES

Acosta Hermoso, Eduardo (1969): *Análisis histórico de la OPEP*, Vol. 1, Mérida: Universidad de Los Andes.

Acosta Hermoso, Eduardo (1971a): *La Comisión Económica de la OPEP*, Caracas: Editorial Arte.

Acosta Hermoso, Eduardo (1971b): *Análisis histórico de la OPEP*, Vol. 2, Caracas.

Adelman, Morris A. (1972): *The World Petroleum Market*, Baltimore: The Johns Hopkins University Press.

Adelman, Morris A. (1964a): 'The World Oil Outlook', in Marion Clawson (ed.), *Natural Resources and International Development*.

Adelman, Morris A. (1964b): 'Efficiency of Resource Use in Crude Petroleum', *The Southern Economic Journal*, vol. 31, no. 2, October.

Aïssaoui, Ali (2001): *Algeria – The Political Economy of Oil and Gas*, Oxford: Oxford University Press.

Al-Otaiba, Mana Saeed (1975): *OPEC and the Petroleum Industry*, New York: John Wiley & Sons.

American Petroleum Institute: *Basic Petroleum Data Book*, twice-yearly publication.

Amuzegar, Johangir (1975): 'The Oil Story: Facts Fiction and Fair Play', *Foreign Affairs*, vol. 53, no. 4, July.

Ashworth, William (1986): *1946–1982: The Nationalised Industry*, with the assistance of Mark Pegg. (National Coal Board (Sponsor): *The History of British Coal Industry*, vol. 5).

Baptista, Asdrúbal (1997): *Bases Cuantitativas de la Economía Venezolana 1830–1995*, Caracas: Fundación Polar.

Baptista, Asdrúbal and Bernard Mommer (1987): *El petróleo en el pensamiento económico venezolano - Un ensayo*, Caracas.

Barbosa Cano, Favio (1989): 'Los gobiernos de la revolución mexicana y la industria petrolera 1914–1936', in Herrera Reyes and San Martín Tejedo (eds).

Barrows (1996): *World Fiscal Systems for Oil*, New York.

Berman, Matthew D. (1997): '*Caveat Emptor*: Purchasing Petroleum Industry Investment with Fiscal Incentives', *Journal of Energy Finance & Development*, vol. 2, no. 1, pp. 25–44.

Blair, John (1978): *The Control of Oil*, New York: Vintage Books.

Blaug, Mark (1968): *Economic Theory in Retrospect*, Homewood (Ill.): Richard D. Irwin.

Bohi, Douglas R. and Milton Russell (1978): *Limiting Oil Imports. An Economic History and Analysis*, Baltimore: The Johns Hopkins University Press.

Boué, Juan Carlos (2002): *The Market for Heavy Sour Crude Oil in the US Gulf Coast: The PEMEX/PDVSA Duopoly*, with Liliana Figueroa, Oxford: Oxford Institute for Energy Studies.

Boué, Juan Carlos (1998): *The Political Control of State Oil Companies. A Case Study of the Vertical Integration Programme of Petróleos de Venezuela (1982–95)*, Oxford: D.Phil. thesis.

Boué, Juan Carlos (1993): *Venezuela – The Political Economy of Oil*, Oxford: Oxford University Press.

Bradley Jr., Robert L. (1996): *Oil, Gas & Government – The US Experience*, 2 vols, Cato Institute, Rowman & Littlefield Publishers, Boston.

Bradley, Paul G. (1967): *The Economics of Crude Petroleum Production*, Amsterdam: The North-Holland Publishing Company.

Breton, Hubert (1972): 'Le pétrole libyen au service de l'unité arabe?', *Revue française de science politique*, vol. 22, no. 6, December.

Brown, Jonathan C. (1992): 'The Structure of the Foreign-Owned Petroleum Industry in Mexico, 1880–1938', in Brown and Knight (eds.).

Brown, Jonathan C. and Alan Knight (eds.) (1992): *The Mexican Petroleum Industry in the Twentieth Century*, Austin: University of Texas Press.

Burgoa Orihuela, Ignacio (1989): 'Aspectos fundamentales del régimen constitucional del petróleo en México', in Herrera Reyes and San Martín Tejedo (eds).

Campbell, Duncan R. G. (1963): 'Public Policy Problems of the Domestic Crude Oil Industry: comment', *The American Economic Review*, vol. 54, April.

Cattan, Henry (1967): *The Evolution of Oil Concessions in the Middle East and North Africa*, New York: Dobbs Ferry.

Chamberlain, Kathlin P. (2000): *Under Sacred Ground – A History of Navajo Oil, 1922–1982*, Albuquerque: University of New Mexico Press.

Church, Roy (1986): *Victorian Pre-eminence*, with the assistance of Alan Hall and John Kanefsky. (National Coal Board (Sponsor): *The History of British Coal Industry*, vol. 3).

Collado H., María del Carmen (1987): 'El régimen porfirista y la privatización del subsuelo petrolero', *Secuencia – Revista Americana de Ciencias Sociales*, Mayo–Agosto, Instituto Mora, Mexico.

Davidson, Paul (1963a): 'Public Policy Problems of the Domestic Crude Oil Industry', *The American Economic Review*, vol. 53, March.

Davidson, Paul (1963b): 'Public Policy Problems of the Domestic Crude Oil Industry: A Reply', *The American Economic Review*, vol. 54, April.

De Chazeau, Melvin G. and Alfred Kahn (1959): *Integration and Competition in the Petroleum Industry*, Newhaven: Yale University Press.

De Gortari Rábiela, Rebeca (1989): 'De Carranza a Cárdenas – la política petrolera en México', in Herrera Reyes and San Martín Tejedo (eds.).

De La Vega, Ángel (1999): *La evolución del componente petrolero en el desarrollo y la transición de México*, Mexico: Universidad Nacional Autónoma de México.

Díaz Dufóo, Carlos (1921): *La cuestión del petróleo*, México: Eusebio Gomex de la Puente.

Duclos, Louis-Jean (1972): 'L'épisode de Téhéran', *Revue française de science politique*, vol. 22, no. 6, December.

Duque Corredor, Román J. (1978): *El derecho de la nacionalización petrolera*, Caracas: Ed. Jurídica Venezolana.

ECT/IEA (1998): *Energy Investment*, joint paper by the Energy Charter Secretariat and the International Energy Agency presented to the G8 Energy Ministerial in Moscow, 1 April.

Egaña, Manuel R. (1979): *Venezuela y sus minas*, Caracas: Banco Central de Venezuela.

Egaña, Manuel R. (1949a): 'Instrucciones de los Ministerios de Relaciones Exteriores y de Fomento para los Doctores Edmundo Luongo Cabello, Luis E. Monsanto y Ezequiel Monsalve Casado, miembros de la Comisión Especial que envía Venezuela cerca de los países del Medio Oriente y el Egipto', personal papers.

Egaña, Manuel R. (1949b): Letter from one of the members of the delegation, written in Tehran on 21 October 1949. Personal papers.

Egaña, Manuel R. (1939): *Memoria del Ministerio de Fomento*, Caracas.

El Nacional, 29-12-1973.

El País, 28-12-1946.

El-Sayed, Mustafa (1967): *L'Organisation des Pays Exportateurs de Pétrole*, Paris.

Elwell-Sutton, Laurence Paul (1955): *Persian Oil: A Study in Power Politics*, London: Lawrence and Wishart.

Energy Exploration & Exploitation (2001): 'The UK Government Cancels Royalties on Mature Oilfield', vol. 19, no. 1.

Engler, Robert (1961): *The Politics of Oil*, New York: Macmillan.

España, Luis Pedro (1993): *La industria petrolera y su relación con el Estado Mexicano 1976–89 – una comparación con Venezuela*, Master thesis, Universidad Simón Bolívar.

Espinasa, Ramón (1999): 'El marco fiscal petrolero venezolano: evolución y propuestas', *Revista del Banco Central de Venezuela*, Foros 3; pp. 260–303.

Espinasa, Ramón and Bernard Mommer (1992): 'Venezuelan Oil Policy in the Long Run', James P. Dorian and Fereidun Fesharaki (eds): *International Issues in Energy Policy, Development and Economics*, Boulder (Colorado): Westview Press.

Fine, Ben (1990): *The Coal Question*, London: Routledge.

Flinn, Michael W. (1984): *1799–1830: The Industrial Revolution*, with the assistance of David Stoker. (National Coal Board (Sponsor): *The History of British Coal Industry*, vol. 2).

Fortune, February 1949.

Frank, Helmut J. (1966): *Crude Oil Prices in the Middle East*, New York: Praeger.

Frankel, Paul H. (1946): *Essentials of Petroleum*, London: Frank Cass.

Fuentes, Carlos (1978): *La cabeza de la hidra*, Mexico: Joaquin Mortiz.

Gately, Dermot (1984): 'A Ten Year Retrospective: OPEC and the World Oil Market', *Journal of Economic Literature*, vol. 22, September.

Giddens, Paul H. (1975): *The Early Petroleum Industry*, Philadelphia: Porcupine Press.

Glassmire, S.H. (1938): *Law of Oil and Gas Leases*, 2nd ed. St. Louis: Thomas Law Book Company

Gobierno de México (1940): *El petróleo de México. Recopilación de documentos oficiales del conflicto de orden económico de la industria petrolera, con una introducción que resume sus motivos y consecuencias*, Mexico.

González-Berti, Luis: (1967): *Ley de Hidrocarburos*.

Grimaud, Nicole (1972): 'Le conflit pétrolier franco-algérien', *Revue française de science politique*, vol. 22, no. 6, December.

Guevara, Rafael M. (1983): *Petróleo y ruina. La verdad sobre el contrato firmado entre PDVSA y la Veba Oel A.G.*, Caracas.

Guigou, Jean-Louis (1982): *La rente foncière – Les théories et leur évolution depuis 1650*, Paris: Economica.

Hall, Linda B. (1995): *Oil Banks and Politics. The United States and Postrevolutionary Mexico, 1917–1924*, Austin: University of Texas Press.

Hamilton Charles W. (1962): *Americans and Oil in the Middle East*, Houston: Gulf Pub.

Hamilton, Nora (1982): *The Limits of State Autonomy: Post-Revolutionary Mexico*, Princeton: Princeton University Press.

Hatcher, John (1993): *Before 1700: Towards the Age of Coal*. (National Coal Board (Sponsor): *The History of British Coal Industry*, vol. 1).

Hawley, P. W., A. D. Bramley and J. M. Castellani (1994): 'Competitive Bidding Tactics for New Exploration Concessions', Thomas W. Wälde and George K. Ndi (eds): *International Oil and Gas Investment – Moving Eastward?*, Centre for Petroleum and Mineral Law and Policy, University of Dundee.

Herrera Reyes, Augustín and Lorea San Martín Tejedo (eds.) (1989): *México a cincuenta años de la expropiación petrolera*, Mexico: Universidad Autónoma de México.

Hoopes, Stephanie M. (1997): *Oil Privatisation, Public Choice and International Forces*, London: Macmillan.

Hotelling, Harold (1931): 'The Economics of Exhaustible Resources', *Journal of Political Economy*, April.

International Monetary Fund (2000): *The Impact of Higher Oil Prices on the Global Economy*, Research Department, December 8.

Ise, John (1926): *The United States Oil Policy*, Newhaven: Yale University Press.

Jevons, W. Stanley (1865): *The Coal Question*, reprint Macmillan 1965.

Jiménez, Andrea (2002): *El Régimen Fiscal en la Política Petrolera*, Facultad de Ciencias Económicas y Sociales, Universidad Central de Venezuela, Master thesis.

Jiménez, Andrea (2001): *The World Trade Organisation*, Oxford Institute for Energy Studies, SP 12, August.

Johany, Ali D. (1980): *The Myth of the OPEC Cartel – The Role of Saudi Arabia*, Chichester: John Wiley and Sons.

Johnston, Daniel (1994): *International Petroleum Fiscal Systems and Production Sharing Contracts*, Tulsa (Oklahoma): Pennwell.

Kahn, Alfred A. (1964): 'The Depletion Allowance in the Context of Cartelisation', *The American Economic Review*, vol. 54, June.

Kautsky, Karl (1899): *Die Agrarfrage*, Stuttgart.

Kemp, Alexander G. and Peter D.A. Jones (1997): 'Reforming the Alaskan Petroleum Fiscal System: A Positive Sum Game', *Journal of Energy Finance & Development*, vol. 2, no. 1.

Kemp, Alexander G., Linda Stephen, and Kathleen Masson (1997): *A Reassessment of Petroleum Taxation in the UKCS*, North Sea Study Occasional Paper No. 65, Department of Economics, University of Aberdeen, United Kingdom.

Kielmas, Maria (1992): 'Venezuela – Little Moves Ahead of an Explosion', *Petroleum Economist*, November.

Kissinger, Henry (1999): *Years of Renewal* (*Memoirs*, vol. 3), Simon & Schuster.

Klein, Michael (1999): 'Energy Taxation in the 21st Century', *Oxford Energy Forum*, Issue 40, Oxford Institute for Energy Studies, Oxford, December.

Knight, Alan (1986): *The Mexican Revolution*; vol. 1: *Porfirians, Liberals and Peasants*; vol. 2: *Counter-revolution and Reconstruction*, New York: Cambridge University Press.

Laffont, Jean-Jacques and Jean Tirole (1993): *A Theory of Incentives in Procurement and Regulation*, Cambridge (Mass.), MIT Press.

Lagoven (1993): *Proyecto Cristóbal Colón*, Caracas, March.

Lecuna, Vicente (1975): 'El historiador Vicente Lecuna y nuestra riqueza petrolera', Publication of the Lecuna Foundation, Supplement of the newspaper *El Nacional*, Caracas, 12 March.

Lenczowski, George (1960): *Oil and State in the Middle East*, Ithaca, N.Y.: Cornell University Press.

Lenin, Vladimir I. (1964): *The Agrarian Programme of Social Democracy in the First Russian Revolution, 1905–1907*, Collected Works, vol. 22, Moscow: Progress Publishers.

Lenin, Vladimir I. (1934): *Imperialism the Highest Stage of Capitalism*, London: Martin Lawrence.

Levy, Walter J. (1973): 'An Atlantic-Japanese Energy Policy', *Foreign Policy*, no. 10, Spring.

Lichtblau, John and Diland P. Spriggs (1952): *The Oil Depletion Issue*, New York: Petroleum Industry Research Foundation.

Logsdon, Charles (1997): 'Oil Revenues and the Response of Government to Reserves Depletion – The Alaskan Experience', *Journal of Energy Finance & Development*, vol. 2, no. 1.

Longrigg, Stephen Hemsley (1968): *Oil in the Middle East*, 3rd. ed. London: Oxford University Press.

Lovejoy, Wallace F. and Paul T. Homan (1967): *Economic Aspects of Oil Conservation Regulation*, Baltimore: The Johns Hopkins University Press.

Lutfi, Ashraf (1968): *OPEC Oil*, Beirut: Middle East Research and Publishing Centre.

Mabro, Robert (1991): *A Dialogue between Oil Producers and Consumers – The Why and the How*, Oxford Institute for Energy Studies, June.

Mabro, Robert *et al.* (1986): *The Market for North Sea Crude Oil*, Oxford: Oxford University Press.

Machlup, Fritz (1949): *The Basing Point System*, Philadelphia: The Blakiston Co.

Madelin, Henri (1973): *Pétrole et politique en Méditerranée occidentale*, Paris.

Majone, Giandomenico (1989): *Evidence, Argument and Persuasion in the Policy Process*, Yale University Press.

Mancke, Richard B. (1978): *The Failure of US Energy Policy*, Washington: Columbia University Press.

Márquez, Ángel J. (ed.) (1977): *El Imperialismo petrolero y la revolución venezolana*, vol. 2, *Las ganancias extraordinarias y la soberanía nacional*, Caracas.

Marshall, Alfred (1961): *Principles of Economics*, vol. 1, London: MacMillan.

Martin, Steve (1997): *Tax or Technology? The Revival of UK North Sea Oil Production*, Oxford Institute for Energy Studies, SP8, October.

Marx, Karl (1974): *Theorien über den Mehrwert*; Marx-Engels-Werke, vol. 26.2, Berlin (DDR).

Marx, Karl (1966): *Das Kapital*, Marx-Engels-Werke, vol. 25, Berlin (DDR).

McDonald, Stephen L. (1979): *The Leasing of Federal Lands for Fossil Fuels Production*, Baltimore: The Johns Hopkins University Press.

McDonald, Stephen L. (1971): *Petroleum Conservation in the United States: An Economic Analysis*, Baltimore: Johns Hopkins University Press.

Mead, Walter (1994): 'Towards an Optimal Oil and Gas Leasing System', *The Energy Journal*, vol. 15, no. 4.

Mead, Walter (1993): 'Oil and Gas Leasing Policy Alternatives' in Richard J. Gilbert (ed.), *The Environment of Oil*.

Mejía Alarcón, Pedro E. (1972): *La industria del petróleo en Venezuela*, Caracas: Universidad Central de Venezuela.

Mény, Yves (ed.) (1993): *Les politiques du mimétisme institutionnel – La greffe et le rejet*. Paris: L'Harmattan.

Meyer, Lorenzo and Isidro Morales (1990): *Petróleo y nación - La política petrolera en México (1900–1987)*, Mexico: Fondo de Cultura Económica.

Mikdashi, Zuhayr (1972): *The Community of Oil Exporting Countries*, Ithaca (New York): Cornell University Press.

Mikdashi, Zuhayr (ed.) (1970): *Continuity and Change in the World Oil Industry*, Beirut: Middle East Research and Publishing Centre.

Mikdashi, Zuhayr (1966): *A Financial Analysis of Middle Eastern Oil Concessions: 1901–1965*, New York: Praeger.

Mirabeau, Honoré-Gabriel Victor de Riqueti Comte de (1792): *Collection complète des travaux de M. Mirabeau l'aîné, à l'assemblée nationale*, vol. 5.

Mitchell, B. R. (1984): *Economic Development of the British Coal Industry 1800–1914*, Cambridge: Cambridge University Press.

Mitchell, John V. (2001) *The New Economy of Oil*, with Koji Morita, Norman

Selley, and Jonathan Stern. London: The Royal Institute of International Affairs.

Mitchell, John V. (1996): *Tribal Movement – Strategies of the International Oil Companies in the 1990s*, Oxford Energy Seminar, September.

Mommer, Bernard (2000): 'Ese chorro que atraviesa el siglo', Asdrúbal Baptista (ed.): *Venezuela siglo XX – Visiones y testimonios (The Twentieth Century of Venezuela – Visions and Testimonies)*, Fundación Polar, 3 vol, Caracas; vol. 2, pp. 529–62.

Mommer, Bernard (1999): 'Oil Prices and Fiscal Regimes', OIES Paper WPM 24, Oxford Institute for Energy Studies.

Mommer, Bernard (1998): *The New Governance of Venezuelan Oil*, Oxford Institute for Energy Studies.

Mommer, Bernard (1994): 'Rôle Politique des compagnies pétrolières nationales dans les grands pays exportateurs: Le cas du Venezuela', *Économies et Sociétés*, Série Économie de l'énergie, EN, vol. 6, septembre, pp.111–35.

Mommer, Bernard (1991): *La distribución de la renta petrolera – El desarrollo del capitalismo rentístico venezolano*, in Omar Bello Rodríguez and Hector Valencillo (eds): *La Economía Contemporánea de Venezuela. Ensayos Escogidos*, Banco Central de Venezuela, vol. IV, Caracas.

Mommer, Bernard (1990): 'Oil Rent and Rent Capitalism: The Example of Venezuela', *Review*, vol. XIII, 4, Fall 1990, Fernand Braudel Center, New York; pp.417–37.

Mommer, Bernard (1988): *La cuestión petrolera*, Asociación de Profesores UCV-TROPYKOS, Caracas.

Mommer, Bernard (1983): *Die Ölfrage*, Institut für Internationale Angelegenheiten der Universität Hamburg, Nomos Verlagsgesellschaft Baden-Baden.

Mommer, Bernard (1981): 'Valores internacionales y los términos absolutos de intercambio del petróleo venezolano, 1917–1977', Guillermo Flichman, Leo Hagedoorn, and Jean Stroom (eds): *Renta del suelo y economía internacional*, CEDLA incidentele Publicaties 19, Amsterdam.

Montel, J. (1970): 'Concession versus Contract' in Mikdashi *Continuity and Change in the World Oil Industry*.

Morales, Isidro, Cecilia Escalante, and Rosía Vargas (1988): *La formación de la política petrolera en México*, El Colegio de México.

National Coal Board (Sponsor) (1984–1993): *The History of British Coal Industry*. Five-volume study. Vol. 1: *Before 1700: Towards the Age of Coal* by John Hatcher, 1993. Vol. 2, 1799–1830: *The Industrial Revolution* by Michael W. Flinn with the assistance of David Stoker, 1984. Vol. 3: *Victorian Pre-eminence* by Roy Church with the assistance of Alan Hall and John Kanefsky, 1986. Vol. 4: 1913–1946: *The Political Economy of Decline* by Barry Supple, 1987. Vol. 5: 1946–1982: *The Nationalised Industry* by William Ashworth with the assistance of Mark Pegg, 1986.

Nef, J.U. (1932): *The Rise of the British Coal Industry*, 2 vols, London: Routledge.

North American Free Trade Agreement (1993).

Offer, Avner (1981): *Property and Politics 1870–1914. Landownership, Law, Ideology and Urban Development in England*, Cambridge: Cambridge University Press.

Ögütçü, Mehmet (1996): 'Eurasian Energy Prospects and Politics: Need for Longer-Term Western Strategy', in Wälde *The Energy Charty Treaty*.

Parker, M. J. (2001): *Thatcherism and the Fall of Coal*, Oxford: Oxford University Press.

Pearton, Maurice (1971): *Oil and the Romanian State*, Oxford: Oxford University Press.

Pechman, Joseph A. (1987): *Federal Tax Policy*, Washington, 5th ed.

Peele, Robert (1918.): *Mining Engineer's Handbook*, New York: John Wiley & Sons.

Penrose, Edith T. (1971): *The Growth of Firms, Middle East Oil and other Essays*, London: Frank Cass.

Penrose, Edith T. (1970): 'OPEC and the changing Structure of the International Petroleum Industry', in Mikdashi *Continuity and Change in the World Oil Industry*.

Pérez Alfonzo, Juan Pablo (1967): *El pentágono petrolero*, Caracas.

Pérez Alfonzo, Juan Pablo (1960): *Venezuela y su petróleo*, Caracas: Imprenta Nacional.

Philby, H.St.J.B. (1964): *Arabian Oil Ventures*, Washington D.C.: Middle East Institute.

Philip, George (1982): *Oil and Politics in Latin America*, Cambridge: Cambridge University Press.

Pierce, David E. *et al.* (1998): *Cases and Materials on Oil and Gas Law*, 3rd ed., American Casebook Series.

Pogue, Joseph E. (1949): *Oil in Venezuela*, New York: Chase National Bank, Petroleum Division, June.

Rasmusen, Eric (1989): *Games and Information – An Introduction to Game Theory*, Oxford: Basil Blackwell.

Revista del Ministerio de Fomento (1939): 'Resumen de los documentos de traspaso de concesiones de hidrocarburos, del año 1920 al año 1938 inclusive', vol. 2, no. 8, January, pp. 162–274.

Ricardo, David (1821): *On the Principles of Political Economy and Taxation*, 3rd ed., London: John Murray.

Rifaï, Taki (1974): *Les prix du pétrole*, Paris: Édition Technip.

Rodríguez, Luis Roberto (2000): *The Political Economy of State-Oil Relations: Institutional Case Studies of Venezuela and Norway*, Oxford, D.Phil. thesis.

Rouhani, Fouad (1971): *A History of OPEC*, New York: Praeger.

Rutledge, Ian (2001): 'Industrial Structure, Profitability and Supply Price in the US Domestic Oil Industry: Implications for the Political Economy of Oil in the 21st Century', Mimeo, Energy Studies Programme, University of Sheffield, July.

Rutledge, Ian and Philip Wright (2000): 'Taxing Petroleum: Don't forget the upstream', *Financial Times Energy, Energy Economist Briefing*, October.

Rutledge, Ian and Philip Wright (1998): 'Profitability and Taxation in the UKCS Oil and Gas Industry: Analysing the Distribution of Rewards between Company and Country', *Energy Policy*, vol. 26, no. 10, pp.795–812.

Schneider, Luis Mario (1989): 'La literatura del petróleo en México', in Herrera Reyes and San Martín Tejedo (eds).

Schurr, Sam H. and Paul T. Homan (1971): *Middle Eastern Oil and the Western World*, New York: American Elsevier Press.

Scott, Richard (1995): *IEA The First 20 Years*. Vol. 1: *Origins and Structure* (1994); Vol. 2: *Major Policies and Actions* (1995); Vol. 3: *Principal Documents* (1995), Paris : OECD/IEA.

Sentíes, Octavio (1989): 'Petróleo y derecho – seguimiento mexicano', in Herrera Reyes and Martín Tejedo (eds).

Shaffer, Edward H. (1968): *The Oil Import Program of the U.S.A.*, New York: Praeger.

Skeet, Ian (1988): *OPEC: Twenty-five Years of Prices and Politics*, Cambridge: Cambridge University Press.

Smith, Adam (1950): *The Wealth of Nations*, 2 vols., London: Methuen & Co.

Société des Nations (1932): *Journal Officiel*, vol. 13.2, July-December.

Sosa Pietri, Andrés (1994): 'Vinculaciones internacionales de la industria petrolera Venezolana: OPEP, AIE, OLADE, ARPEL y bloques económicos regionales en América', paper presented to the *Quinto Congreso Venezolano de Petróleo*, Caracas.

Sosa Pietri, Andrés (1993): *Petróleo y poder*, Caracas.

State of Alaska (2000a): *2000 Annual Report*, Department of Natural Resources, Division of Oil and Gas.

State of Alaska (2000b): *Fiscal Year 2000 Annual Report*, Department of Revenue, Tax Division.

State of Alaska (2000c), *Fall 2000 Revenue Resources Book*, Department of Revenue, Tax Division.

State of Alaska (2000d): *Oil and Gas Revenue From State Leases – Fiscal Years 1990 Through 2000*, Department of Natural Resources, Division of Oil and Gas.

Stobaugh, Robert B. (1978): 'The Evolution of Iranian Oil Policy 1925–1975', in George Lenczowski (ed.): *Iran under the Pahlevis*, Stanford: Bibliotheca Persica Press.

Stocking, George W. (1971): *Middle East Oil*, London: Allen Lane The Penguin Press.

Strange, Susan (1998): *States and Markets*, 2nd ed., London: Pinter.

Strohmeyer, John (1993): *Extreme Conditions: Big Oil and the Transformation of Alaska*, New York: Anchorage Cascade Press.

Sullivan, Robert E. (1955): *Handbook of Oil and Gas Law*.

Supple, Barry (1987): *1913–1946: The Political Economy of Decline*. (National Coal Board (Sponsor): *The History of British Coal Industry*, vol. 4).

The New Palgrave (1998): *A Dictionary of Economics*, London: MacMillan.

Torres, Gumersindo (1920): *Memoria del Ministerio de Fomento*, Caracas.

Torres, Gumersindo (1918): *Memoria del Ministerio de Fomento*, Caracas.

Tugwell, Franklin (1975): *The Politics of Oil in Venezuela*, Stanford: Stanford University Press.

Turgot, Anne Robert Jacques (1898): *The Formation and the Distribution of Riches*, London: MacMillan.

United Nations (1962): *Permanent Sovereignty over Natural Resources*, General Assembly Resolution 1803.

United States Government (2000): Budget of the Fiscal Year 2000.

United States Government (1995): Outer Continental Shelf Deep Water Royalty Relief Act. Public Law 104-58, 43 U.S.C. § 1337.

United States Senate (1952): *The International Petroleum Cartel*, Select Committee on Small Business, Staff Report to the Federal Trade Commission, 82nd. Congress, 2nd Session, Publication of the Committee No. 6, August 22.

Uren, Lester Charles (1950): *Petroleum Production Engineering*. Vol. 3: *Petroleum Production Economics*.

USA-Azerbaijan (1997): Treaty Between the Government of the United States of America and the Government of the Republic of Azerbaijan for the Encouragement and Reciprocal Protection of Investment (1997).

USA-Canada Free Trade Agreement (1989).

Vallenilla, Luis (1995): *La apertura petrolera – un peligrosa retorno al pasado*, Caracas.

Vallenilla, Luis (1973): *Auge, declinación y porvenir del petróleo venezolana*, Caracas.

Venezuela, Ministerio de Energía y Minas: *Petróleo y otros datos estadísticos*, yearbook.

Wälde, Thomas W. (1996b): 'International Investment under the 1994 Energy Charter Treaty', in Wälde (1996).

Wälde, Thomas W. (ed.) (1996a): *The Energy Charter Treaty – An East West Gateway for Investment and Trade*, London: Kluwer Law International.

Williamson, Harold F. and Arnold R. Daum (1959): *The American Petroleum Industry*. Vol. 1: *The Age of Illumination 1859–1899*, Evanston: Northwestern University Press.

Williamson, Harold F. *et al.* (1963): *The American Petroleum Industry*. Vol. 2: *The Age of Energy 1899–1959*, Evanston: Northwestern University Press.

World Petroleum (1959), vol. 30, no. 1, January.

Yamani, Ahmed Zaki (1970): 'Participation versus Nationalisation: A Better Means to Survive', in Mikdashi *Continuity and Change in the World Oil Industry*.

INDEX